D0332973

WITHDRAWN
FROM
STOCK

WORLD MOTORSPORT FACTS & RECORDS

METROPOLITAN BOROUGH OF WIRRAL

THIS BOOK IS FOR REFERENCE
USE ONLY, AND MUST NOT BE
TAKEN FROM THE BUILDING.

WIRRAL LIBRARIES

WIRRAL LIBRARY
SERVICES

600017782037

...rams   20/05/2011

...JON   £6 99

...

Copyright © Carlton Books Limited 2010

First published under the title of World Motor Sport Records 2011 in 2010
Reissued in text-only version in 2011

All rights reserved. No part of this publication may be reproduced,
stored in a retrieval system, or transmitted in any form or by any means,
electronic, mechanical, photocopying, recording or otherwise, without the
prior permission of the copyright owner and the publishers.

A CIP catalogue record for this book is available from the British Library

Carlton Books Limited
20 Mortimer Street
London W1T 3JW

ISBN: 978-1-84732-774-1

Editor: Martin Corteel
Design: Ben Durston
Production: Karin Kolbe

Printed in Great Britain

WORLD MOTORSPORT FACTS & RECORDS

BRUCE JONES

CARLTON

CONTENTS

INTRODUCTION

Welcome to the most all-encompassing book of motor sport records ever. Facts and stats started being laid down the moment that people first raced cars at the end of the 19th century and the sport that we all love has grown and diversified, from Formula One racing on the streets of Monaco, to NASCAR stockers dicing on the banking at Daytona and World Rally Cars rattling down a rutted track in East Africa. Motor sport does not stand still. It is continuously shaped by technological progress, the state of the world economy and often by increased requirements for driver and spectator safety.

Whatever is changed, though, one factor is constant: competition. It's all about the contest and every competitor within every contest has a story, making the statistics and records about more than just a date or a number. *World Motorsport Facts & Records* doesn't provide a chronology of championship results, as there are other books that do that. Instead, its focus is on the achievements of drivers, teams and manufacturers across the years. It highlights the degrees of both success and failure, compares the greats from different eras and lays down the extremes of every category from Formula One to NASCAR, from IndyCar to the World Rally Championships, from sports car and touring car racing to the best of the junior single-seater formula.

The book doesn't only include what has happened in the heat of competition on the road circuits, speed ovals and rally stages, as it looks too at drag racing and the most free-form motor spot of all – the quest for the world land speed record.

So, whether your allegiance is to Ferrari, Chevrolet or Citroën; to Michael Schumacher, Richard Petty or Colin McRae; to the British GP, the Indianapolis 500 or the Le Mans 24 Hours; to Monza, Talladega or the 1000 Lakes Rally, this book will provide you with stories, facts and figures, and inform you about the categories of motor sport that you don't know so well. Hopefully, it will also give you a new respect for the drivers who were in action in the 1950s and 1960s, when they really did lay their lives on the line to satisfy that primal urge to compete. *World Motorsport Facts & Records* was both great fun and, occasionally, infuriating to research and led to many pleasurable but time-consuming off-beat journeys in the quest for information that were only curtailed when the next deadline loomed. There really is so much information out there, so many stories of perseverance and near success. It would take several more books to pack it all in.

After reading this book I hope that you come away with an informed opinion about the merits of different drivers, teams, racing categories and circuits, and how the greats compare across the eras. No one will ever be able to come up with a definitive answer as to whether Jim Clark, Dale Earnhardt, Sébastien Loeb or Mario Andretti were the greatest drivers of all time in their respective categories, but I hope that this book provides you with new food for thought.

Bruce Jones
January 2011

PART 1: FORMULA ONE

Formula One, the world's fastest-moving sport, has been exciting and entertaining fans around the globe since the World Championship began in 1950. The drive to win is as strong as ever, but Formula One has changed dramatically over the past 60 years. The cars have been transformed into high-tech missiles with incredible acceleration, cornering and braking capabilities. The circuits are bigger, better and considerably safer. So, with every grand Prix, the records keep on being added to in a blaze of glamour and speed.

DRIVERS

Michael Schumacher's dominance from 2000 to 2004 means that his name is at the top of virtually every list of driver achievement. However, some of his rivals and those who raced before him certainly made huge contributions to the colourful history of Formula One, including greats such as Alberto Ascari, Juan Manuel Fangio, Stirling Moss, Jim Clark, Jackie Stewart, Niki Lauda, Alain Prost, Ayrton Senna and Nigel Mansell.

CHAMPIONS

⊙ THE LION'S SHARE

Every now and again, a team or a driver, occasionally both, hits the sweet spot and dominates F1. Take Michael Schumacher's run at the beginning of the 21st century, when he was world champion from 2000 to 2004. His team, Ferrari, won a record-equalling 15 grands prix, both in 2002 and 2004. Of those, Michael won 11 in 2002 and all but two in 2004, leaving teammate Rubens Barrichello with the scraps. When McLaren won 15 out of 16 in 1988, the wins were split seven to eight between Alain Prost and Ayrton Senna.

⊙ NUMBER 1 ON THE NOSE

The world champion has the honour of carrying the number "1" on his car for the following season. Michael Schumacher has raced with this number for the longest spell, from the beginning of the 2001 season to the end of the 2005 season.

⊙ BRITISH DRIVERS COME OUT ON TOP

British drivers, teams and engine suppliers top many tables of F1 statistics, which is a fact that would have amazed onlookers in the 1950s as the dark green cars made up the numbers behind the best from Italy and Germany. Yet Britain has claimed more drivers' titles than any other country – 14, and more world champions too, 10, namely Mike Hawthorn, Graham Hill, Jim Clark, John Surtees, Jackie Stewart, James Hunt, Nigel Mansell, Damon Hill, Lewis Hamilton and Jenson Button.

⊙ WINNER BY A FRACTION

Some champions win by a clear margin, others just scrape home. Lewis Hamilton in 2008 and Kimi Räikkönen in 2007 both won by a point. Mike Hawthorn also edged home by the same margin in 1958, but his championship win required an act of fair play from Stirling Moss who stopped Hawthorn from being disqualified from the Portuguese GP, verifying that Hawthorn's Ferrari hadn't been given a push-start. The closest championship finish was in 1984, when Niki Lauda beat his McLaren teammate Alain Prost by half a point.

TOP WORLD CHAMPIONSHIP WINNING DRIVERS

1	Michael Schumacher	7
2	Juan Manuel Fangio	5
3	Alain Prost	4
4	Jack Brabham	3
=	Niki Lauda	3
=	Nelson Piquet	3
=	Ayrton Senna	3
=	Jackie Stewart	3
9	Fernando Alonso	2
=	Alberto Ascari	2
=	Jim Clark	2
=	Emerson Fittipaldi	2
=	Mika Hakkinen	2
=	Graham Hill	2
15	Mario Andretti	1
=	Jenson Button	1
=	Giuseppe Farina	1
=	Lewis Hamilton	1
=	Mike Hawthorn	1
=	Damon Hill	1
=	Phil Hill	1
=	Denis Hulme	1
=	James Hunt	1
=	Alan Jones	1
=	Nigel Mansell	1
=	Kimi Räikkönen	1
=	Jochen Rindt	1
=	Keke Rosberg	1
=	Jody Scheckter	1
=	John Surtees	1
=	Sebastian Vettel	1
=	Jacques Villeneuve	1

⊙ BREAKING CLEAR

In the first 50 years of the F1 World Championship, Nigel Mansell's 52-point gap ahead of Williams teammate Riccardo Patrese in 1992 was the biggest title-winning margin. Michael Schumacher broke that record in 2001, outstripping David Coulthard of Williams by 58 points and, a year later, recorded what remains the largest title-winning margin, 67 points, over Ferrari teammate Rubens Barrichello.

⊙ PRIVATEERS STRIKE A BLOW

Jack Brabham and Cooper struck a blow for the little guys when they won both the 1959 World Drivers' and Constructors' Championships together. This made Cooper the first specialist racing-car manufacturer to beat the established automotive marques such as Alfa Romeo, Ferrari, Mercedes and Maserati, which ran their F1 teams alongside their established road-car business.

⊙ PLAYING DIRTY

Damon Hill had every reason to feel aggrieved in the season-ending finale in Adelaide in 1994. Michael Schumacher seemed to have left a gap; Hill dived for it, not knowing that the German had just damaged his car against the wall. Schumacher then turned his Benetton across into Hill's Williams and the resulting clash caused irreparable damage to Hill's car and he had to retire from the race. Schumacher claimed the World Championship by a point. Damon's father Graham also lost a title through dastardly deeds. This happened at Mexico in 1964 when Ferrari's John Surtees beat him to the title by a point after his teammate Lorenzo Bandini tipped Hill into a spin.

⊙ HOP, SKIP AND A JUMP

Aside from Giuseppe Farina's record in winning the inaugural World Championship in 1950, the smallest total number of grands prix contested by a driver before becoming world champion is Juan Manuel Fangio, who won the title in 1951 for Alfa Romeo after competing in just 12 grands prix. Drivers these days contest many more grands prix than that in just one season alone.

⊙ WORST TITLE DEFENCE

Alberto Ascari won two World Championships in a row in 1952 and 1953. However, his second title defence was a disaster. His Lancia wasn't ready and Ascari didn't race until late in the year, failing to finish any of his five races in 1954 and scoring just 1.14 points by setting one fastest lap and sharing another. More recently, Jody Scheckter had a nightmare defending his 1979 crown. Scheckter's Ferrari 312T5 was uncooperative and his full campaign produced just two points.

◉ JUST ONE WILL DO

Anyone who watched Keke Rosberg race will know that he was a driver who raced to win, a driver full of on-the-limit aggression, yet he claimed his world title for Williams in 1982 with just one win. That was Mike Hawthorn's tally too when he was crowned in 1958. Jack Brabham (1959), Phil Hill (1961), John Surtees (1964) and Denny Hulme (1967) all managed to win the title with just two victories.

◉ WORLD CHAMPION PAIRINGS

The 2010 McLaren partnership of Lewis Hamilton, winner in 2008, and Jenson Button, the current incumbent, is the eighth time that a team has fielded a pair of world champions. The previous occasions were: Alberto Ascari and Giuseppe Farina at Ferrari in 1953 and 1954; Jim Clark and Graham Hill at Lotus in 1967 and 1968; Emerson Fittipaldi and Denny Hulme at McLaren in 1974; Alain Prost and Keke Rosberg at McLaren in 1986; and Alain Prost and Ayrton Senna at McLaren in 1989.

◉ TWO WHEELS TO FOUR

John Surtees – who was the world champion for Ferrari in 1964 – has the distinction of being the only motorcycle world champion to hit world title-winning heights after transferring to car racing. Fellow motorcycle world champions Mike Hailwood and Johnny Cecotto also made the move to four wheels, but "Mike the Bike" peaked with a best finish of second place in the 1972 Italian GP, ironically racing for Surtees's team, while Cecotto's best result was a sixth position at Long Beach for Theodore in 1983.

◉ WITH ROOM TO SPARE

The driver who clinched the World Championship with the most races still to be run was Michael Schumacher during his runaway success for Ferrari in 2002. There were 17 rounds that year and the German was world champion by the 11th race, the French GP at Magny-Cours, which he won.

◉ COMING BACK FROM RETIREMENT

Niki Lauda had two World Championship titles to his name when he quit before the end of the 1979 season. Like many before and after him he couldn't stay away and was back in 1982, racing for McLaren. In winning the title in 1984 he set the record for the longest gap between titles – seven years.

⊙ KEEP IT IN THE FAMILY

The Hill family has a proud boast. Despite F1 being littered with sons following their fathers into the sport, Graham and Damon are the only father and son to both win the F1 title. Graham won in 1962 for BRM and in 1968 for Lotus while Damon was crowned with Williams in 1996. The Andrettis and Scheckters failed to match their feat, while the Piquet and Rosberg dynasties are still aiming to emulate them.

⊙ I'LL TAKE THE FASTEST CAR

Juan Manuel Fangio was undoubtedly a maestro behind the wheel, but he was also a master at making sure he had the right machinery beneath him and he moved teams to ensure this, which explains why he won the World Championship with more teams than any other driver. He was champion with Alfa Romeo, Mercedes, Ferrari and Maserati.

⊙ THE FIRST WORLD CHAMPION

Giuseppe Farina was the first F1 world champion in 1950 at the age of 44. The Italian achieved his final win three years later just a few months short of his 47th birthday and, in so doing, became the second-oldest F1 race winner ever. These days, most of the drivers' fathers are younger than that.

⊙ ADDING TITLES TO TITLES

Fernando Alonso set a record when he won his second consecutive World Championship in 2006, as he became the youngest double world champion at the age of 25 years and 85 days. Ayrton Senna was the youngest triple world champion, at 31 years and 227 days.

RUNNERS-UP

⊙ FIRST OF THE LOSERS

Nobody wants to finish second in a grand prix. In F1 it's referred to as "the first of the losers". So, imagine how drivers gnash their teeth at ending the year as the championship runner-up. It's even worse if they trip up in the final round and let the title slide from their grasp. The most extreme example of this was when Lewis Hamilton blew his chance of winning the title at his first attempt in 2007 at the Brazilian GP when gearbox problems affected his race and he could only finish seventh. Ferrari's Kimi Räikkönen powered to a race victory and the title.

⊙ LAUDA PIPS PROST

Being faster and scoring more wins is one thing, but master tactician Niki Lauda taught his McLaren teammate Alain Prost a lesson in consistency in 1984. Prost settled in quickly after joining from Renault and won the opening round, then added six more wins, including three of the final four races. However, Lauda kept racking up the points, including five race wins. Lauda won the World Championship by half a point, courtesy of only half the points being awarded when the Monaco GP was stopped prematurely because of a heavy rainstorm falling when Prost was leading.

⊙ CHASING THE DREAM

Rubens Barrichello ran second behind Ayrton Senna in the 1993 European GP at Donington Park in his Jordan in only his third grand prix, a month short of his 21st birthday. Yet, for all this promise, Barrichello has now contested the most grands prix without clinching a World Championship title, having raced 306 times by the end of the 2010 season.

⊙ ALWAYS THE BRIDESMAID

Stirling Moss will be remembered as the best driver never to have been world champion. Four times he finished as runner-up, three of those behind Juan Manuel Fangio, his one-time mentor at Mercedes. On the fourth occasion he lost out by one point to Mike Hawthorn, despite winning more races that year. Alain Prost was also runner-up four times, but he did win four World Championships.

⊙ INSTANT IMPACT

Jacques Villeneuve and Lewis Hamilton are the only drivers to end their debut seasons as World Championship runners-up. Villeneuve achieved it for Williams behind Damon Hill in 1996 and Hamilton for McLaren in 2007. However, both drivers won the title a year later.

⊙ SO YOUNG AND SO CLOSE

Lewis Hamilton was fresh-faced when he ended his 2007 F1 campaign one point short of the title, but Sebastian Vettel was almost six months younger still when he finished as runner-up to Jenson Button in 2009. The Red Bull Racing driver was just 22 years and 122 days old, but he put that right in 2010.

⊙ IS SEVEN A LUCKY NUMBER?

Three drivers who became or already had been world champion hold an unwanted record in that they managed to win the most races in a season, seven, without landing that year's title. They are: Alain Prost in 1984 and 1988, Kimi Räikkönen in 2005 and Michael Schumacher in 2006.

⊙ IF AT FIRST YOU DON'T SUCCEED...

Nigel Mansell would have been world champion in 1986 but for his blowout in the Adelaide finale that left him ranked second behind Alain Prost. But he persevered and was runner-up twice more, in 1987 and 1991, before it all came good and he finally landed his World Championship crown for Williams in 1992.

⊙ POINTS DON'T MEAN PRIZES

Rubens Barrichello has the dubious honour of not only the most grand prix starts to his name without winning the World Championship, he has also scored the most points, with a tally of 654. David Coulthard is the next runner-up in the points chart, with a career total of 535.

DRIVERS WITH MOST CAREER RACE WINS WITHOUT WINNING WORLD CHAMPIONSHIP

1	Stirling Moss	16	6	Gerhard Berger	10
2	David Coulthard	13	=	Ronnie Peterson	10
3	Carlos Reutemann	12	8	Jacky Ickx	8
4	Rubens Barrichello	11	9	Rene Arnoux	7
=	Felipe Massa	11	=	Juan Pablo Montoya	7

WINS

⊙ FERRARI TO THE FORE

Combine the fact that Ferrari has been racing in F1 for longer than any other marque (going back to the inaugural season in 1950) with the fact that the most garlanded winner, Michael Schumacher, scored the bulk of his 91 wins with them, and it's not surprising that it tops the charts for the most wins, with a tally of 215 wins by the end of 2010. McLaren lags 46 wins behind, but it did fleetingly nose in front in the late 1990s before Schumacher and Ferrari dominated.

⊙ 13: UNLUCKY FOR EVERYONE ELSE

Michael Schumacher wasn't the sort of driver troubled by superstition. There were no habits such as always getting into the car from the same side or wearing odd boots (like Alexander Wurz), or a lucky pair of underpants or gloves (David Coulthard). But, it seems, 13 was a lucky number for him, as his record of 13 wins from 18 grands prix in 2004 gave him his seventh and final F1 title.

⊙ RULE BRITANNIA

Not only are British drivers the most successful in landing World Championships, they've also won the most grands prix. They have 213 wins shared between 19 of them, with Nigel Mansell at the top of the pile with 31. This is good only for fourth in the overall wins table, though, far behind Michael Schumacher's 91. That said, Britain's overall tally is 100 more than the next most successful country, Germany, with Brazil third on 101.

⊙ ON A ROLL

If one win upsets a driver's rivals, just think what a string of wins does. King of the rolling wins is Alberto Ascari, who hit the most vivid of purple patches in 1952 when he won the Belgian GP and carried on winning through the next eight grands prix, with the last of these being the Belgian GP the following year. Not surprisingly, he was world champion both years. Even the great Michael Schumacher peaked at seven straight wins in 2004.

⊙ MR CONSISTENCY

Perhaps the most impressive of Michael Schumacher's many, many records is that once he started winning in 1992 he kept going, claiming at least one win in each of the following 14 World Championship seasons through to 2006, but he wasn't able to add any on his return in 2010.

⊙ EVERYONE HAS A GO

The 1982 season was extremely competitive as 11 drivers took at least one win in the 16 grands prix. Keke Rosberg ended the year as world champion ahead of Didier Pironi and John Watson (both of whom scored two wins), with Michele Alboreto, Rene Arnoux (two), Elio de Angelis, Niki Lauda (two), Riccardo Patrese, Nelson Piquet, Alain Prost (two) and Patrick Tambay also enjoying victories.

⊙ KEEPING IT TO THEMSELVES

The opposite of sharing around wins is what happened in the 1950 and 1952 World Championship seasons, when only two drivers claimed victories. In 1950 it was Giuseppe Farina and Juan Manuel Fangio, with three each, and in 1952 just Piero Taruffi, once, and Alberto Ascari, six times, were triumphant. (This doesn't include the standalone Indianapolis 500 that was then nominally part of the World Championship.)

⊙ TOO GOOD TO BE A FLUKE

When a driver dominates, a lot of F1 fans point to the merits of the car. So, perhaps one of the best ways to prove that a driver's input is vital is to find the driver who has won for the most different teams. Step forward Stirling Moss, who won for five marques – Mercedes, Maserati, Vanwall, Cooper and Lotus. Juan Manuel Fangio and Alain Prost both won for four teams.

⊙ NO DISCERNIBLE PATTERN

The 1982 World Championship in which 11 drivers won grands prix also produced the longest run of different winning drivers. Riccardo Patrese's surprise win in the sixth round in Monaco triggered a sequence of wins for different drivers that ran through to Keke Rosberg's win in the 14th round in the Swiss GP. There's never been another year like it.

⊙ HOME IS WHERE THE HEART IS

With a little help from having two grands prix held in Germany most years during his career, the inimitable Michael Schumacher holds the record for the most wins at a driver's home race, adding five wins in the European GP at the Nürburgring to his three in the German GP. Alain Prost recorded six wins in the French GP.

TOP 10 DRIVERS WITH MOST GRAND PRIX WINS

1	Michael Schumacher	91	6	Fernando Alonso	26
2	Alain Prost	51	7	Jim Clark	25
3	Ayrton Senna	41	=	Niki Lauda	25
4	Nigel Mansell	31	9	Juan Manuel Fangio	24
5	Jackie Stewart	27	10	Nelson Piquet	23

⊙ THE LAP THAT COUNTS

Jochen Rindt was an expert at leading the final lap rather than the first one and he pulled off the trick to the greatest effect at Monaco in 1970 when he hunted down Jack Brabham and pressured him into a mistake at the first corner of the final lap. Poor Brabham was pipped in another last-lap changeover later that year at Brands Hatch, when again Rindt demoted him as he coasted to the finish line, out of fuel.

⊙ A WONDERFUL YEAR'S WORK

Six wins in any World Championship campaign is an impressive and seldom achieved tally. However, World Championships were considerably shorter in the early 1950s and Alberto Ascari's six wins in his first title-winning year for Ferrari, 1952, came from just seven grands prix, giving him a winning rate of 86 per cent – the best ever. Michael Schumacher's 13 wins from 18 races in 2004 represented a 72 per cent return.

⊙ FIRST IMPRESSIONS

Jacques Villeneuve and Lewis Hamilton share the record for the most grand prix wins in their maiden season of F1. Their tally is four apiece, with Villeneuve scoring the first of these with Williams on his fourth outing, at the Nürburgring, and Hamilton taking his McLaren past the chequered flag first at his sixth attempt, in Canada. Juan Manuel Fangio and Giuseppe Farina both won three grands prix in 1950, the inaugural year of the F1 World Championship.

⊙ DOMINANT PAIRINGS

Michael Schumacher led home Rubens Barrichello on 19 occasions when they raced together at Ferrari. When he had a particular year's World Championship in the bag, Michael would ease off and let Rubens through to head home giving another Ferrari one-two. He did this five times, although one of these was a fumble when he tried to stage a dead heat at Indianapolis in 2002 and failed.

⊙ WINNING NATION

Great Britain's drivers have the greatest aggregate total of grand prix wins, with 19 of them sharing a table-topping 213 victories. The first of these wins was by Mike Hawthorn, when his Ferrari edged out Juan Manuel Fangio's Maserati to win the French GP at Reims in 1953 by a second. Germany rank as runners-up, almost solely due to seven-time world champion Michael Schumacher's tally of 91 wins. Only five of his compatriots have added to the haul.

⊙ COMETH THE HOUR, COMETH THE MAN

There are 22 drivers who have won just one solitary grand prix. How did it all go so right just the once then never again? In the case of Jean-Pierre Beltoise, a former French motorcycle racing champion who showed immense promise, he delivered in extremely wet conditions at Monaco in 1972. His BRM lacked the regular power of the other cars on the grid, but the rain negated this disadvantage and he never again had the equipment to add to that tally.

⊙ A CLOSE SHAVE

A driver's first win is usually a time of celebration and often of relief at having "got the monkey off their back". For John Watson at the 1975 Austrian GP at the Österreichring, it was also a time to meet his side of a wager with his team boss Roger Penske. For winning, Watson had to shave off his beard, and he has never sported one since.

⊙ HIT THE GROUND RUNNING

Nigel Mansell enjoyed the best start to a season when he and his Williams-Renault FW14B won the first five grands prix in 1992. It could have been the first six but for a wheel weight coming loose at Monaco and his subsequent charge just failed to overhaul Ayrton Senna's McLaren.

⊙ ...AND RELAX

You've beaten the conditions – foul weather, the track criss-crossed with streams – and you've certainly beaten the odds. In fact, you've just scored your first grand prix win. It's time to celebrate, punch the air with delight and... lose control, wiping the nose off your car. Welcome to the wild world of March's Vittorio Brambilla at the 1975 Austrian GP. It also proved to be the last victory for the man nick-named the "Monza Gorilla".

⊙ WHEN OVERTAKING IS ESSENTIAL

With overtaking becoming increasingly difficult, the possibility of a driver advancing from the rear of the grid is becoming less likely. Therefore, John Watson's record, set at the 1983 US West GP at Long Beach, California, of winning from 22nd on the grid is probably guaranteed its place in the history books for ever. He also holds the record for the third best charge, from 17th to 1st at Detroit in 1982.

⊙ NO ONE SHALL PASS

Ayrton Senna started from pole position 65 times and he made the most of them as he holds the record for leading the most grands prix from start to finish. He did this 19 times, with Jim Clark next on this list with 13, ahead of Michael Schumacher and Jackie Stewart on 11.

⊙ BY THE SKIN OF HIS TEETH

A last-lap lead change in the Italian GP at Monza in 1971 produced the closest finish in F1 history. Peter Gethin nosed his BRM to the front of a five-car pack after a slipstreaming dash out of the final corner, doing his best to gain the stewards' confidence that he'd secured victory by punching the air ostentatiously as he crossed the line. His margin of victory was 0.01 seconds over March's Ronnie Peterson, with the first five covered by just 0.61 seconds.

TOP 10 COUNTRIES WITH MOST GRAND PRIX WINS

1	Great Britain	213	6	Italy	43
2	Germany	113	7	Austria	41
3	Brazil	101	8	Argentina	38
4	France	79	9	Australia	32
5	Finland	44	10	Spain	26

◉ TAKING THEIR TIME

In 2009 Mark Webber usurped Rubens Barrichello to become the holder of the record for the most grands prix contested before scoring a win. He had 130 races under his belt before he and his Red Bull hit the bull's eye at the Nürburgring. Barrichello's 2009 teammate, Jenson Button (113 starts before winning), ranks fourth in this list behind Jarno Trulli (119).

◉ STARTING WITH A BANG

Two drivers hold the almost unbelievable record of winning a grand prix on their World Championship debut. Giuseppe Farina achieved this in 1950, in the first ever World Championship (he went on to win the title), but the more significant achievement was by Giancarlo Baghetti. Having been promoted through the Ferrari ranks in their search for a young Italian driver, in 1961 he won two non-championship races and then won a slipstreamer by 0.1 secs from Dan Gurney on his World Championship debut in the French GP at Reims. He never won again. Since then, only Jacques Villeneuve has come close to the same achievement, finishing as runner-up in Australia in 1996.

◉ THREE DRIVERS, ONE NATIONAL FLAG

There have only been 16 clean sweeps of drivers of one nationality occupying all three steps on the podium since 1950 and British drivers have accounted for 10 of these. Bumper years were 1958 and 1965, when it happened three times. Mike Hawthorn was on the podium but never a winner in the 1958 trio of clean sweeps and, in 1965, Jim Clark was the winner each time and John Surtees was on the podium.

◉ WHO'D HAVE THOUGHT IT?

Throughout F1 history there have been wins that have surprised everyone. Jo Bonnier's victory in the 1959 Dutch GP is a good example as no one thought that a BRM would ever win. Vittorio Brambilla's win in Austria in 1975 came as a shock as no one expected that the wild Italian would be the one to stay on the track in the wet. However, Giancarlo Baghetti's win on his World Championship debut in France in 1961 was the most surprising as he had to work his way forward from 13th to do it, and it required his teammates to retire to aid his progress.

⊙ WINNING BY A COUNTRY MILE

Jackie Stewart was always an exponent of "winning at the lowest speed possible". Risks weren't something he considered worthwhile but the policy paid dividends as he won 27 grands prix and three World Championships. Stewart also holds the record for the largest winning margin in F1 history of two laps. This was at the 1969 Spanish GP at Montjuich Park when his Matra won by 4.711 miles. Williams's Damon Hill also won by two laps in the 1995 Australian GP at Adelaide, but his winning margin was only 4.698 miles.

⊙ A LITTLE HELP FROM YOUR FRIENDS

Shared wins were allowed until 1957, when a team's lead driver might realize that something was wrong with his car and commandeer one of his teammates' cars with which to complete the race. The points would be split between them. This happened three times for wins, and many more times for lower placings. Juan Manuel Fangio took over Luigi Fagioli's Alfa Romeo to win the 1951 French GP and did the same to Ferrari teammate Luigi Musso in Argentina in 1956.

⊙ LA BELLE FRANCE

Michael Schumacher seemed to have an affinity with the French GP, as he won the race on eight occasions. This is the most times that any driver has won any nation's grand prix. His first success in France came in 1994 at Magny-Cours and his last at the same circuit in 2006.

⊙ BEAT THE CLOCK

In terms of time, rather than laps, Stirling Moss holds the record for the greatest margin of victory. He took the chequered flag with his Vanwall 5 mins and 12.75 secs clear of Mike Hawthorn in the Portuguese GP at Oporto in 1958. Hawthorn half spun on the final lap and Moss, not wanting to embarrass his title rival by lapping him, slowed to let him rejoin, as he himself ambled around his slowing-down lap.

SMALLEST WINNING MARGIN

Margin	Winner	Runner-up	GP	Year
0.010 sec	Peter Gethin	Ronnie Peterson	Italian	1971
0.011 sec	Rubens Barrichello	Michael Schumacher	US	2002
0.014 sec	Ayrton Senna	Nigel Mansell	Spanish	1986
0.050 sec	Elio de Angelis	Keke Rosberg	Austrian	1982
0.080 sec	Jackie Stewart	Jochen Rindt	Italian	1969
0.100 sec	Juan Manuel Fangio	Karl Kling	French	1954
0.100 sec	Giancarlo Baghetti	Dan Gurney	French	1961
0.174 sec	Michael Schumacher	Rubens Barrichello	Canadian	2000
0.182 sec*	Michael Schumacher	Rubens Barrichello	Austrian	2002
0.200 sec*	Stirling Moss	Juan Manuel Fangio	British	1955

* The win was donated to a teammate due to team orders or benevolence.

⊙ A HAT-TRICK OF HAT-TRICKS

A grand slam is when a driver starts from pole, leads every lap and sets the fastest lap en route to victory. Twenty drivers have achieved this, but three stand out for managing it three times in a single season: Alberto Ascari, Jim Clark and Nigel Mansell, and all did it in a world-championship-winning campaign. Ascari did it for Ferrari, in 1952, at Rouen-les-Essarts, the Nurburgring and Zandvoort. Clark was next, for Lotus in 1963, at Zandvoort, Reims and Mexico City. Then Mansell matched them at Kyalami, Catalunya and Silverstone for Williams in 1992.

⊙ HE CERTAINLY TRIED

The unwanted record for the most grands prix without a win belongs to Andrea de Cesaris, who entered 214 races (208 starts) between 1980 and 1994. His best results were two second-place finishes in 1983.

POLE POSITIONS

⊙ THE PERFECT SCORE

Winning from pole position and also setting the race's fastest lap is just a dream for all but a few. The driver who achieved this most recently was Sebastian Vettel for Red Bull Racing in the 2009 British GP. However, the ultimate is to achieve the grand slam – pole position, fastest lap and lead every lap. Fernando Alonso was the last driver to achieve this, when he drove an exemplary race for Ferrari in the 2010 Singapore GP. Jim Clark achieved the grand slam a record eight times.

⊙ AS EASY AS ONE, TWO, THREE

Achieving pole position, setting the race's fastest lap and then winning the race shows a certain style, and guess who has achieved this clean sweep the most times? Yes, Michael Schumacher, on 22 occasions. Jim Clark is next, on 11, meaning that Clark achieved this feat close to one in every six grands prix he entered.

⊙ TURN UP, TAKE POLE

With World Championships in the 1950s having fewer rounds it's hard for drivers from that decade to be at the top of any list, but Juan Manuel Fangio still ranks sixth in the all-time list of pole positions achieved. Fangio also has by far the best pole to race average. His 29 pole positions, from a total of 51 races started, equates to a 57 per cent ratio, with Jim Clark in second place on 46 per cent.

⊙ LUCKY SEVEN

Ayrton Senna clearly loved Imola as he qualified on pole position there for seven years in a row between 1985 and 1991, three times for Lotus and four for McLaren. He put his Williams on pole there in 1994, in the race that was to be his last.

⊙ A FRENCH AFFAIR

Jim Clark qualified his Lotus on pole position for the French GP four years straight from 1962–65 (matching his achievement at the British GP). He achieved this on three markedly different circuits – Rouen-les-Essarts (twice), Reims and Clermont-Ferrand.

⊙ HE WAS THE MAN

Michael Schumacher tops the list for the most pole positions achieved, but his pole to race ratio is nowhere near as good as Ayrton Senna's. The great Brazilian was really the man when it came to a pure, focused, banzai lap. The 1988 Monaco GP is a perfect example; Senna was on pole by 1.4 secs. His tally of 65 poles, just three fewer than Schumacher, gave him a 40 per cent hit rate compared to the German's 27 per cent.

⊙ NIGEL MANSELL'S GOLDEN YEAR

Armed with the dominant Renault-powered Williams FW14B, Nigel Mansell took pole after pole after pole in 1992. In all he claimed pole at 14 of the season's 16 grands prix, missing out only at the Canadian GP, where he lined up behind Ayrton Senna, and the Hungarian GP, where he started second behind teammate Patrese. Senna achieved 13 poles from 16 in both 1988 and 1989, as did Alain Prost in 1993.

⊙ POLE SHOULD EQUAL WIN

Grabbing pole position clearly puts a driver in the best position to win the race, but it's by no means a guarantee of victory. The record number of drives from pole to victory is held by Michael Schumacher, with 40, 11 ahead of Ayrton Senna, showing how on 28 other occasions Michael's poles didn't yield the big prize.

⊙ FOUR IN A ROW

British fans had every reason to expect a home driver to be on pole at the British GP in the 1950s and 1960s. Stirling Moss was on pole for four straight years, 1955–58, as the race alternated between Aintree and Silverstone. Then Jim Clark matched that feat between 1962–65, at Aintree, twice at Silverstone and Brands Hatch. The Scottish Lotus driver didn't manage pole in 1966, but was at the front of the grid in 1967.

⊙ A SHOOTING STAR

Sebastian Vettel holds the record for being the youngest pole-sitter, when he secured his place at the front of the grid at the 2008 Italian GP at the age of 21 years and 73 days. The previous holder of this record was Fernando Alonso, who outqualified the rest of the pack at the 2003 Malaysian GP at the age of 21 years and 236 days.

◉ THERE'S NO PLACE LIKE HOME

Ayrton Senna seemed fated never to win at his home grand prix, although he finally managed it on his eighth attempt in 1991. But setting pole in Brazil came to him far more easily, and he holds the record for the most number of times that a driver has qualified on pole for his home race. He did so six times, in 1986, from 1988–91 and in 1994. The first three came at Rio de Janeiro's Jacarepagua circuit and the others at Interlagos in his home city of São Paulo.

◉ STARTING FROM THE FRONT

Michael Schumacher edges out Ayrton Senna at the top of the all-time number of pole positions table by three, but his advantage is greater when front-row starting positions are considered. Schumacher qualified first or second 115 times, 28 more than Senna. Alain Prost is one behind the Brazilian.

◉ IT'S SENNA AGAIN

Ayrton Senna emphasized his outstanding ability to qualify faster than anyone else when he claimed pole position for a record eight grands prix in a row in his McLaren. The run started at the 1988 Spanish GP and continued through to the 1989 US GP at Phoenix.

◉ POLE AT THE FIRST ATTEMPT

The record books show that Mario Andretti (1968 US GP), Carlos Reutemann (1972 Argentinian GP) and Jacques Villeneuve (1996 Australian GP) all claimed pole on their first World Championship outing, but it was actually Andretti's second appearance for Lotus. He'd qualified 11th for the Italian GP but wasn't allowed to start as he'd raced in an IndyCar event at Indiana State Fairgrounds within 24 hours.

TOP 10 DRIVERS WITH MOST POLE POSITIONS

1	Michael Schumacher	68	7	Mika Hakkinen	26
2	Ayrton Senna	65	8	Niki Lauda	24
3	Jim Clark	33	=	Nelson Piquet	24
=	Alain Prost	33	10	Fernando Alonso	20
5	Nigel Mansell	32	=	Damon Hill	20
6	Juan Manuel Fangio	29			

FASTEST LAPS

⊚ FASTER, FASTER

Michael Schumacher's all-round excellence is shown by the fact that he doesn't just top the record tables in race wins, pole positions, laps led and points scored, he is first in most fastest laps set too, a total of 75. He holds the record by some margin; the second-placed driver on the list, Alain Prost, achieved the feat 41 times.

⊚ HITTING DOUBLE FIGURES

Michael Schumacher and Kimi Räikkönen both gave Ferrari a return of 10 fastest laps in a single season, with the German achieving this impressive tally in 2004 and the Finn doing the same in 2008, both from 18 starts. Räikkönen also claimed 10 fastest laps for McLaren in 2005, although this percentage is slightly lower because there were 19 grands prix that season.

⊚ NO ONE'S AN EXPERT

The Jarama circuit outside Madrid hosted nine Spanish GPs between 1968 and 1991, but not one driver was able to take the fastest lap more than once. A record nine different drivers set fastest lap times, starting with Matra's Jean-Pierre Beltoise in 1968 and ending with Williams's reigning world champion Alan Jones in 1981. Rival Spanish circuit Jerez ended up with a similar record, with seven drivers setting fastest laps there on F1's seven visits.

⊚ WAS IT REALLY?

Every now and again a fastest lap is set by a driver that no one had expected to be so fast. This often happens when a driver with nothing to lose pits for fresh tyres. The most notorious example was Masahiro Hasemi setting the fastest lap on his F1 debut in the 1976 Japanese GP. There were mitigating circumstances in that he knew Fuji Speedway well and it was F1's first visit. Furthermore, it was incredibly wet and his Kojima chassis was on Dunlop wets that were superior to the Goodyears used by the regulars, but still...

⊚ LOVING THE SMOOTH

David Coulthard demonstrated an affinity for the smooth surface and twisting nature of Magny-Cours as he set the fastest lap of the race there five years in a row for McLaren between 1998 and 2002, albeit coming away as the winner on just one of those occasions, in 2000.

⊙ ASCARI'S DOMINANCE

Alberto Ascari's near total dominance of the 1952 World Championship left him with a tally of six fastest laps from seven rounds as he raced to the title for Ferrari. The Indianapolis 500 was also a round of the World Championship then, but he, like other F1 drivers, gave it a miss. So, his tally was even better than the six from eight that some record books show.

⊙ NATIONAL PRIDE

Michael Schumacher is way out in front in the all-time list of drivers who have set the most fastest laps, but as none of his compatriots has even reached double figures it's not surprising that British drivers push the Germans into second place in the overall nationality list of fastest laps. The British have a combined tally of 185 fastest laps to Germany's 103, with French drivers third on 86.

⊙ KEEPING IT ALL GOING

Alberto Ascari set the fastest lap six times from seven rounds in 1952 – he missed the first race, in Swizterland, so he could compete in the Indianapolis 500 – and kept his run going into the 1953 campaign, adding a seventh consecutive fastest lap at the season-opening Argentinian GP. His run was broken by his Ferrari teammate Luigi Villoresi at the Dutch GP.

TOP 10 FASTEST LAPS BY DRIVER NATIONALITY

1	Great Britain	191	6	Italy	51
2	Germany	106	7	Austria	49
3	France	86	8	Argentina	37
4	Brazil	84	9	Australia	31
5	Finland	65	10	USA	25

TOP 10 DRIVERS WHO HAVE SET MOST FASTEST LAPS

1	Michael Schumacher	75	6	Mika Hakkinen	25
2	Alain Prost	41	7	Niki Lauda	24
3	Kimi Räikkönen	35	8	Juan Manuel Fangio	23
4	Nigel Mansell	30	=	Nelson Piquet	23
5	Jim Clark	28	10	Gerhard Berger	21

POINTS

⊙ QUICK NICK, BUT NO WINS

Nick Heidfeld has twice come close to scoring his first grand prix win, most recently in the wet/dry 2009 Malaysian GP, but he has never ascended to the top step of the podium despite notching up a career tally of 225 points by the end of the 2010 season. Martin Brundle is next on the all-time list of points scored without taking a win, with a tally of 98, thus emphasizing Heidfeld's perseverance.

⊙ ALMOST 10 SCORE SCORES

Michael Schumacher had the most remarkable career, almost all of which was spent in competitive cars, and proof of this is not just in his number of wins but in the fact that he was in the points in almost every race, starting with his second outing in 1991, when he moved from Jordan to Benetton. He went on to score in 202 of his 269 starts, achieving an average of 5.38 points per start, thus pipping Juan Manuel Fangio's avearge of 5.34.

⊙ KEEP ON SCORING

Yet another of Michael Schumacher's records is that of consecutive point-scoring drives. His best run is scoring points in 24 grands prix in a row, from the 2001 Hungarian GP to the 2003 Malaysian GP, during which time he won two drivers' titles and scored 191 points, which is a handful more than Stirling Moss managed in his entire F1 career.

⊙ POINTS FOR ALL

Even though points were allocated to only the first six finishers back in 1989, a record 29 different drivers made it on to the scoreboard that year: from world champion Alain Prost on 76, down to Philippe Alliot, Olivier Grouillard, Luis Perez Sala and Gabriele Tarquini on one point apiece. It was an incredible year, as 39 cars turned up for most races and a system of pre-qualifying had to be used to clear out the slowest before qualifying.

⊙ FROM CHAMPION TO SHORT RATIONS

America's first F1 world champion, Phil Hill, had a rapid fall from grace after his 1961 World Championship with Ferrari. Just over a year after winning the title he made a terrible mistake and followed some of Ferrari's staff to ATS, a new Italian team that proved to be a disaster. So, shortly after he peaked, he plummeted and ended up with a career tally of 98 points, the fewest for a world champion.

⊙ GUESS WHO?

If you had to guess who achieved the highest points tally in a season, you'd be a fool to choose anyone other than record scorer Michael Schumacher. However, that all changed in 2010 when the points system was changed to award 25 points for a win rather than 10. So 2010 champion Sebastian Vettel holds the record for now, with 256. Schumacher's largest tally, of 148 points, came in 2004, when it was 10 points for a win.

⊙ SHARED BY MANY

A total of 281 drivers have scored points in the World Championship since 1950 (plus 33 others who scored in the nominally included Indianapolis 500), split between 33 nationalities, with Great Britain producing the most point-scoring drivers – 59. The Italians have a total of 45 drivers in the points, the French 39 and the Germans 20.

TOP 10 DRIVERS WITH MOST GRAND PRIX POINTS

1	Michael Schumacher	1,441
2	Fernando Alonso	829
3	Alain Prost	798.5
4	Rubens Barrichello	654
5	Ayrton Senna	614
6	Kimi Räikkönen	579
7	Jenson Button	541
8	David Coulthard	535
9	Lewis Hamilton	496
10	Nelson Piquet	489.5

Figures are gross, i.e. including scores that were later dropped.

⊙ ADD THEM TOGETHER

Since British drivers hold the highest cumulative tally of wins, it comes as no surprise that British drivers also hold the record for the most combined points scored. Up to the end of 2009, British drivers had scored 5,157.28 points, with Germany second on 3,105.5, Brazil third on 2,654 and France fourth on 2,326.47. Perhaps most impressive is Finland's tally of 1,306.5 points, despite having ever had only six drivers compete in F1.

⊙ JUST WHAT'S THE POINT?

Prior to the start of the 2009 season, Luca Badoer held an unwanted record: after 49 races he had not scored a single point. He hoped to put a stop to the record getting any worse when he stood in at Ferrari for the injured Felipe Massa midway through the season. Unfortunately he didn't, and he has extended that record to 51 races without a point. The closest he has come to a points finish was in the 1999 European GP, when he had to retire his Minardi while in fourth place with just 12 laps to go.

⊙ SCORING A CENTURY FIRST TIME OUT

One hundred points is an impressive points tally for any driver in a World Championship campaign. However, Lewis Hamilton surpassed this figure in his maiden F1 season, amassing a superb 109 points for McLaren. No other rookie has ever scored as many.

⊙ GAPING CHASM

The biggest points gap between a world champion and the runner-up was the 67-point advantage that Michael Schumacher had over his Ferrari teammate, Rubens Barrichello, in 2002.

CAREER DURATION

⊙ OLD FATHER TIME

Graham Hill long held the record for the longest F1 career in terms of the number of years between his first race – the 1958 Monaco GP – and his last start in Brazil in 1975. Hill's F1 career span was 16 years and 253 days. However, Rubens Barrichello broke that when he raced for Williams in 2010, extending the record to 17 years and 245 days.

⊙ EVER YOUNGER

Rubens Barrichello is very much the World Championship's old-timer now, when he embarks upon his 19th F1 campaign in 2011. However, he will still only be the same age that Graham Hill was when he completed his 10th season. Then again, Hill didn't pass his driving test to drive on the road until he was 24 and actually did extremely well to get to F1 by the time he was 29.

⊙ NEVER GIVE UP!

Some drivers just never want to give up. Witness the way in which 40-year-old Michael Schumacher considered standing in for the injured Felipe Massa midway through 2009 but injury intervened, three years after retiring, then he made his return in 2010. This is nothing compared to Jan Lammers, who returned to F1 in 1992 at the age of 36 after a break of 10 years and 114 days. He is still racing.

⊙ LOOKING DOWN FROM ABOVE

All drivers get a kick out of standing on the podium after a race, having finished first, second or third. The thrill is still as great as ever for Rubens Barrichello, who holds the record for the longest spell between his first podium place – at the 1994 Pacific GP – and his most recent appearance at the 2009 Italian GP. His record spans 15 years and 149 days.

⊙ F1: IT'S A CAREER

Graham Hill and Rubens Barrichello are the faces of longevity on the driving front, but their career spans are short next to the number of years put in by those out of the cockpit. Bernie Ecclestone has clocked up 54 years – from his first appearance as a driver-manager to his role as F1's ringmaster.

⊙ TRIED AND TESTED

Michael Schumacher clearly believed in sticking with a winning formula, as his stay with Ferrari was the longest of any driver with one team in F1 history. He turned out for the team in 179 grands prix in 11 seasons between 1996 and 2006. And Schumacher's total would have been higher still, except for the fact that he missed six races in 1999 after breaking a leg in the British GP at Silverstone.

⊙ BLINK AND YOU MISSED IT

Marco Apicella was a decent driver, so it's odd that the Italian's spell in F1 remains the shortest on record. He had one crack at F1, with the Jordan team after Thierry Boutsen had been dropped, in his home race at Monza in 1993. He qualified 23rd out of 26 and, unfortunately, was unable to avoid the melee into the first chicane on the opening lap. His distance covered as an F1 racer was around half a mile.

⊙ EXCELLENCE OVER A DECADE AND MORE

Michael Schumacher holds the record for the most years between his first grand prix victory and his last – 14 years and 32 days. This was between the 1992 Belgian GP at Spa-Francorchamps for Benetton and the 2006 Chinese GP at Shanghai for Ferrari.

⊙ SILVER-HAIRED FLIER

Racer Luigi Fagioli showed that staying power is rewarded. Fagioli raced for Alfa Romeo in 1933, and was still with the team in 1951 when he took his one win in the World Championship, 22 days past his 53rd birthday, making him the oldest person to win an F1 race. The victory came in strange circumstances as he was pulled out of his car when he pitted and was forced to hand it over to team leader Juan Manuel Fangio whose car was having mechanical difficulties. Fangio went on to win, but Fagioli was so unhappy, despite being credited with the win (shared with Fangio), that he quit.

TOP 10 LONGEST SERVERS

1	Bernie Ecclestone (1957–)	54 years	6	Giampaolo Dallara (1970–)	41 years
2	Tyler Alxander (1966–2009)	44 years	=	Jo Ramirez (1961–2001)	41 years
=	Ron Dennis (1966–2009)	44 years	8	Max Mosley (1970–2009)	40 years
4	Herbie Blash (1968–)	43 years	9	Eric Broadley (1960–1997)	38 years
5	Frank Williams (1969–)	42 years	=	Luca di Montezemolo (1973–)	38 years

YOUNGEST AND OLDEST

⊙ YOUNG AND KEEN

The youngest driver to compete in F1 is the Spaniard Jaime Alguersuari, who lowered the mark at the 2009 Hungarian GP driving for Toro Rosso at 19 years and 125 days. He beat Mike Thackwell's long-standing record of competing at the age of 19 years and 182 days at the 1980 Canadian GP. However, Thackwell's record was not universally recognized as he was involved in a first-lap crash and the race restarted without him.

⊙ AFTER YOU, YOUNG SIR

The youngest driver to lead a grand prix is Sebastian Vettel, who led the 2007 Japanese GP during a pit-stop sequence when racing for Toro Rosso. He was just 20 years and 89 days old. Later in the race he showed the impetuousness of youth when he took out Red Bull's Mark Webber when circulating behind the safety car, which put an end to the race for both drivers.

⊙ RACING IS ONE THING...

Some drivers get the lucky break and make it to F1 while still in their teens, but the next step up to getting a drive that offers the chance to win a grand prix is quite another thing. So Sebastian Vettel's record for being the youngest winner at just 21 years and 73 days is a remarkable one. His victory came in the 2008 Italian GP while driving for Toro Rosso.

⊙ A WEALTH OF EXPERIENCE

Luigi Fagioli was just short of 37 when he scored his second to last grand prix win, for Mercedes at Monaco in 1935. So, it must have been for his experience that he was added to Alfa Romeo's line-up at the start of the first World Championship in 1950, in which he ranked third overall. In his one race in 1951, at the French GP, he was forced out of his car mid-race as team leader Juan Manuel Fangio's car had mechanical difficulties. They shared the win. Luigi was aged 53 years and 22 days. Giuseppe Farina was next oldest when he won in Germany in 1953, at 46 years and 276 days.

⊙ DELIVERING UNDER PRESSURE

Qualifying has always been an exacting element of a grand prix meeting, and it takes many drivers years to learn how to squeeze the maximum from themselves and their cars without pushing just that little bit too hard. The mercurial Sebastian Vettel is the youngest ever pole sitter, being just 21 years and 72 days when he took first place on the grid at the 2008 Italian GP. Ferrari's Giuseppe Farina is the oldest pole sitter, aged 47 years and 79 days at the 1954 Argentinian GP.

⊙ FROM FRESH-FACED TO VETERAN

The inaugural winner of the World Championship in 1950, Giuseppe Farina, was just a couple of months short of his 44th birthday. Juan Manuel Fangio soon topped that, taking his final title in 1957 at 46 years and 41 days, making him the oldest driver ever to win the World Championship. At the other end of the scale, Lewis Hamilton lowered the title-winning age even further in 2008 when he was crowned at 23 years and 300 days. Then, just two years later, Sebastian Vettel reduced that to 23 years and 134 days when he triumphed for Red Bull Racing.

⊙ IF YOU'RE GOOD ENOUGH, YOU'RE READY

Nico Rosberg delighted his world champion father Keke on his grand prix debut for Williams at the 2006 Bahrain GP. He set the fastest lap and became the youngest driver ever to achieve this, at just 20 years and 258 days, beating Fernando Alonso's previous record by more than a year. The great Juan Manuel Fangio is the oldest, aged 46 years and 209 days, when he was swiftest in a Maserati in the 1958 Argentinian GP.

⊙ STILL A TEENAGER

Sebastian Vettel was still telling friends what he would like for his 20th birthday when he became the youngest driver ever to score a World Championship point at 19 years and 348 days. His achievement for BMW Sauber in the 2007 US GP came when he was 83 days younger than Jenson Button, the previous record holder. Philippe Etancelin is the oldest, at 53 years and 249 days, when he finished fifth in his Lago Talbot in the 1950 Italian GP.

⊙ DON'T THEY ALL LOOK YOUNG?

The youngest, most fresh-faced trio to appear on the podium was at the 2008 Italian GP when Sebastian Vettel, Heikki Kovalainen and Robert Kubica finished first, second and third respectively. The trio had an average age of just 23 years and 350 days.

10 YOUNGEST DRIVERS IN F1

	Name	Team	GP	Year	Age
1	Jaime Alguersuari	Toro Rosso	Hungarian	2009	19 years 125 days
2	Mike Thackwell	Tyrrell	Canadian	1980	19 years 182 days
3	Ricardo Rodriguez	Ferrari	Italian	1961	19 years 208 days
4	Fernando Alonso	Minardi	Australian	2001	19 years 218 days
5	Esteban Tuero	Minardi	Australian	1998	19 years 320 days
6	Chris Amon	Lola	Belgian	1963	19 years 324 days
7	Sebastian Vettel	BMW Sauber	US	2007	19 years 348 days
8	Jenson Button	Williams	Australian	2000	20 years 52 days
=	Eddie Cheever	Theodore	South African	1978	20 years 52 days
10	Tarso Marques	Minardi	Brazilian	1996	20 years 72 days

10 OLDEST DRIVERS IN F1

	Name	Team	GP	Year	Age
1	Eitel Cantoni	Maserati	Italian	1952	55 years 337 days
2	Louis Chiron	Lancia	Monaco	1955	55 years 292 days
3	Philippe Etancelin	Maserati	French	1952	55 years 190 days
4	Arthur Legat	Veritas	Belgian	1953	54 years 232 days
5	Luigi Fagioli	Alfa Romeo	French	1951	53 years 21 days
6	Adolf Brudes	Veritas	German	1952	52 years 292 days
7	Hans Stuck	AFM	Italian	1953	52 years 260 days
8	Bill Aston	Aston	German	1952	52 years 127 days
9	Clemente Biondetti	Ferrari	Italian	1950	52 years 15 days
10	Louis Rosier	Maserati	German	1956	50 years 273 days

⊙ FROM ANOTHER CENTURY

Apart from Luigi Fagioli, Louis Chiron is the only other driver over the age of 50 to step up on to the podium. He was aged 50 years and 289 days when he finished third for Maserati in his hometown of Monaco in 1950. Both drivers were born in the 19th century.

RACE STARTS

⊙ CHOPPING AND CHANGING

Jo Bonnier and Johnny Claes share the record for driving for the most teams in a World Championship season – four. Claes turned out for Gordini, Ecurie Belge, HWM and Vickomtesse de Walckiers in 1952. Bonnier raced for his own team, Giorgio Scarlatti's, Scuderia Centro Sud and BRM in 1958.

⊙ I'VE BEEN HERE BEFORE

Seven-time world champion Michael Schumacher has led no fewer than 141 grands prix for a minimum of one lap; this is far more than any other driver in F1 history. Ayrton Senna is next on the list, albeit way behind on 86 races led, and this is two more than the 84 achieved by his arch-rival and sometime teammate Alain Prost.

⊙ THE WRONG MOTTO

BAR was asking for trouble when the team was launched with the motto "A tradition of excellence". Firstly, it had no tradition. Secondly, its lead driver Jacques Villeneuve's run of retirements in the first 11 grands prix of the team's maiden season in 1999 set a record that is anything but excellent.

⊙ A FLYING START

Two drivers, Tiago Monteiro and Heikki Kovalainen, share the record for the most consecutive races finished from the first race of their F1 careers – 16 grands prix. Monteiro achieved it driving for Jordan in 2005, and Kovalainen repeated the feat as a member of the Renault team two years later.

⊙ STARTING AND FINISHING

Nick Heidfeld is often considered unremarkable as he has tended to operate under the radar, starting neither at the front nor the back of the grid, but usually in with the pack. The German, however, does own one remarkable record. From the 2007 Chinese GP until the 2009 Singapore GP, Heidfeld achieved 33 consecutive finishes. Heidfeld's exceptional run came to an end when his BMW Sauber was hit by Adrian Sutil and he was forced to retire.

⊙ A NATIONAL SPORT

British drivers have the most appearances in grands prix. In total, 143 have qualified and raced. The next most prodigious country in getting its drivers on to an F1 grid is Italy, with 84 drivers, then France with 67 and 47 from the USA.

⊙ MANY AND FEW

In 1952 a mind-boggling total of 75 drivers contested the seven grands prix that season. In 2008, just 22 drivers went head-to-head in 18 grands prix.

⊙ FIRST ON THE START LINE

British drivers have between them racked up a table-topping 3,393 grand prix starts since the World Championship began at Silverstone in 1950. Italy's drivers are next on the all-time starts list with 2,884.

⊙ 36 AND RISING

By the end of the 2010 Formula 1 World Championship, drivers from 36 nations have taken part since its inception in 1950. Over those 60 seasons, there have been drivers from all of the world's continents, apart from Antarctica.

⊙ PODIUMS, BUT NO WINS

Despite starting 174 F1 grands prix across 11 seasons, from 2000 to 2010, Nick Heidfeld has still to claim a grand prix victory. He did clock up another second place at the Malaysian GP at Sepang in 2009 to bring his tally of podium results to 12 without taking a win. The German driver also equalled the record for podiums without a win, set by Stefan Johansson between 1985 and 1989.

⊙ F1'S CENTURIONS

The first driver to contest 100 grands prix was Jack Brabham driving for his own team at the 1968 Dutch GP. The first to break the 200 grands prix barrier was Williams racer Ricardo Patrese at the British GP at Silverstone in 1990. In 2010, Rubens Barrichello duly became the first driver to contest 300 grands prix, achieving this at the Belgian GP.

⊙ BANG, SPLUTTER, PHUT!

So promising early in his career, it all started to go wrong for Ivan Capelli when he retired from the 1990 Italian GP. He retired his Leyton House from the next 15 grands prix, making this the longest run of retirements in F1 history.

◉ MAKING IT TO THE END

Nick Heidfeld's record run of 33 consecutive finishes includes all 18 grands prix in the 2008 season. However, he is matched in making 18 finishes in a single year by Portuguese driver Tiago Monteiro. Monteiro achieved this tally for Jordan in his rookie season in 2005, failing to finish only once, at the Brazilian GP, the 17th of that year's 19 races.

TOP 10 DRIVERS WITH MOST GP STARTS

1	Rubens Barrichello	306	6	Giancarlo Fisichella	231
2	Michael Schumacher	269	7	Gerhard Berger	210
3	Riccardo Patrese	256	8	Andrea de Cesaris	208
4	David Coulthard	247	9	Nelson Piquet	204
5	Jarno Trulli	238	10	Jean Alesi	201

◉ CLOSE, BUT NO CIGAR

Gabriele Tarquini holds the unenviable record of the most grand prix appearances that didn't result in a start. Forty times he turned up then failed to qualify. This was the price he paid for driving for uncompetitive teams such as Coloni and AGS in the late 1980s, when 39 cars fought for 26 grid spots and a pre-qualifying session was necessary to decide which were even worthy of a chance to qualify. Luckily, he qualified on 38 other occasions.

◉ HIGHEST WIN RATE

Juan Manuel Fangio won 24 times from 51 starts to give him a record win rate of 0.471. Second on the list is Alberto Ascari, who dominated for Ferrari in the early 1950s and ended up with a rate of 0.419 after winning 13 of his 31 races. Michael Schumacher's tally of 91 wins was spread across 269 grands prix, a strike rate of 0.338. Jim Clark ranks fourth and would certainly have ranked higher but for his Lotus often suffering from mechanical problems.

◉ NOT FOR WANT OF TRYING

Italian driver Andrea de Cesaris holds the record for the most grands prix contested without a win. In all, his F1 career stretched from 1980 (with Alfa Romeo) to 1994 (with Sauber), yet he did not produce one win from his 208 starts. His best results were a pair of second-place finishes in 1983.

⊙ WHAT'S A CHEQUERED FLAG?

From his 208 starts, Andrea de Cesaris failed to reach the finish of the race 137 times. There were certainly numerous mechanical failures when he raced for Alfa Romeo in the early 1980s, but he was equally responsible as there were many crashes too. Compatriot Riccardo Patrese clocked up 130 retirements from his 256 starts, but at least he scored six wins.

⊙ WELL, HE TRIED...

Claudio Langes seldom sported a smile in the paddock and his one and only campaign in F1, in 1990, gave him every reason to look forlorn. The Italian had stepped up from F3000 to drive for the EuroBrun Racing team. But the car was not up to scratch and he failed to pre-qualify for all 14 races he entered. And that was the end of his F1 career.

⊙ NEW SEASON, NEW TEAM

Chris Amon is described as the best driver never to win a grand prix. One look at his F1 career shows that he wasn't worried about changing teams to chase his dream, as he raced for 12: Reg Parnell Racing, Ian Raby Racing, Cooper, his own team, Ferrari, March, Matra, Tecno, Tyrrell, BRM, Ensign and Walter Wolf Racing. In total he drove 13 different makes of car. Andrea de Cesaris, Stefan Johansson, Stirling Moss and Maurice Trintignant raced 10.

⊙ HOW NOT TO DO IT

Andrea de Cesaris retired from all 16 grands prix in 1987 while racing for Brabham; a record for F1's hall of shame. He was actually running third in Monaco, but was stationary when the chequered flag fell, his car having run out of fuel; and he was in eighth place in the Adelaide season finale, but spun off with four laps to go.

⊙ MICHAEL LOVES FERRARI

Michael Schumacher made Ferrari a team to fear again in 1996 when he shook it by the scruff of its neck with the Scuderia CEO Jean Todt. Their success triggered the longest stay any driver has had with a team in F1 history and stretched to 201 starts before Schumacher retired at the end of 2006. It would have been six more had he not broken a leg at the 1999 British GP. David Coulthard has the next longest stay, racing 150 times for McLaren.

⊙ THE RISKIEST LAP

All the efforts exerted to develop a car through practice and then to qualify it as far up the grid as possible can come to naught on the opening lap, when the cars are racing at their closest. Take the 1978 Italian GP, the worst ever example of wastage, as 10 cars were eliminated before they had reached the first corner. Sadly, Lotus ace Ronnie Peterson died of his injuries.

⊙ TRY, TRY AND TRY AGAIN

While Nick Heidfeld of Germany holds the record for the most starts without a win by a driver (he had 174 before breaking his duck), Arrows hold the team record. Founded by Jackie Oliver in 1978, the British-based team took part in 383 grands prix without achieving a victory. Arrows ran out of money and bowed out of F1 with five races remaining in the 2002 season.

⊙ THAT'S HOW TO DO IT!

Jody Scheckter was enticed by Canadian industrialist Walter Wolf to join his new team, Wolf, for 1977. The move paid off immediately as Scheckter won the first race of the season in Argentina and went on to win two more. No team has made such an instant impact since. (Some might suggest Brawn GP in 2009, but this team was developed from Honda Racing, and did not start from scratch.)

TOP 10 TEAMS WITH MOST STARTS

1	Ferrari	812
2	McLaren	685
3	Williams	604
4	Lotus	509
5	Toro Rosso (née Minardi)	430
6	Tyrrell	418
7	Prost (née Ligier)	409
8	Brabham	394
9	Arrows	383
10	Force India (née Jordan – Midland – Spyker)	339

DRIVER RECORDS

⊙ THE DARKEST DAYS
Death was a regular feature of F1 in the early years, with driver safety scarcely considered in the 1950s. Six drivers died at the wheel in both 1957 and 1958, with five being killed in other events and one in F1 testing in 1957. In 1958, Luigi Musso died in the French GP, Peter Collins in the German GP and Stuart Lewis-Evans from burns received in the Moroccan GP, with three others being killed in non-F1 events.

⊙ THE MOST COSMOPOLITAN YEAR
The 1970s proved to be the decade when the most different nations had drivers competing in F1, with 18 countries being represented in 1978. They were: Argentina, Australia, Austria, Brazil, Canada, Finland, France, Germany, Great Britain, Holland, Ireland, Italy, Mexico, South Africa, Spain, Sweden, Switzerland and the USA.

⊙ NOT AHEAD WHEN IT COUNTED
Neither Jean Behra nor Chris Amon ever won a grand prix, but they both led races seven times. Nick Heidfeld equalled their record tally, but his situation is perhaps more easily explained as racing in the 21st century is peppered with pit stops and different race strategies mean that a driver can have a moment of glory before dropping out of the reckoning.

⊙ LET'S ALL TAKE TURNS
In the days before tyre and fuel pit stops, a driver leading the race really was leading the race, not just leading for a short period until the "two-stoppers" made their next pit call. In the light of this the 1971 Italian GP stands out as it holds the record for the number of race leaders on merit – eight. They were Clay Regazzoni, Ronnie Peterson, Jackie Stewart, François Cevert, Mike Hailwood, Jo Siffert, Chris Amon and winner, Peter Gethin.

◉ SHOWING WHO'S BOSS

Michael Schumacher's 2004 world title-winning campaign was one of dominance as he outscored his closest rival, teammate Rubens Barrichello, by 34 points. Such was his speed in his Ferrari that Schumacher led 16 of the year's 18 grands prix, totalling 683 laps (2,085 miles) in front, which equates to 61 per cent of all the laps. Nigel Mansell's swagger to the 1992 title came close, as he led 693 laps (2,043 miles).

◉ FEW FLAGS TO WAVE

The lowest number of different driver nationalities competing in a season was in 1954, 1966, 1999 and 2008, when just 10 were represented. This is less surprising in the latter years, as despite the fact that the sport is global, drivers tended to stay with their teams throughout the season rather than changing.

◉ THE LONG AND WINDING ROAD

Fernando Alonso set a new record in 2005 when he claimed his first world title. That season was 19 grands prix long, totalling a distance of 3,592 miles. Alonso and his Renault covered 3,312 of them. He then extended that in 2010 when there were again 19 grands prix but this time representing 3,601 miles in all, and he set a new record for distance covered, managing 3,564 miles. Had he not crashed at Spa, it would have been further still.

◉ HE LOOKS A LITTLE FAMILIAR

From the early 1990s to the mid-2000s, it felt odd if there wasn't one particular face grinning down from the podium – Michael Schumacher's. He was usually second or third if he didn't win and so made 154 podium appearances in his 250 starts. He was on the podium at all the races in 2002, completing a record run of 19 podium appearances that began at Indianapolis in 2001.

◉ FAMILY MATTERS

There are many familiar family names in F1. Brothers and fathers and sons have competed in F1, with Graham and Damon Hill the only father and son to have both become world champions. Other world champions – Mario Andretti, Jack Brabham, Nelson Piquet and Keke Rosberg – have had sons that have competed in F1, as did grand-prix winner Gilles Villeneuve. There have also been uncles and nephews and even brothers-in-law.

⊙ NO BROTHERLY LOVE

Quite a few brothers have competed in F1 at the same time, such as the Fittipaldis, the Scheckters, the Villeneuves and the less well-known Whiteheads. However, the Schumachers are the best known, with Michael taking 91 wins and Ralf six. Michael never cut Ralf any slack on track and was once accused of "trying to kill" him when he edged Ralf towards the wall.

⊙ YOU DON'T HAVE TO BE MALE

Only five female racers have entered World Championship grands prix, and only Lella Lombardi and Maria-Teresa de Filippis managed to qualify. Giovanna Amati, Divina Galica and Desire Wilson failed to make it on to the starting grid. Lombardi scored too, finishing sixth for March in the 1975 Spanish GP at Montjuich Park. The race was stopped after 29 laps (out of 75) because of a major accident.

⊙ CHOPPING AND CHANGING

The most lead changes in a grand prix came in one of the cut and thrust races at Monza, where drivers slipstreamed the car in front down the long straights then dived out to overtake. The record isn't from the classic 1971 encounter, in which the lead changed 25 times, but the race in 1965 when it changed a staggering 41 times, the last time when Jackie Stewart passed Graham Hill on the final lap to win.

TOP 10 DRIVERS WITH MOST LAPS IN LEAD

1	Michael Schumacher	5,108	6	Jackie Stewart	1,918
2	Ayrton Senna	2,931	7	Nelson Piquet	1,633
3	Alain Prost	2,683	8	Niki Lauda	1,590
4	Nigel Mansell	2,058	9	Mika Hakkinen	1,490
5	Jim Clark	1,940	10	Damon Hill	1,363

TOP 10 DRIVERS WITH MOST MILES IN LEAD

1	Michael Schumacher	14,992	6	Juan Manuel Fangio	5,789
2	Ayrton Senna	8,345	7	Jackie Stewart	5,692
3	Alain Prost	7,751	8	Nelson Piquet	4,820
4	Jim Clark	6,282	9	Mika Hakkinen	4,475
5	Nigel Mansell	5,905	10	Niki Lauda	4,386

CONSTRUCTORS

Alfa Romeo, Maserati, Vanwall, Cooper, BRM, Lotus, Tyrrell, Brabham, Benetton and Honda have all shone then disappeared. McLaren, Williams and Red Bull Racing are still in there competing. Yet, however the Formula One landscape changes, as it does continually, Ferrari continues to win grands prix and attracts unswerving support. It is the only team to have been racing since Formula One began.

TEAM WINS

⊙ FERRARI – TITLES AND MORE TITLES

The team with the most constructors' titles to its name is Ferrari. It has 16, compared with Williams's nine and McLaren's eight. Ferrari would have had a couple more, but the Constructors' Cup wasn't awarded until 1958, therefore its dominant seasons in 1952 and 1953 don't count.

⊙ McLAREN'S FIRST XI

McLaren holds the record for the most successive grand prix wins, with a run of 11 in the first 11 races of the 1988 season. Ayrton Senna and Alain Prost dominated, but they tripped up when Ferrari came good at the place that mattered most to them, Monza, with Gerhard Berger winning the Italian GP. McLaren closed the season by winning the final four races.

⊙ THE RISE AND FALL

Ferrari's position at the top of the all-time grand prix wins list is assured thanks to its longevity, but it hasn't been the most successful team in each of the six decades in which it has raced. Take the 1960s: Lotus led the way in technical innovation and scored 36 wins. Ferrari was second, but with a tally of only 13, just one ahead of both Brabham and BRM.

⊙ DECADE BY DECADE

If you add up team grand prix wins and look at them decade by decade the 1950s belonged to Ferrari with 29 wins, the 1960s to Lotus with 36 wins, the 1970s to Ferrari with 37 wins, the 1980s to McLaren with 56 wins, the 1990s to Williams with 61 wins and the 2000s to Ferrari with a huge 85 wins. Almost all of the 85 were achieved by Michael Schumacher as he raced to five drivers' titles.

⊙ HOME ADVANTAGE

Ferrari has scored the most wins at its home grand prix, its drivers winning the Italian GP 17 times between Alberto Ascari's win at Monza in 1951 and Fernando Alonso's in 2010. Ferrari has also won Italy's second race, the San Marino GP, eight times.

⊙ A HUNGRY WOLF

Walter Wolf had backed Williams in 1976, but he wanted his own team and set one up for the following year. What an impact his team made when the 1977 World Championship opened in Argentina. After front-row starters James Hunt and John Watson faltered, Jody Scheckter came through to take the only maiden team win in F1 history.

⊙ THE JOY OF SIX

It's debatable whether Brawn GP can be viewed as a new team in 2009, as it was effectively a continuation of Honda Racing after the Japanese manufacturer quit at the end of 2008. Even if it was more of a new team name rather than a new team, its six wins were the best haul from a team in its first season.

⊙ PERSEVERANCE PAYS OFF

Scuderia Toro Rosso hold the record for the most races contested by a team before scoring its first win. It started life in 1985 as Minardi and never looked likely to score points on a regular basis let alone have its drivers mount the podium or take a win. It took a change of ownership in 2007 and an injection of money into its coffers to turn its fortunes around. Sebastian Vettel did the rest, winning in the wet at Monza in 2008, the team's first victory out of 372 starts.

⊙ WINNING FOR YOUR COUNTRY

Looking at stats in terms of the nationality of the team, or the country out of which it operated, there can be no denying that Britain is the home of F1, with an "arc of excellence" around London from Cambridgeshire to Surrey in which the vast majority of the teams and suppliers are located. Even if the owners are not British, the majority of F1 teams have long been based in Britain. As a result of this, British-based teams had won 557 of the 839 grands prix held by the end of 2010, with Italy next, almost entirely down to Ferrari, on 235.

⊙ CLEAN SWEEPS AS RARE AS HENS' TEETH

Only two teams have achieved 100 per cent win rates across a season. Alfa Romeo was the first to achieve this, winning all six grands prix in the inaugural World Championship in 1950. Then, two years later, Ferrari matched its national rivals, who quit the World Championship after 1951, and won seven from seven. The closest any team has come since is when McLaren won 15 from 16 in 1988.

⊙ MANY WINS, NO PRIZE

As the Constructors' Championship wasn't started until 1958, Alfa Romeo goes down in the history books as the marque with the most grand prix wins without a title. It dominated the 1950 and 1951 seasons, taking 10 wins. Mercedes-Benz and Maserati, with nine wins apiece, were also short-changed in 1955 and 1957. Ligier also scored nine wins, but they were scattered across several seasons.

⊙ THE *TIFOSI'S* FAVOURITE

Michael Schumacher was admired rather than liked by the *Tifosi* when he joined Ferrari in 1996, but they soon warmed to him when he and the team started winning on a regular basis. He is by far the most successful Ferrari driver, having won 72 times for the Scuderia. The next most successful is Niki Lauda on 15, just ahead of another Ferrari double champion, Alberto Ascari, who took 13 wins.

TOP 10 TEAMS WITH MOST GRAND PRIX WINS

1	Ferrari	215	=	Renault	35
2	McLaren	169	7	Benetton	27
3	Williams	113	8	Tyrrell	23
4	Lotus	79	9	BRM	17
5	Brabham	35	10	Cooper	16

MOST WINS IN ONE SEASON

15	Ferrari	2002	10	Ferrari	2000
=	Ferrari	2004	=	McLaren	2005
=	McLaren	1988	=	McLaren	1989
12	McLaren	1984	=	Williams	1992
=	Williams	1996	=	Williams	1993
11	Benetton	1995			

TEAM POLE POSITIONS

⊙ FOR THE *TIFOSI*

It almost feels like a birthright that a Ferrari should take pole position in the Italian GP and the team has achieved this on 19 occasions, rising to the challenge even in years when its form has been patchy elsewhere. After Ferrari's qualifying glories at Monza, the next most pole positions set by a team at an individual circuit is shared by a trio of teams: Ferrari at the Nürburgring; McLaren at Hockenheim and Monaco; and Williams at Silverstone.

⊙ FROM POLE TO POLE

British or British-based teams dominate the records for pole positions, largely thanks to McLaren, Williams and Lotus, with an overall record of 542 poles split between 25 teams. The Italian teams are second on 227 (205 set by Ferrari), then the French teams are on 44 and the German teams on 11.

⊙ KEEP ON RUNNING

McLaren enjoyed glory years at the end of the 1980s. Had it not been for the Ferraris filling the front row at the 1988 British GP, the run of poles that started at the 1988 opener in Brazil would have stretched to 25 races before Ricardo Patrese put his Williams on pole position in Hungary in 1989. As it was, McLaren managed a 17-race streak.

⊙ ALL BUT PERFECT

The record for the most poles in a year is shared between McLaren and Williams. The "red and white fliers" grabbed 15 poles from 16 races in 1988 and then did precisely the same in 1989, courtesy of Ayrton Senna and Alain Prost. Williams achieved the same record in 1992 (principally as a result of Nigel Mansell's exploits) and 1993 (13 to Prost, two to Damon Hill).

⊙ FROM ZERO TO HERO

A number of teams have taken their first win without having previously achieved a pole position, including debutants Alfa Romeo in 1950, Mercedes in 1954 and Wolf in 1977, plus others who'd been racing a while, such as Cooper, Honda, Matra, McLaren and Porsche. Some teams, including BRM, Ferrari, Lotus, Toro Rosso, Vanwall and Williams, hit form and claimed their first pole and first win at the same race.

⊙ A DEAD HEAT

When Lewis Hamilton claimed pole position and then raced to victory at the 2010 Canadian GP, he moved McLaren one ahead of Ferrari at the top of the table for teams with the most pole/win doubles, claiming the British team's 37th double. Lotus remain ranked third in this category, largely due to the efforts of Ayrton Senna in 1986 when his car was fast but fragile.

⊙ INCREDIBLE TREBLE

Taking pole then winning is an achievement, but even more prestigious than that is adding the fastest lap to make it a treble. Ferrari has achieved this an incredible 82 times, with Michael Schumacher the main driving force. Williams is next up on 50, edging McLaren out by one. Lotus is ranked fourth on 26, with Renault fifth on 11.

⊙ McLAREN'S YEAR OF YEARS

McLaren had it all in 1988: its MP4/4 chassis was supreme; its Honda engine mighty; and in Alain Prost and Ayrton Senna it had the two best drivers. Between them, Prost and Senna took pole at every race except one, when Gerhard Berger took pole for Ferrari at the British GP. McLaren's record for the year was 15 poles from 16 grands prix, with Senna taking 13. McLaren repeated the feat in 1989 and Williams matched it in 1992 and 1993.

⊙ AND, AT LAST...

The most pole positions achieved by a team before its first victory is just three. Shadow was on pole three times in 1975 through Jean-Pierre Jarier (twice) and Tom Pryce. However, the first win, in fact the team's only win, came two years later when Alan Jones raced from 14th to first on a damp track in the Austrian GP.

⊙ THE MORE THE MERRIER

The record for the greatest number of different teams to achieve pole position in one season is six. The ever-increasing number of rounds favours teams competing in recent years over those who raced in the early 1950s when there were sometimes only seven races in a season, in addition to the fact that there were only a handful of competitive teams in the early years. So the record was first set in 1972, but then matched in 1976, 1981, 1985, 2005 and in 2009. In 2009 Brawn and Red Bull led the way in terms of the number of poles achieved, ahead of McLaren, Force India, Renault and Toyota.

TOP 10 TEAM POLES

1	Ferrari	205
2	McLaren	146
3	Williams	126
4	Lotus	107
5	Renault	51
6	Brabham	39
7	Red Bull Racing	21
8	Benetton	16
9	Tyrrell	14
10	Alfa Romeo	12

TEAM FASTEST LAPS

⊙ SPEED OVER RESULTS

Ferrari has set the most fastest laps of any team at any circuit, with 16 at Monaco, but it would gladly swap that record for McLaren's table-topping figure of 15 wins around the street circuit. McLaren's drivers, it seems, have kept the cooler heads and delivered what every team boss wants most, especially in front of friends and sponsors on the yachts in the harbour.

⊙ WHO'S FASTEST?

Since the 1960s most of the F1 teams have been British or based in Britain, so it's not surprising that their combined tally of 519 fastest laps exceeds the best that Italy (largely Ferrari) and other countries have managed. Italy's combined attack includes Ferrari, Alfa Romeo, Maserati and Lancia, with a total of 253.

⊙ FERRARI LEADS THE WAY

Ferrari has been racing in the World Championship since it began in 1950 and has been competitive in the vast majority of seasons. So it's no surprise that Ferrari tops the table as the team that has set or equalled the fastest lap at the most circuits, having done so at 50 of the 68 circuits used up to the end of 2010. McLaren is the next most successful in its spread of fastest laps, being top or equal top at 46.

⊙ FERRARI FLIES

Michael Schumacher was peerless in 2004, setting 10 fastest laps from 18 rounds. But Ferrari's number-two driver, Rubens Barrichello, was also able to reel off fastest laps in his F2004, helping the Italian team to a record 14 fastest laps in a season. This is one more than its 2008 line-up of Felipe Massa (3) and Kimi Räikkönen (10) managed.

⊙ FAVOURING AMERICA

With a need to sell road-going sports cars as well as its range of racing cars, Lotus boss Colin Chapman was always delighted that his F1 cars seemed to shine in North America. The team has the most or equal most fastest laps at Detroit, Riverside and, most importantly, Watkins Glen in New York State.

⊙ ALMOST IDENTICAL

Being in pole position is thought to have more bearing on whether a team wins than if it sets the fastest lap, but the correlation between the two can't be ignored. British or British-based teams had started from pole 542 times by the end of 2010 and set the fastest lap on 538 occasions. Italian teams have 254 fastest laps, with French teams next best on 31.

⊙ A BRITISH BONANZA

Italian teams started F1 with a bang, with Alfa Romeo, Ferrari or Maserati setting the fastest lap at each of the first 30 grands prix. However, this is no longer the record for the most successive fastest laps set by teams from one country. It was finally bettered between 1991 and 1995 when British teams Williams, McLaren, Benetton and Jordan set fastest laps for an incredible 62 races in a row.

⊙ STRONG ON THE DAY

A host of teams have had drivers who have been qualifying experts – such as Ayrton Senna, who took 65 poles from his 161 starts, but unless the car is resilient enough to last the race this speed does not necessarily translate into a race win. Across the first 61 years of F1, Ferrari holds the record for the most win/fastest lap doubles, at 52. McLaren is the next most successful team at this, with 35, and Williams is in third place, having achieved it on 22 occasions.

⊙ RENAULT'S GLORY DAYS

Renault struggled when it arrived in the World Championship midway through 1977. The team had F1's first turbocharged engine, and while power wasn't a problem, reliability was. However, within two years the team's yellow and black cars were flying. Jean-Pierre Jabouille took the marque's first win at Dijon-Prenois and René Arnoux set the race's fastest lap. Renault again bagged the fastest lap on its return visit to the circuit in 1981.

TOP 10 TEAMS WITH THE MOST FASTEST LAPS

1	Ferrari	223	6	Benetton	35
2	McLaren	143	7	Renault	31
3	Williams	130	8	Tyrrell	20
4	Lotus	71	9	BRM	15
5	Brabham	40	=	Maserati	15

TEAM POINTS

⊙ RAKING THEM IN

The change of the World Championship points system – awarding points from first place to 10th from 2010, with 25 for a win whereas it had previously been 10 – meant that Red Bull Racing achieved a new record tally when Sebastian Vettel raced to the title and teammate Mark Webber backed him up by being ranked third for a joint tally of 498 points. This worked out at an average of 26.21 points at each of the campaign's 19 grands prix.

⊙ ONE AND TWO

F1's most successful teams aren't always at the top, but they all have periods when they manage to have the best chassis, the best engine, the best tyres and the best drivers at the same time; then the one-two finishes flow. McLaren exemplified this when Ayrton Senna and Alain Prost dominated in 1988 and they scored 10 one-twos that year alone, with Senna in front in seven of them.

⊙ POINTS ALL THE WAY

Several teams have scored points in every grand prix of the year. This was easier to do in the 1950s when there were fewer teams and fewer grands prix. The most recent teams to achieve this was Brawn GP, which managed to score in each of the 17 races of its maiden season in 2009, and then McLaren in 2010 when either Lewis Hamilton or Jenson Button proved effective in all of the 19 grands prix.

⊙ CLOSEST TO PERFECTION

The scoring system has changed five times since the World Championship began in 1950* but, even taking this into account, Alfa Romeo achieved the highest points average ever in that inaugural season, as its drivers finished first and second in every race except two. This gave the Italian marque a points score of 90.476 per cent of the maximum. In recent years, McLaren's 1988 tally is the best, with an 82.917 per cent hit rate, edging out Ferrari in 2002 (81.250 per cent) and 2004 (80.864 per cent).

Points from 1950–57 counted only towards the drivers' tally, but have been added here for comparative purposes.

⊙ BY THE THOUSANDS

British and British-based teams lead the way in points accrued, with their combined tally being 14,729.5 at the end of the 2010 World Championship. Italian teams rank second, on 4,673.5 points, with French teams on 777 and Swiss-based Sauber and BMW Sauber accumulating 547 points between them.

⊙ SCORING AT HOME

Not only because of its speed and success, but also its longevity, Ferrari is the team that has scored the most points at its home race. From 1958, the first year of the Constructors' Cup, to 2010, Ferrari collected 354 points from the Italian GP at Monza. Ferrari's record in Italy's second race, the San Marino GP that ran from 1981 to 2006, is not as strong, although it did record eight victories.

⊙ SO LITTLE REWARD

You could never criticize Minardi for its effort, but a lack of finance left it struggling to be competitive. The team's record of 38 points from 340 starts is poor, equal to a return of 0.112 points per race. Still, that is impressive compared to both the Zakspeed, which accumulated just two points in 53 starts (0.0377), and Osella, five points from 132 (0.0379). Needless to say, none of the teams managed a single podium finish.

⊙ COMING GOOD IN THE END

Red Bull Racing took over a record in 2010 that had long been held by the Benetton team. This was for scoring the most points before landing its first constructors' title. Benetton had had 663.5 to its name across 15 campaigns when it landed its first title in 1995. Red Bull Racing had scored 813.5 points when it wrapped up the 2010 constructors' crown a round early at Interlagos.

⊙ MAXIMUM POINTS HAULS

The best way for a team to rack up points is obviously to have its cars finish first and second, and Ferrari is the most successful team at this, having achieved it 78 times, starting all the way back at the Italian GP in 1951. McLaren, the next most successful team in taking one-two results, with 47, didn't score its first one until 17 years later in Belgium when Denny Hulme led home team owner Bruce McLaren.

⦿ LOOKING DOWN FROM ABOVE

Ferrari holds the record for the most consecutive top-three finishes which, largely thanks to the might of Michael Schumacher, resulted in podium finishes at an incredible 53 straight grands prix between the 1999 Malaysian GP and the final grand prix of 2002 in Japan. The team kept the stream of points flowing into 2003, but only for the next two grands prix. Disaster struck in the third race of the season at Interlagos when Ferrari went home empty-handed as both Michael Schumacher (crashed) and Rubens Barrichello (fuel shortage) retired. They bounced back to finish first and third next time out.

⦿ SOMETHING FOR ALMOST EVERYONE

In 1989 16 different teams scored points in the World Championship, the most ever. This statistic is even more remarkable when you note that points were awarded down to only sixth rather than eighth place, as was the situation from 2003. The scoring teams were, in points order: McLaren, Williams, Ferrari, Benetton, Tyrrell, Lotus, Arrows, Dallara, Brabham, Onyx, Minardi, March, Rial, Ligier, AGS and Lola. Only the Coloni, EuroBrun, Osella and Zakspeed teams failed to score.

TOP 10 TEAMS WITH MOST POINTS

1	Ferrari	4,473.5	6	Benetton	877.5
2	McLaren	3,816.5	7	Brabham	854
3	Williams	2,675	8	Red Bull Racing (née Stewart)	842.5
4	Lotus	1,352	9	Mercedes (née BAR)	710
5	Renault	1,309	10	Tyrrell	617

TOP 10 TEAMS WITH MOST ONE-TWO FINISHES

1	Ferrari	78	=	Red Bull Racing	7
2	McLaren	47	8	BRM	5
3	Williams	32	=	Mercedes	5
4	Brabham	8	10	Alfa Romeo	4
=	Tyrrell	8	=	Brawn	4
6	Lotus	7			

TEAM TITLES

⊙ FORZA FERRARI

Ferrari's head start in the 1950s and its incredibly strong run of success from 2000 onwards – with Michael Schumacher leading the way – ensure that the Italian team has more constructors' titles than any other, with 16 to Williams's nine and McLaren's eight. Had the constructors' title been awarded before 1958, it would be closer to 20.

⊙ GLORY IS HARD TO COME BY

British or British-based teams rule in terms of race wins, with 557 to Italy's 235. In fact, such is the centralization of expertise that teams based in only six countries have won a grand prix. France's Renault (in its first iteration), Ligier and Matra help the country rank third on 33, while Mercedes won 10 for Germany. At the foot of the table on one win apiece are the Netherlands, home of the Honda team from 1964–66, and Switzerland, with BMW Sauber's one and only win coming at Montreal in 2008.

⊙ FERRARI'S FLOP

There's no doubt that the worst follow-up season by a champion team was that of the inaugural constructors' champions, Vanwall, as they scaled down their involvement to almost nothing due to patron Tony Vandervell's ill health. However, of those who returned to defend their titles, Ferrari has had the worst time, scoring just eight points in 1980. As there was no driver change, 1979 world champion Jody Scheckter and Gilles Villeneuve staying on, the blame fell on the car.

⊙ CROWNS FOR COUNTRIES

British or British-based teams hold sway in terms of the most constructors' titles won, with their combined forces achieving 37 titles, largely thanks to Williams and McLaren, to Italy's 16. France, the country that hosted the first road races starting in 1894, and the first grand prix in 1906, has three titles (one from Matra and two from Renault), but its claims to titles are debatable as in each case the teams were run out of Great Britain.

⊙ TAKE THAT

Ferrari had its most dominant seasons when Michael Schumacher was leading the driver line-up. In 2004, he and Rubens Barrichello guided the team to a winning margin of 143 points in the Constructors' Championship over BAR's Jenson Button and Takuma Sato. McLaren's Ayrton Senna and Alain Prost achieved the second-largest title-winning margin, when their 15 wins from 16 starts in 1988 meant that the team was 134 points clear of Ferrari.

⊙ GETTING BY, JUST

The team that has won the Constructors' Championship with the fewest grand prix wins is Ferrari, with just three wins proving sufficient both in 1964 and in 1982. The latter of these two championships was won in the most extraordinary year for the drivers' title. Keke Rosberg of Williams was crowned the world champion with just one win to his name, in the 14th of the year's 16 grands prix.

⊙ A SIGN OF EXCELLENCE

To wrap up the constructors' title before the final round is always the sign of a team in control and 11 teams have managed this since the Constructors' Championship began in 1958. They are: Benetton, Brabham (two), Brawn, Cooper (two), Ferrari (nine), Lotus (five), McLaren (four), Red Bull Racing, Tyrrell, Vanwall and Williams (eight).

⊙ SAVING IT FOR THE FINALE

There have been 43 Constructors' Championships since the first one in 1958 and the title has been decided at the final round on 17 occasions, most recently when Ferrari beat McLaren to the title in 2008. In years of clear dominance, the title has been won before summer is out.

⊙ NEVER AT HOME

Despite the Italian GP taking place towards the end of the F1 racing calendar, not once has the *Tifosi* seen Ferrari claim the constructors' title on home ground, even in the years of Michael Schumacher's dominance. However, in two of those years – 2002 and 2004 – Ferrari had already won the title before heading for Monza, wrapping it up several rounds earlier at the Hungarian GP.

⊙ SQUEAKING HOME

The narrowest title-winning margin is just three points, which was the result back in 1964 when Ferrari edged out BRM thanks to John Surtees and Lorenzo Bandini getting the better of the British team's Graham Hill and Richie Ginther. However, that season was contested across only 10 rounds, making Ferrari's victory over McLaren by four points after 16 grands prix in 1999 statistically closer.

⊙ ECONOMIES OF SCALE

The teams that won the constructors' titles in the early years have the best record in terms of having the fewest race starts to their name before landing the title. The first constructors' champions, Vanwall, had made a total of just 27 starts when it took the 1958 title, only to be trumped by Cooper in 1959, who became champions with just 25 starts.

MOST CONSTRUCTORS' TITLES

1	Ferrari	16
2	Williams	9
3	McLaren	8
4	Lotus	7
5	Brabham	2
=	Cooper	2
=	Renault	2
8	Benetton	1
=	Brawn GP	1
=	BRM	1
=	Matra	1
=	Red Bull Racing	1
=	Tyrrell	1
=	Vanwall	1

PARTICIPATION

⊙ I'LL START, SO I'LL FINISH

Someone always retires, well, except in three of the 820 grands prix held between 1950 and the end of 2009. At the 1961 Dutch GP, all 15 starters finished. Then every car on the starting grid finished the 2005 US GP, but that was just six, as the other 14 had pulled off after the formation lap protesting over tyre safety. However, all 20 starters finished at Monza later that year, showing just how much car reliability has improved.

⊙ YOUR NAME ON THE NOSE

Winning is wonderful, and a handful of drivers have sought to do it in a car bearing their name. Most successful by far is Jack Brabham, who won seven grands prix in 1966 and landed both the drivers' and constructors' titles. His former teammate Bruce McLaren founded a successful dynasty, although it flourished mainly after his death in 1970.

⊙ WHY MOVE WHEN YOU'RE WINNING?

Michael Schumacher turned Ferrari back into a winning machine and so saw no reason to move elsewhere. He landed 72 of his 91 grand prix wins and five of his seven world titles while driving for the Italian team, before retiring from racing after a record 162 grand prix for the team from Maranello. David Coulthard is the next most long-staying driver, clocking up 150 races for McLaren.

⊙ KEEP IT SHORT

Which is the most successful team if you pit wins against starts: Ferrari or McLaren? Answer: Mercedes when it raced in F1 for the first time in 1954–55. The German team arrived with a competitive car, raced for a season and a half, and left with a strike rate of 0.75 after winning nine times in 12 starts. Add in its 2010 rebirth, though, and that falls to 0.290. Had Alfa Romeo not returned in 1979, its 1950–51 strike rate would have been 0.769. For the record, long-serving multiple winners Ferrari and McLaren have strike rates of 0.265 and 0.246 respectively.

⊙ STICKING TOGETHER

David Coulthard and Mika Hakkinen raced together more times than any other teammates in the history of F1, totalling 99 grands prix as a duo. They had a six-year stretch together at McLaren between 1996 and 2001 before Hakkinen took what he'd planned to be a sabbatical, which by mid-2002 had become full retirement from F1.

⊙ WHICH MICHAEL SCHUMACHER?

The crash-strewn 1996 Monaco GP was confusing enough, but it was all the more puzzling to those spectators who weren't listening to the commentary as there appeared to be two Michael Schumachers in the race, one driving for Ferrari, the other for McLaren. This was because David Coulthard's own helmet was misting up in the rain, so he borrowed one of Michael's spares.

⊙ TO FINISH FIRST, FIRST YOU MUST FINISH

The 1996 Monaco GP was an odd one. The Minardis took each other out before the first corner; Michael Schumacher took himself out further around the lap; and Rubens Barrichello spun out in his Jordan before the lap was over. At the end of it all, Olivier Panis scored his one and only win, for Ligier, and there were just four classified finishers, only three of which were still running at flag-fall. No race has come close to being as destructive.

⊙ ROLL UP, ROLL UP

The desire to race in F1 in the 1950s was incredible. A staggering 76 different drivers turned up across the seven rounds in 1952, with 73 reporting for action in 1953, and neither of these tallies includes the drivers who raced in the Indy 500 that was a round of the World Championship but had no crossover. Ironically, F1 teams and drivers only started competing at Indianapolis after it was dropped from the World Championship.

⊙ FAMILY HONOUR, CAREER SUICIDE

Emerson Fittipaldi was a two-time world champion by 1974. In 1975, his brother Wilson set up an F1 team. Despite the fact that the team was struggling, Emerson felt the pull of family ties and left McLaren to join his brother for the 1976 season. He persevered too, and stayed for 84 grands prix before quitting, with a best result of second in the 1978 Brazilian GP.

TEAMS THAT HAVE LED MOST LAPS

1	Ferrari	13,247
2	McLaren	9,966
3	Williams	7,497
4	Lotus	5,498
5	Brabham	2,717

TEAMS THAT HAVE LED MOST MILES

1	Ferrari	42,888
2	McLaren	29,331
3	Williams	21,622
4	Lotus	16,263
5	Tyrrell	4,186

⊙ POINTS, BUT NO PRIZES

The Arrows team is no more, but at least it will never extend its record of being the team with the most grand prix starts without winning a grand prix – 382. It came close twice. Riccardo Patrese was leading until 15 laps before the end of the team's third race, in South Africa in 1978, before the engine failed and Damon Hill led the 1997 Hungarian GP until a lap before the finish when Jacques Villeneuve swept past to win and Hill came second.

TEAM PRINCIPALS

⊙ PASSION HIDDEN BEHIND DARK GLASSES

Enzo Ferrari was drawn to the sport by a desire to compete. In the 1930s, he was put in charge of Alfa Romeo's racing activities. Fired in 1939, Enzo started building his own cars after the Second World War. His team's first World Championship win came at the 1951 British GP and the legend grew from there. Enzo was famously unemotional about his cars, which were broken up after they were superseded. He remained enigmatic in the extreme, and by the end of his career would no longer watch races at the track.

⊙A SHARP BRAIN AND A STERN LOOK

Alfred Neubauer was the man who made the Mercedes team tick during its one-and-a-half-year stint in F1 in the mid-1950s. He joined Mercedes as a racing driver in 1923, but he quit after a teammate was killed at the 1924 Italian GP and turned to team management. He guided the "Silver Arrows" through their glory years of the late 1920s and 1930s. Portly, never without a jacket and tie, and usually with a serious expression, he was still at the helm after the Second World War and he encouraged the team back into racing in 1954 when it set new standards.

⊙ A RESTLESS, DRIVEN GENIUS

Colin Chapman probably shaped F1 more than any other team principal through his restless quest to find an engineering advantage. In 1962 his Lotus team was the first to use a monocoque chassis, and Jim Clark started to win. He made ground effects work for the 1978 season and Mario Andretti duly did the same. He tried to introduce a double chassis, but it was banned, infuriating this effervescent character. He died of a heart attack in 1988, leaving memories of a man dressed in black hurling his cap in the air when his drivers won.

⊙ A DRIVEN MAN

Guy Ligier's first love was rugby and he was a top-class player, but he had an even greater drive to become rich, and he achieved this by building up a successful construction firm. This financed forays into motorcycle racing before Guy tried cars, moving into sports cars before driving in F1 in 1966. His best result was sixth in Germany in 1967. After retiring from driving he turned to building racing sports cars and, in 1976, an F1 car. The team won nine times. Guy sold up in 1992.

⊙ TIMBER MERCHANT TURNED CHAMPION CHIEF

Ken Tyrrell was a racing driver, financed by his family's timber business. Following the end of his driving career he ran the Cooper Formula Junior team in 1960, and advanced, with Jackie Stewart, to F2 in 1965. They switched to a Matra chassis for F2 and Ken moved into F1 with his own team in 1968, running a Matra-Ford for Stewart. They won races and improved to win the 1969 title. The first Tyrrell car appeared in 1970, and Stewart won titles in 1971 and 1973, but the team struggled financially after sponsor Elf quit, being taken over by BAR in 1998. Ken died of cancer in 2001.

⊙ CAPTAIN AMERICA

Roger Penske started racing when at university and was competitive enough to enter the US GP in 1961 and 1962, ranking eighth at his first attempt. However, his skills as a businessman soon became more apparent as he built up a chain of car dealerships that is now the second largest in the USA. He also set up a team and ran Mark Donohue to success in TransAm in 1968 before branching into single-seaters. This was mainly in IndyCars, but he tried F1 from 1974–77 and took one win, with John Watson, at the Österreichring in 1976.

⊙ ONE BIG TEDDY BEAR

Lord Hesketh made quite a splash in F1 in the mid-1970s when he rolled in with a plain white car daubed with patriotic red and blue stripes and a teddy bear on the nose. There was no sponsorship to be seen. "The Good Lord", as driver James Hunt called him, was bankrolling his foray into F1 from his considerable inheritance. They raced a March in 1974, but soon built their own car, and had their day of days when Hunt won the Dutch GP at Zandvoort in 1975, then Hesketh sold the team and moved into politics, leaving F1 all the poorer without his flamboyance.

⊙ FERRARI'S FIERCE LITTLE NAPOLEON

Jean Todt was a successful rally co-driver through the 1970s before being given his break in management in 1982 when he was asked to set up Peugeot Talbot Sport. Wins and world titles soon followed through Ari Vatanen, before Peugeot sought success in sports car racing, and got it in 1992. After Peugeot declined to enter F1, Todt joined Ferrari in 1993 and stabilized the team, making it more clinical in its approach. The team won its first constructors' title under Todt's leadership in 1999 and then, in conjunction with Michael Schumacher, won title after title from 2000 until 2004. Todt became FIA president in 2009, replacing Max Mosley.

⊙ FRANCE'S FIXER

Gerard Larrousse came to prominence in rallying, then turned to racing in 1966 and made his name by finishing second in the 1969 Le Mans 24 Hours. He went on to win this race in 1973 and 1974 for Matra. He then set up an F2 team and Jean-Pierre Jabouille won the 1976 crown, after which Gerard became Renault's competitions manager, managing its entry into F1 in 1977. After Renault closed in 1985, he set up his own F1 team for 1987, running Lola chassis. The team's best result was a third place in Japan in 1990 but it folded at the end of 1994.

⊙ McLAREN'S METICULOUS MAN

Ron Dennis started as a race mechanic with Cooper. He moved to Brabham in 1968, before starting a team, Rondel, with Neil Trundle in 1972. They were successful in F2 and built an F1 car that they had to sell when their sponsor pulled out. Back in F2, Ron gained management experience and, with backing from Marlboro, he returned to F1 in 1981, taking over McLaren. Through his legendary attention to detail he turned it into the second most successful team in F1 history. In 2009 he took a step back from F1 to concentrate on the rest of the McLaren Group business.

⊙ A TECHNICAL AND TACTICAL BRAIN

Ross Brawn joined March from the atomic industry. From there, he moved to Williams and learnt to be an aerodynamicist. After spells at Beatrice and Arrows, Ross designed Jaguar's sports cars then went back to F1 to join Benetton. It was at Benetton that he started working with Michael Schumacher, displaying his tactical as well as his technical skills. The pair moved to Ferrari and claimed five more titles before Ross took a sabbatical. He came back with Honda, which, of course, became Brawn GP. The team with his name took both the drivers' and constructors' titles in 2009 before being renamed as Mercedes GP for 2010.

⊙ MID-ENGINES TO MINIS

John Cooper's father Charles got him interested in racing and they started building small chassis powered by motorbike engines after the Second World War. Stirling Moss gave Cooper its first F1 win in 1958 and Jack Brabham claimed the next two drivers' and constructors' titles for the team before Lotus stole its thunder. John took over the running of the team in 1964 after his father died, but was then injured in a car crash and decided to sell the company, moving on to create the high-performance Mini Cooper. John died in 2000.

⊙ DRIVEN BY PATRIOTIC FERVOUR

A racer first and foremost, up to F3 level, Frank Williams never had the money to go any higher and turned to running cars for others, most notably for Piers Courage in 1969 and 1970, until Courage died at the Dutch GP. Some lean years followed as Frank fought on in F1, always short of money. In 1977 he formed Williams Grand Prix Engineering with Patrick Head. It developed into F1's third most successful team, winning nine constructors' titles, despite the setback of Frank being paralysed in a car crash in 1986.

⊙ FROM RACER TO PRESIDENT

Max Mosley has spent his life being referred to as the son of fascist politician Sir Oswald Mosley, precluding any dreams of a political career. Instead, Max tried racing, reaching F2 before becoming one of the founder members of March in 1969. He quit March in 1977 and moved into helping the teams form a united front through the Formula One Constructors' Association (FOCA), working with Bernie Ecclestone. He then became president of the Fédération Internationale de l'Automobile (FIA) in 1986, and held the position until late 2009 when he stood down and was replaced by the newly elected Jean Todt.

⊙ AN INDUSTRIALIST DEMANDING SUCCESS

Sir Alfred Owen inherited the family's industrial empire on his father's death. He was only 21, but continued its expansion across the globe. Disappointed by the BRM team's floundering attempts to put Britain on the map in F1, he bought it in 1952, running it under the Owen Racing Organization banner. After a weak 1961 campaign he demanded success in 1962 or he would close the team. It responded and won the constructors' and drivers' title, but he tired of its form after that and gave the team to his sister, to be run by her husband, Louis Stanley.

⊙ THE ULTIMATE ENTREPRENEUR

Bernie Ecclestone made his first fortune selling motorbike parts. A club-level car racer, Bernie was busier away from the tracks, establishing a multi-pronged business empire. He bought the Connaught F1 team in 1958 and even tried to qualify a car himself at Monaco. His attempt was unsuccessful so he settled for driver management. After the death of his charge Jochen Rindt in 1970, he bought Brabham in 1972 and ran that until he sold it in 1987. But it's his role as the F1 rights holder through his Formula One Management company that has given him both power and considerable wealth.

◉ FLAMBOYANT BUT FLAWED

Flavio Briatore had no love of racing, but became involved through the Benetton family after he'd headed up its clothing chain's push into the USA. He was asked to be commercial director of their team in 1988 and brought in Tom Walkinshaw to help run it. Signing Michael Schumacher was the key to success and titles followed in 1994 (drivers') and 1995 (drivers' and constructors'). He has since been involved with supplying teams with Renault engines and then ran Renault's F1 return until he was banned from the sport in 2009 for his role in "Singaporegate", the race-fixing scandal that arose as a result of the 2008 Singapore GP.

◉ THE FACE OF FERRARI

Aristocrat Luca di Montezemolo was a rally driver, but quit to pursue a business career, as every Agnelli family member was expected to do. His family firm – Fiat – snapped up Ferrari in 1969 and he became Enzo Ferrari's right-hand man in 1973. By 1974, he was running Ferrari's F1 team and titles followed quickly from 1975. By 1977, he was in charge of the entire Fiat group. He ran Italy's hosting of the 1990 FIFA World Cup before taking over Ferrari in 1991 and, recently, he became head of the teams' governing body, Formula One Teams' Association (FOTA).

◉ LOOKING FOR THE DEAL

Eddie Jordan is one of motor sport's great wheeler-dealers. He raced, up to F2 level, but turned to running cars for others, with Eddie Jordan Racing becoming a key player in British F3 in the 1980s. The team stepped up to F3000 and took Jean Alesi to the 1989 title. However, F1 was the dream of this fast-talking Irishman and Jordan's team made an instant impact on its arrival in 1991. Eddie had to keep doing deals to sustain the team, revelled in its first win in 1998 and then sold the team in 2005. He is now a TV pundit.

◉ A MODEL PROFESSIONAL

Jackie Stewart achieved far more in F1 than winning 27 grands prix and three World Championships. He pushed for driver safety when it was far from fashionable to do so, his efforts no doubt saving many lives. He also sought a more professional level than his contemporaries and, after a spell commentating for American TV, returned to F1 as a team owner in 1997, in conjunction with older son Paul. Stewart GP won once, at the Nürburgring in 1999, but was sold on to Ford, who rebranded it as Jaguar Racing and it later became Red Bull Racing.

TYRE MANUFACTURERS

⊙ MADE TO LAST

Goodyear holds the record as the tyre company with the longest association with F1. It started its involvement in 1959 and was involved until the end of the 1998 season, in which time its tyres had been used in just short of 500 grands prix. Bridgestone edged past Michelin during the 2009 season, to become the second most used tyre, at 244 grands prix to Michelin's 215 by the end of 2010, with both overhauling Pirelli, which stopped its involvement in F1 in 1991 after 200 starts.

⊙ GOODYEAR'S BREAKTHROUGH

F1's most successful tyre supplier, Goodyear, had no clue to what lay ahead when it did a deal with Honda in 1965 and driver Richie Ginther guided the combination to its first win in the last round of the World Championship in Mexico City. No one then would have predicted that this famous American tyre manufacturer would go on to become F1's leading supplier, achieving a further 367 wins.

⊙ HANDLING THE PRESSURE

There can be no doubt that considerably more is asked of F1 tyres than those fitted to a road car. They have to handle as much as a ton of downforce and, more tellingly, lateral forces of up to 4Gs during cornering. There is even greater pressure on them longitudinally (front to back) during acceleration and under braking. Small wonder the teams are happy that they are allowed to change them during the races.

⊙ YET ANOTHER GOOD YEAR

Cars fitted with Goodyear tyres have started more grands prix than those fitted with any other tyre brand by a factor of two. Goodyear-shod cars have claimed 24 titles between 1966 and 1997, which is also more than twice the tally of its closest rival, Bridgestone, which has 10 titles.

⊙ IN THE BLACK CORNER

The most tyre manufacturers to go head-to-head in a World Championship season is six. This happened in 1958 when Avon, Continental, Dunlop, Englebert, Firestone and Pirelli all sought glory. Dunlop took the most wins.

⊙ FORMULA FARCE

The 2005 US GP at Indianapolis remains the biggest farce in F1 history. Following tyre failure on Ralf Schumacher's Toyota as it went through Turn 13, the only high-speed banked turn on an F1 circuit, during Friday practice, Michelin declared that it couldn't guarantee the safety of the identical tyres that it was supplying for BAR, McLaren, Red Bull, Renault, Sauber and Williams. So, the 14 cars on Michelin tyres peeled into the pits after the formation lap and refused to start, leaving just the six Bridgestone-tyred cars to race.

⊙ THERE'S A PATTERN

If you look at the records for the number of starts, pole positions, fastest laps and wins, the order is the same in each. Goodyear is top, usually by a factor of roughly two and a half, which equates to its proportional number of starts, followed by Bridgestone and Michelin. Pirelli has the fourth most starts, but Dunlop was more successful by ranking fourth for wins, poles and fastest laps, with Firestone demoting Pirelli to sixth in poles and fastest laps.

TYRE MANUFACTURER WITH MOST POLE POSITIONS		
1	Goodyear	358
2	Bridgestone	168
3	Michelin	111
4	Dunlop	76
5	Firestone	49
6	Pirelli	46
7	Englebert	12
8	Continental	8

TYRE MANUFACTURER WITH MOST WINS		
1	Goodyear	368
2	Bridgestone	175
3	Michelin	102
4	Dunlop	83
5	Pirelli	44
6	Firestone	38
7	Continental	10
8	Englebert	8

⊙ MAKING HAY

There have been several spells in F1 history when there has been just one tyre supplier, and this is obviously when the companies such as Goodyear and Bridgestone have made hay, boosting their tallies of wins, poles, fastest laps and points scored. Impressively, considering its strong record, Michelin has never been the sole supplier.

⊙ THEY SHOOT, THEY SCORE

By sheer weight of numbers, Goodyear scored more World Championship points than any other tyre manufacturer, its tally standing at 9,474.5 when it packed up its tyre trucks for the final time after the 1998 Japanese GP, two races after Michael Schumacher gave the American company its final F1 win at Monza. That tally represents just over 19 points for each grand prix that it attended. Don't forget, this would have been higher still had the current 10-8-6-5-4-3-2-1 system been in operation in those years when usually only the top six scored.

⊙ SOME MORE NEW TYRES PLEASE

The record number of pit stops made in a single grand prix is an almost unbelievable 75, for the 22 cars contesting the European GP at the Nürburgring in 2007. With weather conditions changing almost by the lap, the teams just didn't know what sort of tyres to fit. Fernando Alonso guessed best and won for McLaren after making four pit visits, which was two fewer than three of his rivals.

ENGINE MANUFACTURERS

⊙ STRAIGHT EIGHT OR IN A VEE?

When F1 began in 1950, the dominant Alfa Romeos were powered by supercharged straight-eight engines, with their rivals using straight-six or even four-cylinder engines. Since then the V8 engine has been most successful, with 314 grand prix wins, and the more recently popular V10 next on 240.

⊙ GO, GO, GO!

Believe it or not, F1 cars are not the quickest racing cars in the acceleration stakes, as their exposed wheels make them less aerodynamically efficient than larger-engined competition sports-prototype cars with their enclosing bodywork. However, they still hit 100mph from a standstill in around four seconds and keep on accelerating to 200mph and beyond.

⊙ MORE THAN JUST A BADGE

Some road cars bore the legend "turbo" on their boot lids, but the engine performance wasn't vastly different. Not so in F1, after Renault's pioneering years in the late 1970s. As more and more horsepower was produced by these engines, the arbitrary 1.5-litre equivalency allowed against the 3.0-litre normally aspirated engines soon gave the turbo teams a big advantage and they won race after race.

⊙ THE MOST BANGS FOR YOUR BUCK

F1 technical regulations have changed constantly since the World Championship began in 1950 and the most recent engines are not the most powerful. That honour goes to the turbocharged engines when their boost was wound up for qualifying for a burst of one lap. The BMW turbo used by Benetton racers Gerhard Berger and Teo Fabi in 1986 is estimated to have pushed out 1400bhp, rather than the 900bhp without the boost cranked up.

⊙ STOP NOW!

The acceleration capability of a contemporary F1 car is phenomenal, therefore the braking performance has to be sensational too. It's hard to equate it to a normal road car's braking, but imagine travelling at 200mph as a tight corner approaches. An F1 car can slow to 50mph in just three seconds, which equates to 109 yards.

⊙ FERRARI LEADS THE WAY

Ferrari's engines have claimed the most wins (215), set the most pole positions (205), fastest laps (223) and scored the most championship points (4,473.5) up to the end of the 2010 World Championship.

⊙ SPINNERS CAN BE WINNERS

BMW took peak revolutions per minute to a new level in 2003 when its V10-format P83 engines revved up to 19,200rpm and pushed out more than 900bhp in the back of Juan Pablo Montoya's and Ralf Schumacher's Williams. Within two years, engine capacity was cut back from 3.0 litres to 2.4 to reduce performance in the name of driver safety.

THE PACE OF CHANGE

There is no more testing arena for technical development than the world of F1, and it's not surprising that there have been developments almost every year since the World Championship began. The most visible ones have been to the car, but engines have changed greatly too:

Year	Change
1950	Cars allowed 4500cc normally aspirated or 1500cc super-charged engines.
1952	Engine capacity restricted to 2000cc or 500cc supercharged engines as F2 rules adopted.
1954	Capacity boosted to 2500cc or 750cc supercharged engines.
1958	Use of commercial fuel made mandatory.
1961	Supercharged engines banned and engine size reduced to 1500–1300cc.
1966	Engine capacity enlarged to 3000cc.
1972	Maximum of 12 cylinders imposed.
1987	Engine capacity enlarged to 3500cc.
1989	Turbocharged engines banned.
1995	Reduction of maximum engine capacity to 3000cc.
2006	Engines restricted to eight cylinders and 2400cc.

TOP 10 ENGINE MANUFACTURERS WITH MOST STARTS

1	Ferrari	812
2	Ford	587
3	Renault	461
4	Honda	340
5	Mercedes	301
6	BMW	269
7	Alfa Romeo	222
8	BRM	189
9	Mugen Honda	147
10	Hart	128

⊙ THE HEARTBEAT OF AMERICA

The V8 engine is still the heartbeat of America, ticking over through the suburbs in Fords and Chevrolets. However, the first winning V8 in F1 was fitted to Luigi Musso's Lancia Ferrari in the 1956 Argentinian GP. That said, the Ford Motor Company put its name to F1's most successful V8 of all, the Cosworth DFV.

TOP 10 ENGINE MANUFACTURERS WITH MOST WINS

1	Ferrari	215
2	Ford	176
3	Renault	130
4	Mercedes	80
5	Honda	72
6	Coventry Climax	40
7	Porsche	26
8	BMW	20
9	BRM	18
10	Alfa Romeo	12

TRACKS

The names of the great grand prix circuits flow off the tongue mellifluously: Monaco, Monza, Spa-Francorchamps, Silverstone and Suzuka. They are temples to high speed and their toughest corners a real challenge to the drivers. Most have been changed out of all recognition in the name of safety, but they all retain the soul that marks them out from the bright new circuits that have yet to earn their spurs.

TRACK LENGTHS

⊙ KING OF THE STREETS

For decades, Graham Hill held the record for the most wins in the Monaco GP. He achieved five wins between 1963 and 1969. However, Ayrton Senna usurped him by scoring his sixth Monaco win in 1993. This could have been Senna's seventh win, but in 1988 he crashed out of the lead at Portier, then subsequently disappeared to sulk for a few hours.

⊙ GOING ROUND AND ROUND

The greatest number of laps in a grand prix was the 110 laps covered by the winning entrants in the US GP at Watkins Glen between 1963 and 1965. This equated to a race distance of 258.5 miles. In 1966, maximum race distances were cut back to 248.5 miles.

⊙ NOT THE BEST OF STARTS

The Monaco street circuit had been hosting races since 1929, but its World Championship debut in 1950 was a near disaster as there was an accident at Tabac at the end of the opening lap after Giuseppe Farina lost control and triggered a shunt that eliminated nine cars. The wreckage was spread across the track, but Juan Manuel Fangio was able to thread his way through and race clear to score his first win for Alfa Romeo.

⊙ WILL IT BE OVER SOON?

Grands prix up to 1957 were run to a target time of three hours, although some went on for even longer. The 1954 German GP held at the 14.167-mile-long Nürburgring Nordschleife holds the record as the longest grand prix in terms of time. It took race winner Juan Manuel Fangio 3 hrs 45 mins 45.8 secs to cover the allotted 22 laps, and he was rewarded with victory by 1 min 36.5 secs.

⊙ WORST LINE INTO FIRST CORNER

Irish driver Derek Daly will always be remembered for getting his approach to the first corner, Ste Devote, horribly wrong at the start of the 1980 Monaco GP. His Tyrrell clipped Bruno Giacomelli's Alfa Romeo under braking, vaulted clean over it and landed on top of the car in front, that of his teammate Jean-Pierre Jarier. None of the drivers was seriously hurt.

⊙ JUST FOUR LEFT RUNNING

It seems inconceivable, but two grands prix since 1950 have
finished with just four cars still running. Less hard to imagine is that
both of these were at Monaco, where the walls can bite. The first
occasion was in 1966 when Jackie Stewart won for BRM, albeit with
two further finishers not being classified as they were so far behind.
The second was 30 years later when Olivier Panis won a wet/dry
race for Ligier as others crashed out.

⊙ ARE YOU GOING VERY FAR SIR?

Discounting the 500-mile Indianapolis 500 that was nominally a
round of the World Championship from 1950–60, the longest grand
prix in terms of distance was the 1951 French GP at Reims, with its
77 laps equating to 373.912 miles. It's no surprise that Juan Manuel
Fangio's Alfa Romeo started to fail, forcing him to take over the
sister car that started the race in the hands of Luigi Fagioli. Fangio's
winning time was 3 hrs 22 mins 11 secs.

⊙ GOING ON AND ON

Almost every F1 fan will tell you that the Nürburgring Nordschleife, at
more than 14 miles, is the longest ever circuit used by F1. It isn't: the
longest is the Pescara circuit on Italy's Adriatic coast, which held a
grand prix in 1957. The 15.894-mile lap ran uphill, through villages and
over level crossings before returning for a blast along the seafront.
Stirling Moss beat Juan Manuel Fangio by more than 3 minutes.

⊙ OVER IN A FLASH

Because the Monza circuit produces such a high average speed, it
is usually the shortest race on the F1 calendar in terms of duration.
Whereas most modern-day grands prix take around 1 hr 30–40 mins,
drivers know that, in the Italian GP, if they don't clash and the safety
car doesn't have to be involved they can have their afternoon's work
completed in just 1 hr 15 mins.

TRACKS WITH SHORTEST LAP LENGTHS

1	Monaco	1.954 miles
2	Zeltweg (Austria)	1.988 miles
3	Long Beach (USA)	2.020 miles
4	Dijon-Prenois (France)	2.044 miles
5	Jarama (Spain)	2.058 miles

MONACO

Grand prix years:	1950, 1955–present
No. of grands prix held:	57
Lap length:	From 1.976 miles to current 2.075 miles
Fastest qualifying lap:	1 min 13.826 secs, Mark Webber (Red Bull), 2010
Fastest race lap:	1 min 14.439 secs, Michael Schumacher (Ferrari), 2004
Driver with most wins:	Ayrton Senna – six (1987, 1989, 1990, 1991, 1992, 1993)

⊙ OVER ALMOST BEFORE IT STARTED

Heavy rain made the Adelaide street circuit almost undriveable at the 1991 Australian GP and it had to be called to a permanent halt after just 24 mins 34.899 secs, with 14 laps (32.858 miles) covered. McLaren's pole-starter Ayrton Senna was the winner from Nigel Mansell's Williams, with Gerhard Berger third in the second McLaren.

TRACKS WITH LONGEST LAP LENGTHS

1	Pescara (Italy)	15.894 miles
2	Nürburgring (Germany)	14.189 miles
3	Spa-Francorchamps (Belgium)	8.774 miles
4	Monza (Italy)	6.214 miles
5	Sebring (USA)	5.200 miles

LOCATIONS

⊙ STILL LOOKING FOR A HOME

F1 and the USA have never really gelled. This is shown by the fact that the nation's grand prix has bounced around the country, being held at nine different circuits to date: Sebring, Riverside, Watkins Glen, Long Beach, Las Vegas, Detroit, Dallas, Phoenix and Indianapolis. The French GP is the second most unsettled, having used seven circuits, which is one more than Spain has used.

⊙BANKING ON SUCCESS

Racing on banked oval circuits is the domain of American IndyCar racing, but the World Championship has also occasionally taken to the banking, at least in sections of five circuits. These are Monza (using the banked section as part of the lap most years between 1955 and 1961), Avus, Interlagos (Turn 1 on the old layout until 1979), Mexico City (the lightly banked Peraltada) and Indianapolis (using the full oval when the Indy 500 was a World Championship round from 1950–60, then just a section combined with an infield loop from 2000–07).

⊙ ITALY LEADS THE WAY

As a result of being among the founding group of countries that held grands prix in the World Championship's inaugural year (1950) and having hosted two grands prix per year (the Italian and San Marino) for several decades, Italy has hosted more grands prix than any other nation. It leads the way after 2010 with 88, Germany is second with 71 (its tally boosted by hosting the additional European GP for many years), then Great Britain third on 64 and France fourth on 59.

⊙ WORTH A GAMBLE

Two F1 former circuits have horse racing connections – Aintree, and Adelaide's street circuit which wrapped around the Victoria Park Racecourse. The Las Vegas, Montreal and Monaco circuits all passed a casino.

⊙ DOES ANYONE WANT TO FINISH?

A heavy burst of rain that hit the far side of the circuit led to carnage in the 1975 British GP, when car after car aquaplaned off into the catch fencing at Stowe and Club to bring the race to a premature halt. Race leader Emerson Fittipaldi managed to pussyfoot his McLaren through the corners, but Carlos Pace and Jody Scheckter, who were classified second and third, did not, along with 10 others.

⊙ MIND THE WATER!

A crash at every twist and turn around the streets of Monaco is a possibility. However, there is also the additional danger of crashing into the harbour, which the 1952 and 1953 world champion Alberto Ascari did in 1955. He emerged unscathed, but unbelievably experienced the reverse side of fortune four days later when he turned up at Monza to test a sports car, crashed and was killed.

⊙ A CHANGE OF TACK

Several circuits that hosted grands prix have disappeared under urban sprawl. Riverside, in California – home to the 1960 US GP – is now under a housing development. The upper reaches of Kyalami (South Africa) are now a part of an industrial estate, while the far end of the Zandvoort circuit in the Netherlands is a complex of holiday chalets in the sand dunes.

⊙ EUROPE LEADS THE WAY

Europe has hosted grands prix at 37 circuits. They are: A1-Ring, Aintree, Anderstorp, Avus, Brands Hatch, Bremgarten, Catalunya, Clermont-Ferrand, Dijon-Prenois, Donington Park, Estoril, Hockenheim, Hungaroring, Imola, Jarama, Jerez, Le Mans Bugatti, Magny-Cours, Monaco, Monsanto, Montjuich Park, Monza, Nivelles, Nürburgring, Österreichring, Paul Ricard, Pedralbes, Pescara, Porto, Reims, Rouen-les Essarts, Silverstone, Spa-Francorchamps, Valencia, Zandvoort, Zeltweg and Zolder.

⊙ ALL THE FUN OF THE FAIR

Suzuka is the only circuit built in an amusement park, although the Le Mans Bugatti circuit had a famous funfair on its flanks when it was used for the only time by F1 in 1967. The Yas Marina GP circuit in Abu Dhabi, which made its championship debut in 2009, has the Ferrari World theme park right alongside it.

⊙ HOTSPOT LOCATIONS

Three F1 circuits have volcanic connections: Japan's Fuji Speedway is situated on the side slopes of Mount Fuji; Clermont-Ferrand, in France, is built among volcanic outcrops; and the Mexico City circuit is actually located in a volcanic basin, along with the rest of the city.

⊙ HOW NOT TO FINISH THE FIRST LAP

Jody Scheckter was looking to impress when he made his fourth grand prix appearance for McLaren at the 1973 British GP. Starting sixth, he was up to fourth when he ran wide out of Woodcote at the end of the first lap, went on to the grass, then took out a third of the field as he scattered the cars behind. Only 19 of 28 starters were able to take the restart 90 minutes later.

⊙ PLAYING AWAY

The Europe-centric World Championships of old have well and truly been consigned to history and the burgeoning interest from South-East Asia has helped Formula One break new ground when it held a race in South Korea for the first time in 2010, at the Yeongam circuit. Asia's tally is set to be boosted to 11 in 2011 when India will host a grand prix for the first time, at a new track just outside Delhi.

NUMBER OF F1 CIRCUITS BY CONTINENT

1	Europe	37
2	North America	13
3	Asia	10
4	Africa	3
=	South America	3
6	Australasia	2

SILVERSTONE

Grand prix years:	1950–54, 1956, 1958, 1960, 1963, 1965, 1967, 1969, 1971, 1973, 1975, 1977, 1979, 1981, 1983, 1985, 1987–present
No. of grands prix held:	44
Lap length:	From 2.866 miles to current 3.666 miles
Fastest qualifying lap:	1 min 29.615 secs, Sebastian Vettel (Red Bull), 2010
Fastest race lap:	1 min 30.874 secs, Fernando Alonso (Ferrari), 2010
Driver with most wins:	Alain Prost – five (1983, 1985, 1989, 1990, 1993)

TRACK LAP RECORDS

⊙ RED-HOT RUBENS
Qualifying inevitably produces the fastest laps of a grand prix meeting. These laps are often set with special rubber or next to no fuel on board, and the fastest ever of these was set at Monza by the Brazilian Rubens Barrichello in his Ferrari as he secured pole for the 004 Italian GP in front of the Tifosi. His pole time was 1 min 20.089 secs, equating to 161.802mph.

⊙ FAST, FASTER, FASTEST
Monza and Spa-Francorchamps used to vie for the fastest average race-winning speed – a mind-boggling 150mph. Then chicanes were inserted. But the cars kept getting faster and faster and the winning average speed for Michael Schumacher's Ferrari in the 2003 Italian GP at Monza was 153.842mph. The fastest Spa average dates back to 1970 on the old circuit, when Pedro Rodriguez lapped his BRM in a race-winning average of 149.942mph.

⊙ MONZA, THE FASTEST OF THEM ALL
The home of the Italian GP, Monza, remains the circuit with the highest race lap speed recorded – 159.909mph set in 2004. Those circuits ranked behind Monza in terms of lap speed are: Silverstone, Spa-Francorchamps, the Österreichring, Hockenheim, Avus, Suzuka, A1-Ring, Reims and Melbourne. Of these, only Monza, Suzuka and Melbourne have a similar track configuration to when these fastest laps were set.

⊙ GET A MOVE ON
Not all circuits produce average lap speeds that are double what you'd normally travel at in the fast lane of a motorway. The tight confines of Monaco limit drivers to average speeds in double rather than treble figures, as do many of the other street circuits used, notably in the USA. However, the slowest fastest lap in a grand prix was set by Juan Manuel Fangio at Monaco in 1950, at 64.085mph. Detroit's track is second on this list.

⊙ A DOUBLE DISASTER

The 1960 Belgian GP at Spa-Francorchamps had already bared its teeth before the race; Stirling Moss broke his legs in practice and Mike Taylor received considerable injuries in another crash. Worse was to follow in the race as first Chris Bristow crashed to his death while dicing with Willy Mairesse at Burnenville, then five laps later Alan Stacey was hit in the face by a bird and was killed by the resulting crash.

⊙ A MEDAL FOR BRAVERY

Gilles Villeneuve famously spun at almost every corner in practice at his first grand prix, at Silverstone in 1977. This was his way of finding the maximum. Always wanting to run right on the ragged edge, he put on a masterclass of driving in the wet in practice at the 1979 US GP when he went out and lapped all but 10 secs faster than anyone else. As it was only practice it counted for nothing, but it certainly laid down a marker.

⊙ MIND THE WALLS

Street circuits are almost invariably a bit "point-and-squirt", with tight turns surrounded by walls or barriers rather than fast, open sweeps. However, the Valencia circuit, which has hosted the European GP since 2008, breaks the mould with a more open layout and has an appreciable straight. This resulted in a lap record of 122.837mph, set by Toyota racer Timo Glock in 2009.

⊙ ALMOST ALL STRAIGHTS

The Avus circuit in Berlin had a remarkably simple layout. It was an up-and-down dual carriageway, with a corner at its southern end that made its shape like a hairclip and at the northern end there was a high, banked corner. These were its only features. As a consequence lap speeds were high, with Tony Brooks's winning average speed for Ferrari being 143.342mph all the way back in 1959.

⊙ SUSTAINED SPEED

The full-length 8.755-mile Spa-Francorchamps circuit was a case of pedal to the metal for the drivers, along with prayers on the straights that a rain shower wouldn't arrive and render the next corner impossible. Chris Amon set the lap record on this classic circuit through the Ardennes forests in his March, lapping in 152.049mph in 1970, the last year that F1 used the full circuit. It returned to a 4.312-mile circuit in 1983.

TOP 10 CIRCUITS WITH FASTEST LAP RECORDS

	Circuit	Avg. speed
1	Monza	159.909mph
2	Silverstone	153.053mph
3	Spa-Francorchamps	152.049mph
4	Österreichring	150.509mph
5	Hockenheim	150.059mph
6	Avus	149.129mph
7	Suzuka	141.904mph
8	A1-Ring	141.606mph
9	Reims	141.424mph
10	Melbourne	141.009mph

⊙ ENTERING NEW TERRITORY

Official fastest laps are recorded during the race only and are exceeded almost always by single, flying laps in qualifying, when the tyres are fresh and the fuel load often optimum. For 19 years, the fastest ever lap in qualifying was set by Keke Rosberg when he lapped Silverstone in his Williams at 160.925mph in 1985. Rubens Barrichello driving a Ferrari at Monza in 2004 beat it by just under 1mph.

SPA-FRANCORCHAMPS

Grand prix years:	1950–56, 1958, 1960–68, 1970, 1983, 1985–2002, 2004–present
No. of grands prix held:	43
Lap length:	From 9.060 miles to current 4.352 miles
Fastest qualifying lap:	1 min 45.778 secs, Mark Webber (Red Bull), 2010
Fastest race lap:	1 min 47.263 secs, Sebastian Vettel (Red Bull), 2009
Driver with most wins:	Michael Schumacher – six (1992, 1995, 1996, 1997, 2001, 2002)

VICTORY ROLLS

⊙ HOME SWEET HOME

If you are going to set the record for the most wins in a particular country's grand prix by drivers from a particular nation, then you may as well do it at home. This is what British drivers have managed, winning the British GP 21 times, first with Stirling Moss at Aintree for Mercedes in 1955 and most recently with Lewis Hamilton's wet-track masterclass for McLaren in 2008.

⊙ ALL BUT A FEW

British teams have won more races than teams based in other countries, in every country that the World Championship has visited since 1950 bar two. These are Switzerland, where Ferrari has won three of the five grands prix held, and Korea where it has won the only one.

⊙ GIMME FIVE

Ferrari and McLaren have claimed five wins in succession in a particular grand prix. The British team achieved this first, winning the Belgian GP at Spa-Francorchamps each year from 1987 to 1991, with a win for Alain Prost followed by four for Ayrton Senna. Ferrari took its sequence in the Japanese GP at Suzuka between 2000 and 2004, with four going to Michael Schumacher, and one to Rubens Barrichello in 2003.

⊙ STREETS AHEAD

British teams experienced significant success in Monaco in the 1950s, 60s and 70s. Sure, there was extra work for the mechanics as they repaired the damage from brushes with the barriers, and worn gearboxes had to be changed, but the drivers tended to come up trumps, winning there 16 times in a row from Maurice Trintignant's win in Rob Walker's Cooper in 1958 to Ronnie Peterson's victory for Lotus in 1974.

⊙ FERRARI'S MONZA MAGIC

The Italian GP is one of the originals and it is here above all other venues that Ferrari wants to win, right in front of its fans (the *Tifosi*). The team, whose scarlet cars bear the famous prancing horse emblem, has done just that on 18 occasions, from Alberto Ascari's victory in 1951 to Fernando Alonso's in 2010.

⊙ HIGH FIVE

Ayrton Senna rose to the challenge of the Monte Carlo street circuit like no other driver and won there five times in a row for McLaren from 1989 to 1993. He also won there for Lotus in 1987. He led the first 66 laps in 1988 before crashing out with 12 laps to go, and if things had turned out differently that day his run at Monaco would have been a predominant seven. Jim Clark (twice), Juan Manuel Fangio and Michael Schumacher (twice) have all won a particular grand prix four times in a row.

⊙ THAT SPECIAL RELATIONSHIP

British drivers grew to love their forays across the Atlantic to the US GP not only because they spoke the same language and the largest winner's cheque of the year was up for grabs, but because they enjoyed remarkable success there. There was a run of nine straight wins for British drivers between Stirling Moss's triumph in 1960 and Jackie Stewart's in 1968.

⊙ BEATING THE ELEMENTS

Jackie Stewart's first Nürburgring win in 1968 came not only in torrential rain but also in fog and so it is regarded as one of the greatest wins ever. Not only did the Scot win around the mighty Nordschleife by just over 4 minutes in his Matra, with Graham Hill's Lotus finishing second, but he achieved all this nursing an injured wrist.

⊙ ACHIEVING ACROSS THE BOARD

Michael Schumacher, the setter of so many records, proved his versatility by winning at 22 circuits. They were, in the order he conquered them: Spa-Francorchamps, Estoril, Interlagos, TI Circuit, Imola, Monaco, Montreal, Magny-Cours, the Hungaroring, Jerez, Barcelona, Hockenheim, the Nürburgring, Suzuka, Monza, Buenos Aires, Silverstone, Melbourne, Indianapolis, Sepang, the A1-Ring and Bahrain.

⊙ BRAVERY REWARDED

The Nürburgring Nordschleife was so testing and, frankly, dangerous that to complete a race here was an achievement, especially as wet weather was not unusual. To win, then, is something to be treasured and both Juan Manuel Fangio and Jackie Stewart managed it three times, with the Argentinian's charge back to the front in the 1957 German GP one of the all-time epics.

⊙ THE MOST DANGEROUS PLACE TO RACE

The Nürburgring Nordschleife had the reputation as the sport's most deadly circuit, as it claimed the lives of seven F1 drivers: Onofre Marimon in practice in 1954, Erwin Bauer in a sports car race in 1958, Peter Collins in the 1958 grand prix, Carel Godin de Beaufort in practice in 1964, John Taylor in 1966, Georges Berger in an endurance race in 1967 and Gerhard Mitter in practice in 1969. Niki Lauda was almost added to that list in 1976.

TOP 10 TEAMS WITH MOST WINS AT ONE CIRCUIT

1	18	Ferrari	Monza
2	15	McLaren	Monaco
3	14	Ferrari	Nürburgring
4	12	Ferrari	Silverstone
=	12	Ferrari	Spa-Francorchamps
=	12	McLaren	Silverstone
7	10	Ferrari	Hockenheim
=	10	Ferrari	Montreal
9	9	McLaren	Hungaroring
=	9	Williams	Hockenheim

NÜRBURGRING

Grand prix years:	1951–58, 1960–69, 1971–76, 1984–85, 1995–2007, 2009
No. of grands prix held:	38
Lap length:	From 14.167 miles to current 3.199 miles
Fastest qualifying lap:	1 min 28.351 secs, Michael Schumacher (Ferrari), 2004
Fastest race lap:	1 min 29.468 secs, Michael Schumacher (Ferrari), 2004
Driver with most wins:	Michael Schumacher – five (1995, 2000, 2001, 2004, 2006)

NUMBER OF RACES HELD

⊙ BEFORE SPECTATORS HAD PROTECTION

F1 spectators sometimes complain that they are kept back from
the action, but there is a very good reason for this – their safety.
Back in 1961 there was little protection for them and certainly no
chain-link fencing. Had there been, then 14 fans at Monza probably
wouldn't have perished after Jim Clark and Wolfgang von Trips
touched and von Trips's Ferrari was sent cartwheeling into the
crowd, killing the German aristocrat as well.

⊙ BUSY, BUSY

The 2005 World Championship set a new record for comprising
the most grands prix, at 19. However, this tally was equalled in
2010 and the 2010 season was actually longer by three weeks
as it stretched from the opening round in Bahrain on 14 March
through until the Abu Dhabi finale on 14 November, with its duration
stretched by the summer break that now has to be built in to give
the team personnel a well-earned rest.

⊙ EASY GOING

When the World Championship began in 1950 there were only seven
grands prix, the fewest ever, in Great Britain, Monaco, Switzerland,
Spa-Francorchamps, Reims and Monza. The seventh was the
Indianapolis 500, which remained a standalone event. So really
there were six grands prix, just as there were in 1955 when the
French, German, Swiss and Spanish GPs were cancelled after more
than 80 people were killed when a car crashed into the crowd at
the Le Mans 24 Hours.

⊙ HONOUR OF OPENING THE SEASON

Argentina holds the record for hosting the most opening grands prix
of the season, having done so 15 times at its Buenos Aires circuit.
Australia's Melbourne circuit is next with 13, and South Africa's
Kyalami circuit is the third most popular place to kick off the action,
having held the opening race eight times.

⊙ SOMETHING ON THE SIDE

The World Championship was augmented by non-championship races in the early years, with the six championship grands prix in 1950 supported by no fewer than 16 non-championship events in which the drivers raced for prize money. Juan Manuel Fangio won four of them.

⊙ VARIETY APLENTY

The Long Beach street circuit in California has been used just eight times as a second US GP, but its tricky, bumpy course is one that no individual driver conquered as pole position went to a different driver each time, from Clay Regazzoni in 1976 to Patrick Tambay in 1983, both driving for Ferrari.

⊙ AND SO TO BED

Countries fight over who will hold the final grand prix of the year as this more often than not has the added drama of being the title battle decider. Brazil has hosted it most of late, but the USA edges Australia overall, 12 to 11, with Sebring, Riverside, Watkins Glen and the Caesar's Palace circuit in Las Vegas all having brought the curtain down on the season. Australia's closers were all held on the Adelaide street circuit.

TOP 10 MOST-USED CIRCUITS

1	Monza	60
2	Monaco	57
3	Silverstone	44
4	Spa-Francorchamps	43
5	Nürburgring	38
6	Hockenheim	32
7	Montreal	31
8	Zandvoort	30
9	Interlagos	28
10	Imola	26

⊙ A CLASH WITH TRAGIC CONSEQUENCES

Ronnie Peterson was a driver admired around the world for his spectacular style. Sadly, he was not to survive the 1978 Italian GP as his Lotus was caught up in a shunt as the cars accelerated away from the start, with 10 cars left battered and Peterson's on fire. Vittorio Brambilla was knocked out and Peterson had to be taken to hospital with leg injuries. He died during the night.

MONZA

Grand prix years:	1950–79, 1981–present
No. of grands prix held:	60
Lap length:	From 6.214 miles to current 3.6 miles
Fastest qualifying lap:	1 min 20.089 secs, Rubens Barrichello (Ferrari) 2004
Fastest race lap:	1 min 21.046 secs, Rubens Barrichello (Ferrari), 2004
Driver with most wins:	Michael Schumacher – five (1996, 1998, 2000, 2003, 2006)

⊙ DOUBLING UP

Italy is the country that has hosted the most grands prix since the World Championship began in 1950. The reason that it has outstripped Great Britain, Monaco and Belgium, which all hosted races in 1950 and are still hosting races today, is that it held a second race each year from 1981 to 2006 under the nominal title of the San Marino GP. By the end of 2010 Italy had hosted 87 grands prix, 16 ahead of Germany, which has hosted the European GP 12 times and the Luxembourg GP twice, to boost its tally to 71.

HIGHEST AND LOWEST
TOP SPEEDS

⊙ CIRCUIT BOUND
David Coulthard was something of an expert at getting cars to fly in a low downforce setting when he raced for McLaren, as he proved when he recorded F1's fastest speed-trap figure of 224.8mph at Monza in 1999. This exceeded the previous record of 221.5mph that he'd set just a year earlier in practice for the German GP at Hockenheim. (This was when the Hockenheim layout had a long loop through the forest before it was cut back.)

⊙ TAKING IT TO EXTREMES
Honda Racing decided to show what its F1 car could do if it was given every opportunity to go for the max, not constrained by the limits of circuits. In 2006, test driver Alan van der Merwe drove its RA106 on the Bonneville Salt Flats and clocked a top speed of 246.908mph on an early morning run over the flying mile, making it the fastest F1 car ever, but falling just short of its 248.5mph target.

⊙ SURPRISE, SURPRISE
One glance at the tight layout of the Monte Carlo street circuit and it comes as no surprise that it's the slowest circuit used by F1. Its first World Championship grand prix in 1950 was won by Juan Manuel Fangio in his Alfa Romeo, doing an average speed of just 61.331mph. There have been circuit modifications since, but not ap-preciable ones, yet the highest winning average rose to 96.655mph when Fernando Alonso won for McLaren in 2007.

⊙ STOP AT THE RED LIGHT
The highest speed recorded through a speed trap on a street circuit by an F1 car was at the third race on the Valencia circuit around the city's docks in 2010. Swiss driver Sebastien Buemi clocked 195.421mph at the end of the back straight just before Turn 12 in his Ferrari-powered Scuderia Toro Rosso.

⊙ GOING LIKE A ROCKET

The highest average speed over the duration of a grand prix was set by Michael Schumacher, when he won the Italian GP at Monza in 2003 – 153.842mph. He drove so fast that he completed the 53 laps (190.8 miles) in just 1 hr 14 mins 19.838 secs, with Juan Pablo Montoya just over 5 secs behind at the chequered flag.

⊙ MIKEY LIKES IT

Interlagos is a circuit that provides more than its share of race incidents, which is why it isn't one of those circuits where one driver has managed to produce a string of wins. Ayrton Senna managed to win only twice here, but Michael Schumacher kept out of trouble at the tricky first corner enough to win four times, in 1994, 1995, 2000 and 2002.

⊙ FOR THE FANS

Interlagos has a proud boast of being a good track for Brazil's F1 stars, as both Emerson Fittipaldi and Carlos Pace won there during the circuit's first spell of hosting the Brazilian GP in the 1970s, sending the wildly partisan crowd home happy. Ayrton Senna and Felipe Massa have won there since it took over the race again from Rio de Janeiro's Jacarepagua circuit in 1990, but Rubens Barrichello still has not managed a victory

⊙ SHOW US THE NUMBERS

Arab petrolheads love performance cars and F1 too, but enticing them to watch it in the flesh has proved a problem, with Bahrain failing to draw in large crowds for its grand prix. Perhaps with this in mind, Abu Dhabi's incredible Yas Marina circuit was built with a straight that could produce speeds in excess of 200mph, the sort of figure that really impresses car nuts and hopefully encourages them to turn up rather than watch it on TV.

⊙ STILL WAITING

Rubens Barrichello's childhood home overlooked the Interlagos circuit. It was always his dream that, one day, he would stand on top of the podium there as winner of the Brazilian GP. However, Barrichello seems to be "cursed" at his home race and, by the end of 2010, had a best result of only third, despite having led the race in 1999, 2000, 2002, 2003, 2004 and 2009.

TOP 10 HIGHEST SPEEDS IN 2010

1	Monza	215.429mph
2	Montreal	201.759mph
3	Istanbul	199.708mph
4	Yas Marina	198.901mph
5	Hockenheim	198.528mph
6	Shanghai	197.596mph
7	Bahrain	195.607mph
8	Valencia	195.421mph
9	Interlagos	195.110mph
10	Barcelona	193.992mph

All figures recorded at speed trap.

INTERLAGOS

Grand prix years: 1973–77, 1979–80, 1990–present
No. of grands prix held: 28
Lap length: From 4.946 miles to current 2.677 miles
Fastest qualifying lap: 1 min 10.646 secs, Rubens Barrichello (Ferrari), 2004
Fastest race lap: 1 min 11.473 secs, Juan Pablo Montoya (Williams), 2004
Driver with most wins: Michael Schumacher – four (1994, 1995, 2000, 2002)

PART 2: NASCAR SPRINT CUP

With as many as 36 races every year, with 43 cars in each race, NASCAR's top-level Sprint Cup Series is a monster. It gets mind-boggling TV-viewing figures and attracts massive crowds. As a sport, it's huge. As a business, it's even bigger. It's a juggernaut that can't be stopped as sport's loudest show criss-crosses the USA.

NASCAR's premier series, the Grand National Championship, was streamlined for 1972 and cut back from 47 races to 30. It was also given a new title, the Winston Cup, in deference to one of the series' new sponsors' cigarette brands. The period since is known as NASCAR's modern era, with historians dividing NASCAR events into before and after this watershed. Since 2004, the series has been called the Sprint Cup Series.

1949 STRICTLY STOCK CHAMPIONSHIP • 1950 GRAND NATIONAL CHAMPIONSHIP • 1972 WINSTON CUP • 2004 NEXTEL CUP SERIES • 2008 SPRINT CUP SERIES.

DRIVERS

Although Sprint Cup Series events never have much daylight between the winner and the driver in second place, a few drivers have risen above the masses and become superstars. Jimmie Johnson is very much the man of the moment and so joins the likes of Richard Petty, David Pearson, Bobby Allison, Darrell Waltrip, Dale Earnhardt and Jeff Gordon in the pantheon of top-level series NASCAR greats.

CHAMPIONS

⊙ UNDERDOG SQUEAKS HOME

Alan Kulwicki, nicknamed the "Polish Prince", upset the formbook when he landed the 1992 Winston Cup title. Driving his Ford "Underbird" (so-called as he was convinced he was the underdog), he pipped Bill Elliott despite scoring two wins to Elliott's five. He was the first northerner to win the title since Bill Rexford in 1950. His "Polish victory lap" was his trademark. Kulwicki would drive the circuit in reverse (clockwise) so that he was sitting on the side of the car closest to the grandstands and could acknowledge the applause. He died in a plane crash in 1993.

⊙ BUS-DRIVER BAKER

Buck Baker was NASCAR's first top-level series back-to-back champion, pulling off this feat in 1957. He was among the NASCAR pioneers, starting in its inaugural season in 1948, when he would park his bus by his garage and prepare his car. However, Buck proved that he was at his best when driving without passengers and took his first win in 1952. He added 45 more during his career. Remarkably, while his 1957 title was won driving a Chevrolet, he drove three different marques in his first title year in 1956 – a Ford, a Chrysler and a Dodge.

⊙ LUCKY 13

Jeff Gordon equalled Richard Petty's 1975 modern-era top-level NASCAR record of 13 wins in a championship campaign when he claimed the 1998 drivers' crown in his Hendrick Motorsports Chevrolet Monte Carlo. Darrell Waltrip won 12 times in his Junior Johnson Buick Regal on the way to 1981 and 1982 titles.

⊙ DECADE DOMINATORS

Lee Petty edged out Buck Baker in the 1950s, David Pearson took one more title than Richard Petty (Lee's son) in the 1960s, but Richard was king of the 1970s ahead of Cale Yarborough. In the 1980s, Darrell Waltrip and Dale Earnhardt claimed three titles apiece and Earnhardt carried that momentum into the 1990s. Records show that six different drivers won the first seven championships of the 2000s before Jimmie Johnson took control.

⊙ CALE'S TOP TREBLE

Cale Yarborough outdid arch-rival Richard Petty in 1978 when he became the first driver to win three Winston Cup titles in succession. Driving for Junior Johnson's team in 1975–77, with the first two years in a Chevrolet, he guided his Oldsmobile Cutlass to the 1977 title 386 points clear of Petty after claiming nine wins compared to Petty's five.

⊙ PLAYING MIND GAMES

Dale Earnhardt wasn't known as "The Intimidator" for nothing. His aggressive driving style won him races (76) and titles (7) galore, but few friends among his fellow competitors. Many of the fans loved him and looked out for his black Chevrolet around the circuit as this driven man from North Carolina hunted down his rivals then time and time again bettered them. He was still competitive when he crashed and died on the last lap of the 2001 Daytona 500.

⊙ FROM SECOND TO FIRST

To date, only Bobby Labonte has stepped up from being champion in NASCAR's second-division Nationwide Series to become champion in its top-level series. He was Nationwide (or Busch Series as it was then known) champion in 1991 and top-level champion nine years later with his Joe Gibbs Racing Pontiac Grand Prix.

⊙ FANS' FAVOURITE

There has never been a driver more loved by the fans than modest Bill Elliott. He won the Winston Cup just once, when racing a Melling Racing Ford Thunderbird in 1988, but he was voted NASCAR's Most Popular Driver 16 times between 1984 and 2002. In 2005, the governor of the state of Georgia declared 8 October to be Bill Elliott Day.

⊙ POINTS AHEAD OF WINS

David Pearson did everything except win the drivers' championship in 1973 in his Wood Brothers Mercury Montego as he won 11 rounds. However, showing that consistency can beat flashes of speed, Benny Parsons was crowned Grand National champion after winning just once in his LG DeWitt Chevrolet. More recently, Terry Labonte won twice to take the 1996 title ahead of 10-time winner Jeff Gordon while Matt Kenseth won just once in 2003 yet still outscored Ryan Newman, who won eight races.

MOST TITLES

1	Dale Earnhardt	7		=	Joe Weatherly	2
=	Richard Petty	7		16	Bobby Allison	1
3	Jeff Gordon	4		=	Kurt Busch	1
=	Jimmie Johnson	4		=	Red Byron	1
5	David Pearson	3		=	Bill Elliott	1
=	Lee Petty	3		=	Bobby Isaac	1
=	Darrell Waltrip	3		=	Dale Jarrett	1
=	Cale Yarborough	3		=	Matt Kenseth	1
9	Buck Baker	2		=	Alan Kulwicki	1
=	Tim Flock	2		=	Bobby Labonte	1
=	Ned Jarrett	2		=	Benny Parsons	1
=	Terry Labonte	2		=	Bill Rexford	1
=	Tony Stewart	2		=	Rusty Wallace	1
=	Herb Thomas	2		=	Rex White	1

⊙ GORDON CONFOUNDS THE CRITICS

Jeff Gordon was on a roll in the second half of the 1990s, following up his 1995 Winston Cup title success at Hendrick Motorsports with back-to-back championships in 1997 and 1998. In 2001 the California-born resident of Indiana responded to criticism that he couldn't win without former crew chief Ray Evernham by winning six rounds – including his third Brickyard 400 win on his home patch – to outscore Tony Stewart and claim his fourth title. This moved him up to third place on the titles won list, behind only seven-time winners Dale Earnhardt and Richard Petty.

⊙ FOUR IN A ROW

Jimmie Johnson knows how to control the show, as his outstanding run of four straight Sprint Cup titles from 2006–09 demonstrates. In his fourth, in 2009, he didn't take the points lead until the Chase for the Cup, finally taking the points lead with six races to run. Teammate Jeff Gordon has an interest in Jimmie's car as he co-owns the entry with Rick Hendrick, the owner of the successful Hendrick Motorsports team.

RUNNERS-UP

⊙ YOU HAVE TO FEEL FOR MARTIN

He's easily good enough to have been a champion by now, yet Mark Martin has never managed it. Instead, he has finished as the runner-up five times. The first of these occasions was in 1990 behind Dale Earnhardt, followed by disappointment in 1994, 1998, 2002 and most recently behind Jimmie Johnson in 2009.

⊙ BUCK'S TITLE SANDWICH

Buck Baker "hit his straps" in 1956 when he was crowned NASCAR Grand National champion for the first time. He held on to his title in 1957. However, he came close to the title in 1955, when he was runner-up to Tim Flock. Then, completing the sandwich of his two titles, Buck was runner-up again in 1958, finishing second overall to Lee Petty. Following his retirement from racing, he ran NASCAR driving schools at North Carolina Speedway (now Rockingham Speedway) and in Atlanta, as well as passing his love of racing on to son Buddy, who won 19 races.

⊙ MAKING POINTS COUNT

Dave Marcis was not the most heralded of drivers, in fact he won only five races, but he was still able to finish runner-up in 1975 despite claiming only one win that year. Driving Nord Krauskopf's K&K Dodge Charger, he didn't win a round until the 24th of the year's 30 races, coming good at the Old Dominion 500 at Martinsville. Yet through consistent placing, with 16 top-five finishes, he was able to end the year second overall, although he was a whopping 722 points behind Richard Petty.

⊙ FAST IN THOUGHT AND DEED

Fast-talking Darrell Waltrip from Nashville was someone many of the NASCAR fans loved to hate, but the race promoters certainly loved him. He was high profile and any meeting he attended had "extra bite". As well as landing three Winston Cup titles, he also finished second in 1979, just 11 points behind Richard Petty. Proof of Darrell's competitiveness in the early 1980s is in the fact that he led the most laps between 1981 and 1984.

⊙ MORE WINS BUT NO TITLE

Rusty Wallace, Winston Cup champion in 1989, finished second in his first Winston Cup race in 1980, but didn't run full time until 1984. He was runner-up to Bill Elliott in 1988, losing out by just 24 points but, a year later, he was champion. He was also runner-up in 1993, when he won 10 of the 30 rounds in his Raymond Beadle-owned Pontiac Grand Prix. This was four more wins than champion Dale Earnhardt managed.

⊙ WHO NEEDS WINS?

James Hylton was some sort of magician, as he managed to finish runner-up on three occasions, in 1966, 1967 and 1971, despite collecting not one win. He was exceptionally consistent in 1966 and 1967, finishing in the top five in 46 out of the 87 races. In 1966, David Pearson wasn't that far ahead on points, but had won 15 races. In 1967, Richard Petty took 27 wins to James's zero. In 1970 he took his first win, but his third time as runner-up in 1971, this time behind Petty again, was another win-free year. He scored his second and final race win in 1972.

⊙ CHASE KEEPS IT CLOSE

The advantages of the Chase for the Cup were shown to good effect in Jimmie Johnson's first title-winning year – 2006. His final advantage over Matt Kenseth was 56 points, but the fact that Denny Hamlin and Kevin Harvick, third and fourth, were both within 78 points of the champion proved the value of putting the top 10 back to equal points with 10 races to go

⊙ BEST OF THE REST

Junior Johnson was dubbed the "Last American Hero" and was certainly that in the eyes of many NASCAR fans. He was a true southern hero who earned his spurs running illegal moonshine spirit down the backroads of Wilkes County, North Carolina. He was one of the best drivers on the ovals too, yet became the holder of an unwanted record in that he is the driver with the highest number of wins, 50, never to have been champion. In fact he never even finished as runner-up. His best ranking was sixth in 1955 and 1961.

⊙ AFTER YOU, SIR...

To emphasize his incredible run of success, Richard Petty not only jointly holds the record of seven titles, he also holds the record for finishing second in the championship. He has done this six times, one more than 1980s' front-runner Bobby Allison and Mark Martin.

⊙ CHASING THE TASTE OF SUCCESS

Bobby Allison was champion in 1983, but he also experienced what it was like to be runner-up five times. He was in second place in 1970 behind Bobby Isaac, in 1972 behind Richard Petty, in 1978 behind Cale Yarborough, then in 1981 and 1982, both behind Darrell Waltrip, before reversing the order the following year in his DiGard Racing Buick Regal.

⊙ SO NEAR AND YET SO FAR

Now that he has four straight Sprint Cup titles to his name, Jimmie Johnson can probably let this one go, but falling short by just eight points – the smallest losing margin ever – in 2004 will have vexed him as he sought his first title. Driving his Hendrick Motorsports Chevrolet, he took eight wins to champion Ford driver Kurt Busch's three.

MOST TIMES AS RUNNER-UP

1	Richard Petty	6	=	Tim Flock	1
2	Bobby Allison	5	=	Harry Gant	1
=	Mark Martin	5	=	Dick Hutcherson	1
4	Dale Earnhardt	3	=	Bobby Isaac	1
=	Bill Elliott	3	=	Dale Jarrett	1
=	James Hylton	3	=	Ned Jarrett	1
=	Lee Petty	3	=	Matt Kenseth	1
=	Darrell Waltrip	3	=	Bobby Labonte	1
=	Cale Yarborough	3	=	Dave Marcis	1
10	Buck Baker	2	=	Cotton Owens	1
=	Jeff Gordon	2	=	Marvin Panch	1
=	Jimmie Johnson	2	=	Fireball Roberts	1
=	Herb Thomas	2	=	Ricky Rudd	1
=	Rusty Wallace	2	=	Tony Stewart	1
15	Greg Biffle	1	=	Rex White	1
=	Carl Edwards	1			

WINS

⊙ SET THE BALL ROLLING

The first name on NASCAR's list of winners is Robert "Red" Byron, a flight engineer who suffered leg injuries when his Boeing B24 was hit during the Second World War. He was first home in the inaugural NASCAR-sanctioned race at Daytona Beach's beach/road course in 1948, in a 1939 Modified Ford owned by Raymond Parks. He went on to win 10 more times that year. He became the first champion in 1949.

⊙ SENSE OF OCCASION

Richard Petty scored his 199th win at Dover Downs in 1984. Being the ultimate showman, where better to score his 200th than in the Firecracker 400 at Daytona on Independence Day? Petty was leading Cale Yarborough with three laps to go when Doug Heveron crashed. Knowing that a caution period would follow, Petty just kept his Pontiac ahead of Yarborough's Chevrolet as they raced back to the finish-line flag to score the win.

⊙ THORN IN PETTY'S SIDE

David Pearson sits second in the list of drivers with the most top-level NASCAR race wins and was the driver that seven-time champion Richard Petty respected most. Petty said that losing to Pearson didn't hurt as much as losing to anyone else. The first of David's 105 wins came at Charlotte Motor Speedway in his second season, 1961, and he continued to win until 1980 at Darlington, 11 years after the last of his three titles.

⊙ FROM DAYTONA TO DAYTONA

Bobby Allison made his Grand National debut at the Daytona 500 in 1961. He didn't take his first win until five years later, perhaps suggesting a driver who wasn't a quick learner. However, he clearly got the hang of it as he sits equal third in the all-time race wins list. He collected the last of his 84 wins 22 years after the first, at Daytona in 1998.

⊙ KEEP ON WINNING

Tony Stewart is the modern era driver with the longest current streak of seasons with at least one race win. By the end of the 2009 Sprint Cup Series his streak stood at 11 years, stretching his record from his maiden season in 1999. Kurt Busch is next up among drivers still competing, on eight years in a row, but the all-time record is 18 years on the trot, set by Richard Petty, 1960–77.

⊙ LIMPING TO THE FINISH

Richard Petty and David Pearson, first and second in the list of all-time race winners, had their most famous battle in the 1976 Daytona 500. They swapped the lead twice around the final lap then, entering the final corner, touched and hit the wall. Petty's Dodge kept on spinning towards the finish line but stopped short and stalled, allowing Pearson to fire up his Mercury's engine and drive back on to the track from the infield to take victory.

⊙ TIGHTER THAN TIGHT

The 1992 Winston Cup finale was a nail-biter as six drivers went to the last round at Atlanta with a chance of being champion. Davey Allison was leading, 30 points ahead of Alan Kulwicki, with Bill Elliott, Harry Gant, Kyle Petty and Mark Martin also in with a shot. Petty and Martin retired with engine problems, Gant was off the pace and Allison was taken out when Ernie Irvan spun into his path. In the end, Elliott won, but Kulwicki took the title as a result of having led one more lap than Elliott, and took the five-point bonus that accounted for the eventual 10-point difference in their overall totals.

⊙ TIMED TO PERFECTION

The smallest margin of victory in top-level NASCAR history was just 0.002 secs. This was the margin by which Ricky Craven pipped Kurt Busch to victory in the Carolina Dodge Dealers 400 at Darlington Raceway in 2003. Craven came through to push the nose of his PPI Motorsports Pontiac Grand Prix in front of Busch's Roush Racing Ford Taurus for the first time in the race in the final few yards.

⊙ THE ONE THAT NEARLY GOT AWAY

Dale Earnhardt had won it all. He had seven titles to his name, but something bugged him: he had never managed to win the Daytona 500. Finally, in 1998, starting his 20th season, he laid that ghost to rest. He did it in style, dominating the final quarter of the race in his Richard Childress Racing Chevrolet Monte Carlo.

⊙ AN EMOTIONAL VICTORY

Just five months after Dale Earnhardt's fatal crash on the final lap of the 2001 Daytona 500, his son, Dale Jr, won on the Winston Cup Series' return to the Florida superspeedway, with teammate Michael Waltrip riding shotgun behind him in the final laps to ensure the victory in the Pepsi 400.

⊙ A MASTER STROKE

David Pearson went by the nickname "The Silver Fox" and he showed his wily ways when he realized that arch-rival Richard Petty was in position to slingshot by on the final lap of the 1974 Firecracker 400 at Daytona. He pulled to the inside and Petty thought Pearson's Mercury must have blown its engine, then was shocked as he discovered that Pearson had no problem and was now latched to his bumper. Pearson did to Petty what he feared Petty would do to him – slingshot past for victory.

⊙ INSTANT IMPACT

Of all NASCAR's Rookies of the Year, Tony Stewart made the biggest impact in 1999. The 1997 Indy Racing League champion finished eighth on his debut at the Daytona 500 and progressed to take his breakthrough win in the 25th round in his Joe Gibbs Racing Pontiac Grand Prix at Richmond, then added two more wins at Phoenix and Homestead at the end of the year.

⊙ IT'S GOT TO BE GORDON

Richard Petty's 1975 record for the most wins in a season in the modern era was equalled by Jeff Gordon in 1998. Gordon won the second round at North Carolina Speedway at Rockingham in his Hendrick Motorsports Chevrolet Monte Carlo, then won 12 more times, taking the last of these at Atlanta in the final round, ending the year with the third of his four drivers' titles.

⊙ JUNIOR BY NAME, NOT BY NATURE

Among the 19 drivers who have won a streak of three straight wins is Junior Johnson, a large and colourful character who rattled off wins at Columbia, Bradford and Reading in 1958 in Paul Spaulding's Ford Fairlane. This was all the more remarkable as he had just spent 11 months in prison for being caught firing up the family still to make illegal moonshine. He was a master of the art of drafting – running close behind another car to gain a tow – and won 50 races in total.

⊙ LEAVING IT LATE

One of the beauties of the Sprint Cup Series is the way that the cars run really close to each other and that drivers are aware that the last lap is the most important one to lead. The most recent occasion that a race was won by a driver who didn't lead until the last lap was when Mark Martin came through for victory in the Lifelock 400 at Michigan International Speedway in June 2009. Driving a Hendrick Motorsports Chevrolet, Martin passed Greg Biffle in a Rousch Fenway Racing Ford.

⊙ THREE ON THE TROT

Winning a race in NASCAR's top series is hard. Winning two in a row is harder still. So it's not surprising that only 19 drivers have managed to win three races in succession. Herb Thomas was the first to do this in 1951 and Jimmie Johnson the most recent in 2007. Richard Petty has achieved a three-race run a record nine times.

⊙ LET'S MAKE IT FOUR

Every now and then a driver hits a rich vein of form. This happened to Bill Elliott in 1992 when he followed up finishing 27th in the season-opening Daytona 500 with four successive wins in his Melling Racing Ford Thunderbird. In so doing he became one of only 10 drivers in NASCAR history who have achieved this feat. The others are Billy Wade (1964), David Pearson (1966 and 1968), Cale Yarborough (1976), Darrell Waltrip (1981), Dale Earnhardt (1987), Harry Gant (1991), Mark Martin (1993), Jeff Gordon (1998) and Jimmie Johnson (2007).

⊙ MOST WINNERS IN A SEASON

Four campaigns have resulted in 19 different drivers taking one win or more. This happened for the first time in 1956, followed by 1958 and 1961 then, most recently, 2001. The winners in 2001 were, in sequence: Michael Waltrip, Steve Park, Jeff Gordon, Kevin Harvick, Dale Jarrett, Elliott Sadler, Bobby Hamilton, Rusty Wallace, Tony Stewart, Jeff Burton, Ricky Rudd, Bobby Labonte, Sterling Marlin, Ward Burton, Dale Earnhardt Jr, Ricky Craven, Joe Nemechek, Bill Elliott and Robby Gordon.

⊙ KEEP IT IN THE FAMILY

The Petty family can lay claim to the proud boast that they have the highest number of wins of any of NASCAR's families. They have won 262 races between them, with Richard taking the lion's share: 200. His father Lee won 54 and Richard's son Kyle won eight times.

⊙ BROTHER FOLLOWS BROTHER

The most successful brothers in the Sprint Cup Series today are the Busch brothers. Kyle won at Las Vegas in the third round of the 2009 Sprint Cup in his Joe Gibbs Racing Toyota Camry, Kurt took his Penske Racing Dodge Charger to victory at Atlanta the next time out and then Kyle made it three in a row for the brothers by winning the fifth round at Bristol. The Flock brothers, Bob and Fonty, won four races in a row in 1952.

⊙ WINNING START

Five drivers have won the opening two rounds of a campaign. They are Marvin Panch (1957), Bob Welborn (1959), David Pearson (1976), Jeff Gordon (1997) and, most recently, Matt Kenseth. Kenseth won at Daytona and California Speedway in his Roush Fenway Racing Ford Fusion to start his 2009 championship run in style. By the season's end, however, he'd failed to win any of the next 34 races and slipped to 14th in the rankings.

⊙ NOT JUST ONE OF THE FLOCK

Tim Flock claimed two titles, in 1952 and 1955, but it was the second of these that stands out. He started all 45 races in a Carl Kiekhaefer Chrysler 300 and came away with 18 wins, giving him the second greatest winning average for a season – 40 per cent. It wasn't until Richard Petty's epic 1967 campaign that this record was beaten. "The King" won 27 of his 49 starts for a 55.10 per cent record.

⊙ LEE PETTY GETS HIS WIN BACK

NASCAR's first photo finish caused controversy. In 1959 race officials judged that Johnny Beauchamp had won the first ever Daytona 500 by a fraction of a second from Lee Petty after surging out of the final corner in his Ford Thunderbird. Petty protested and it took three days of photo analysis before the decision was reversed and the Oldsmobile 88 driver Petty was given the win.

⊙ 10 IN A ROW

Richard Petty's run of 10 wins in consecutive races set in the second year he became drivers' champion, 1967, will probably never be beaten. He started the run in his Petty Enterprises Plymouth Belvedere at Winston-Salem then won at Columbia, Savannah, Darlington, Hickory, Richmond, Beltsville, Hillsboro and Martinsville before rounding it off at North Wilkesboro. The next greatest run is five wins in a row, set by Richard Petty and Bobby Allison in 1971.

⊙ YOU'RE NOT FROM AROUND HERE

Few non-American drivers have won races. Colombian Juan Pablo Montoya is the most recent driver to achieve this, in 2007. However, the first to do so was Mario Andretti, who was born in Italy before becoming a naturalized American. In 1967, he took his win in the Daytona 500 no less, in a Holman-Moody Ford Fairlane.

⊙ A BAKER'S DOZEN

In the modern era the record for the most wins in a season is shared by Richard Petty and Jeff Gordon. Petty won 13 from 30 rounds in 1975 in his Petty Enterprises Dodge Charger, and Gordon 13 from 33 rounds in 1998 in his Hendrick Motorsports Chevrolet Monte Carlo.

MOST RACE WINS

1	Richard Petty	200	9	Lee Petty	54
2	David Pearson	105	10	Ned Jarrett	50
3	Bobby Allison	84	=	Junior Johnson	50
=	Darrell Waltrip	84	12	Herb Thomas	48
5	Cale Yarborough	83	13	Jimmie Johnson	47
6	Jeff Gordon	82	14	Buck Baker	46
7	Dale Earnhardt	76	15	Bill Elliott	44
8	Rusty Wallace	55			

MOST WINS IN A SEASON IN MODERN ERA

1	Richard Petty (1975)	13
=	Jeff Gordon (1998)	13
3	Darrell Waltrip (1981)	12
=	Darrell Waltrip (1982)	12
5	David Pearson (1973)	11
=	Bill Elliott (1985)	11
=	Dale Earnhardt (1987)	11
8	Bobby Allison (1972)	10
=	Richard Petty (1974)	10
=	Cale Yarborough (1974)	10
=	David Pearson (1976)	10
=	Rusty Wallace (1993)	10
=	Jeff Gordon (1996)	10
=	Jeff Gordon (1997)	10
=	Jimmie Johnson (2007)	10

POINTS

⊙ COUNTED IN THEIR THOUSANDS

An F1 win is worth 25 points. In comparison, a NASCAR win is worth 185, with only marginally fewer awarded for those finishing in second place and below. The scoring goes 185 – 170 – 165 – 160 – 155 – 150, then the points increment drops to four down to 11th, then to three from there down. There is also a five-point bonus for leading a lap and a further five-point bonus for the driver who led the most laps in the race. Therefore, with 36 races in a season, the champion's tally is usually over 6,000 points.

⊙ POINTS GALORE

Jimmie Johnson might have only been racing at NASCAR's top level since 2001 when he competed in three races, but he has been accruing points hand over fist. By the end of the 2009 campaign, with four drivers' titles to his name, he had scored 49,180 points at a remarkable average of 169 points per race from a possible maximum of 195. He has also collected a cool $52,220,894 in prize money.

⊙ JOHNSON'S TARGET – HIMSELF

Jimmie Johnson's imperious form through the late 2000s is such that he is sure to keep adding to and improving the records that he has already set, but one mark he achieved in 2007 has proved beyond him since. This is the record for the most points in a Sprint Cup campaign. He scored 6,723 points that year, winning 10 times in his Hendrick Motorsport Chevrolet.

⊙ PERILS OF COMPETITION

Alan Kulwicki won by just 10 points in his one and only Winston Cup title in 1992. Such was the level of competition that his winning points total, 4,078, was the lowest ever, as each of the six drivers that could have clinched the title at the final round kept taking points off each other.

⊙ CHAMPION, BY A WHISKER

The gap between first and third place is 10 points. After the 36-race Sprint Cup in 2004, Kurt Busch lifted the drivers' title by less than that. His winning margin over Jimmie Johnson was just eight points. He took just three wins in his Roush Racing Ford Taurus to Johnson's eight and led 746 laps to Johnson's 1,312.

⊙ CLAIMING THE BONUSES

Bonus points are there to be collected, for leading a lap and leading the most laps, and Jeff Gordon did just that in 2001 when he added 180 bonus points to his regular points to land his fourth title in a Hendrick Motorsports Chevrolet. He would have actually won the title without them, as he beat Tony Stewart to the title by 349 points.

⊙ A NEW SYSTEM

The Chase for the Cup was introduced in 2004 and is still in place today. With 10 races to go, the top 12 drivers are put on the same number of points (save for a 10-point bonus for any win achieved to that stage) before letting them fight it out to the end of the season. In 2004, five drivers were still in with a shot at the title at the final race. Jimmie Johnson had won four of the previous five races, but Kurt Busch was clinging to an 18-point lead. A late puncture looked to have ruined Kurt's chances, but his tyre flew off, triggered a caution period and he was able to race on to fifth to claim the title by eight points, the smallest margin ever.

⊙ MOST POINTS EVER

The point-scoring system was different in the 1960s and the number of rounds differed from year to year. For example there were as many as 61 rounds in 1964. The greatest points haul for a season was achieved by Richard Petty in his epic 27-victory 1967 campaign, when he scored 42,472 points. There were 49 races in that season.

⊙ ONWARDS AND UPWARDS

It became possible for drivers to surpass 6,000 points in a season in 2004 after the introduction of the Chase for the Cup. The first driver to achieve more than 6,000 points was Kurt Busch, who ended his campaign with a new record tally of 6,506 points.

MOST POINTS IN A YEAR

1	Jimmie Johnson (2007)	6,723
2	Jimmie Johnson (2008)	6,684
3	Jimmie Johnson (2009)	6,652
4	Jeff Gordon (2007)	6,646
5	Carl Edwards (2008)	6,615
6	Tony Stewart (2005)	6,533
7	Mark Martin (2009)	6,511
8	Kurt Busch (2004)	6,506
9	Greg Biffle (2005)	6,498
=	Carl Edwards (2005)	6,498
=	Jimmie Johnson (2004)	6,498
12	Jeff Gordon (2004)	6,490
13	Jimmie Johnson (2006)	6,475
14	Jeff Gordon (2009)	6,473
15	Greg Biffle (2008)	6,467

⊙ SCOOPING THE PRIZE FUND

Bill Elliott was one of the sport's most popular drivers and he took his popularity to new heights in 1985. He produced a dazzling run of wins on NASCAR's fastest tracks, winning at Daytona, Atlanta, Darlington and Talladega in his Coors Ford Thunderbird. With a special prize fund of $1 million put up by sponsor Winston for any driver who won three of the four superspeedway races, "Awesome Bill from Dawsonville" was renamed "Million Dollar Bill".

⊙ 5,000 CLUB

Cale Yarborough broke new ground in 1977 when he became the first driver to score 5,000 points in a season after the points system was overhauled in 1975. He scored exactly 5,000 points that year for team owner Junior Johnson after capturing nine race wins in his Chevrolet. He beat Richard Petty to the title by a healthy 386 points.

POLE POSITIONS

⊙ QUALIFYING MASTER

The most successful exponent in the modern era of the one-at-a-time qualifying system is Jeff Gordon, who qualified on pole position on 68 occasions by producing the lowest lap time across two flying laps (or one on the road courses as the laps are generally longer). Richard Petty leads the all-time chart on 126.

⊙ FLIER FLOCK SETS ALL-TIME RECORD

Tim Flock was the youngest of the three racing Flocks, after Bob and Fonty, and they all used the driving experience gained as bootleggers to good effect on the racetrack. In 1955, Tim hit an incredible streak in qualifying in his Kiekhaefer Chrysler 300, setting what was then an all-time record of poles in a season of 19 poles from the 45 rounds. Perhaps he pretended that he was being chased by the law in his old role as the decoy. His record was broken in 1969.

⊙ THE KING REMAINED REGAL

At first, age did not seem to weary Richard Petty. He was still fast enough to claim his 126th and final pole position in 1979 at the age of 42 at "The World's Fastest Half Mile" at Bristol, Tennessee. He raced on for another 13 years but increasingly relied on his wily race craft for success.

⊙ ALONG CAME ISAAC

Bobby Isaac had an outstanding season in 1969 when he outdid Tim Flock's 1955 most poles in a season record of 19. Isaac claimed 20 in his K&K Dodge Charger. The 20 pole positions were achieved in 36 rounds, Flock's in 45. He carried this form into 1970, when he gathered fewer poles, but raced to 11 wins and ended the year as champion. Sadly, a heart attack claimed him at the age of 45 in 1977.

⊙ FAST APPROACHING 50

Bobby Allison's career was a long one, spanning 25 years. He was still fast enough to take his final pole position in his 24th year at the age of 49 at Rockingham in 1987, driving the Miller Buick. The following year he led son Davey home in a one-two at the Daytona 500, but shortly after that he was injured in a major accident at Pocono, which forced his retirement from racing.

⊙ QUICK TO BE QUICK

By the end of the 2009 Sprint Cup season, Jeff Gordon had started from pole position on 68 occasions. He didn't take long to get going, as he achieved the first of these back at Charlotte in 1993, shortly after his 22nd birthday in only his second season in the Winston Cup, driving a Chevrolet for Hendrick Motorsports.

⊙ YARBOROUGH'S FLYING YEAR

Cale Yarborough still holds the proud boast that he has scored the most pole positions in a season in the modern era. In 1980 he placed his Junior Johnson Chevrolet Monte Carlo on pole 14 times in 31 attempts. Closest to this are three drivers who managed 11 in a campaign: Darrell Waltrip (1981), Bill Elliott (1985) and Ryan Newman (2003).

⊙ VICKERS: MAN IN A GROOVE

One of the drivers with the best recent form in claiming pole positions is Brian Vickers, who claimed six poles in 2009. He was certainly the man setting the pace, with poles in his Red Bull Racing Toyota Camry at California Speedway, Richmond, Michigan (twice), Sears Point and Chicagoland. However, Mark Martin outstripped him later in the season and started from the front of the grid on seven occasions.

⊙ REMINDER OF WHO'S THE BOSS

David Pearson, with three drivers' titles to his name, tended to participate selectively in the mid-1970s, but "The Silver Fox" was still mightily effective, taking more poles than any of his rivals in both 1975 and 1976, with seven and eight respectively. Not taking in all of the races left him down the order, but he proved a point.

	TOP 10 DRIVERS WITH MOST POLE POSITIONS IN MODERN ERA	
1	Jeff Gordon	68
2	Darrell Waltrip	59
3	David Pearson	55
4	Bill Elliott	54
5	Cale Yarborough	51
6	Mark Martin	48
7	Ryan Newman	45
8	Geoff Bodine	37
9	Bobby Allison	36
=	Rusty Wallace	36

CAREER DURATION

⊙ FOR THE LOVE OF RACING

"Awesome Bill from Dawsonville", aka Bill Elliott, is a man who can't give up racing. His selective 20§ Sprint Cup programme was his 36th at NASCAR's top level, one more than the previous record career duration of Dave Marcis and Richard Petty.

⊙ SELF-RUN, SELF- MOTIVATED

Dave Marcis was an old-school driver. At the end of 1978, after racing for 10 years, he predominantly ran his own cars after parting company with Osterlund Racing. Having made his debut in 1968, he raced on and on, despite scoring just five wins in 883 starts across 35 years. His final race was in the 2002 Daytona 500 a fortnight before his 60th birthday.

⊙ DURATION OF SUCCESS

Following in the wheel tracks of a successful grandfather (Lee) and a legendary father (Richard) wasn't easy for Kyle Petty, but he spent 30 years trying to emulate their success. By the time he retired in 2008, he'd added eight wins to the family haul.

⊙ MR CONSISTENT

After dabbling in 1975 and 1976, Ricky Rudd became a regular in 1977 and, apart from half campaigns in 1978 and 1980, he just kept on racing, usually picking up a win or two every year until the wins thinned out at the beginning of the 21st century. He pocketed more than $40 million in prize money along the way by the time he retired at the end of the 2007 season.

⊙ MOST MODERN MAN

Darrell Waltrip burst into NASCAR's top series in 1972 and was a winner by 1975 before going on to land three titles. He finally decided that it was time to retire after the 2000 season and hung up his helmet at the age of 53, after what was then the longest career of any driver in NASCAR's modern era. He had spent 29 seasons at the top, in which he won 85 races and claimed drivers' titles in 1981, 1982 and 1985. Bill Elliott has since surpassed him.

⊙ LIVING THROUGH HISTORY

Elmo Langley's NASCAR career stretched from 1954 to 1981, and the changes experienced during those 27 years must have been extraordinary, from racing on the many dirt ovals and pocketing $450 prize money in his first season to managing just six laps in his last race, at Dover Downs in 1981.

⊙ THREE DECADES AND MORE

James Hylton had a lengthy, if not exceptionally successful career, as he won but twice in his 30 years at NASCAR's top level between 1964 and 1993. Amazingly, the competitive fire still burned into his seventies and he attempted to qualify for the Daytona 500 in 2007 at the age of 72, and was then thwarted in a further attempt in 2009 that would have stretched his career across a 46-year timespan.

⊙ PRACTICALLY PART OF THE FURNITURE

Richard Petty raced at NASCAR's top level for so long that he seemed to be part of the fixtures and fittings. He raced for 35 years, between 1958 and 1992. Remarkably, he won at least one race from 1960 all the way through to 1977, achieving an 18-year winning streak.

⊙ NEVER GIVE UP

JD McDuffie, who raced from 1975–91, holds a record that he would rather belonged to someone else: the most starts without a win. His winless run stretched to 653 starts. Buddy Arrington – who raced from 1964–88 – tried 563 times without success and Neil Castles hit 501 for zero. Of the current drivers, Dave Blaney has 333 starts and still no win since he hit NASCAR's biggest stage in 1992, just behind Kenny Wallace (344), who quit after 2008.

⊙ TEXAN TOUGHIE

AJ Foyt drove at the top level of NASCAR across 30 seasons, between 1964 and 1994, although he managed only 128 races in that time as he concentrated primarily on IndyCar events, with further outings in sports cars. However, the aggressive Texan managed nine wins, showing his talent across all categories of the sport.

⊙ PUTTING OFF RETIREMENT

The fact that Terry Labonte's two drivers' titles are 12 years apart – 1984 and 1996 – shows that he's a driver with longevity and he has a career that stretches from 1978 to 2011. However, like Bill Elliott, he's finding it hard to stand down completely, although he started running part-time from 2005, and he joined Elliott in competing for 34 seasons when ran 15th for FAS Lane Racing at the 2011 Daytona 500.

MOST YEARS IN COMPETITION

1	Bill Elliott	36
2	Dave Marcis	35
=	Richard Petty	35
4	Terry Labonte	34
5	Buddy Baker	33
6	Ricky Rudd	32
7	Cale Yarborough	31
8	AJ Foyt	30
=	James Hylton	30
=	Kyle Petty	30
11	Mark Martin	29
=	Darrell Waltrip	29
13	Dale Earnhardt	27
=	Elmo Langley	27
=	JD McDuffie	27
=	David Pearson	27

YOUNGEST & OLDEST

⊙ STILL ON THE UP

Mark Martin turned 50 just before the start of the 2009 Sprint Cup, but he was still very much a threat. He duly bagged seven poles and five wins with his Hendrick Motorsport Chevrolet Impala and finished the year as runner-up to Hendrick Motorsport teammate Jimmie Johnson. The skill for a sportsman is to know when to retire and not drag a career on too long. Clearly, Martin doesn't have to worry about this just yet.

⊙ OLD FATHER TIME

Bobby Allison became the oldest champion in 1983 at the age of 45. It was certainly a long time coming, as he had made his debut 22 years earlier. He continued racing until 1988, when injuries resulting from an accident at Pocono Raceway forced his retirement.

⊙ YOUTH BEATS EXPERIENCE

NASCAR's youngest champion was Bill Rexford, who was only 23 when he was crowned in 1950 after winning just one of the 19 Grand National Series rounds, at Canfield, in his Julian Buesink-entered Oldsmobile 88. He still outscored Curtis Turner, a fellow Oldsmobile driver, despite the fact that Turner won four times.

⊙ FIRST OF THE YOUNG GUNS

Donald Thomas was very much the young gun when he scored his first victory, at the age of 20 years 129 days in 1952, at Lakewood in Atlanta. However, it proved to be the only win for the younger brother of 1951 and 1953 Grand National champion Herb Thomas. It was achieved after Donald saw that Herb was in trouble and pulled over to let him take over his car.

⊙ FAST IN A CAR AND ON SKATES

In 1993 Morgan Shepherd proved that he was more than making up the numbers 23 years after his debut when he won the Motorcraft 500 at Atlanta in his Wood Brothers Ford Thunderbird. This means that he became the second oldest winner of a race at the age of 51 years 150 days. He continued racing until he was 64. Not content with the speed he generated in the car, he also has a little-known hobby – rollerskating.

⊙ OLDEST POLE SITTER

Harry Gant was a quinquagenarian prodigy, as he claimed eight of his 18 career wins after his 50th birthday. Therefore, it wasn't much of a surprise when he extended the record for being the oldest pole position qualifier, which he achieved at Bristol Motor Speedway in his Leo Jackson Chevrolet Lumina in 1994 when he was 54 years old.

⊙ THE NEW BOYS ARE COMING

NASCAR's top-level competition has experienced a gradual lowering of the average age of its competitors, but there are still drivers racing and winning in their forties. At the other end of the scale, Joey Logano recently became the youngest winner in NASCAR's Sprint Cup when he took his Joe Gibbs Racing Toyota to victory at New Hampshire International Speedway in 2009 only 35 days after his 19th birthday. This took more than a year off Kyle Busch's record set four years earlier.

⊙ STILL UP FOR THE CHALLENGE

The oldest winner of a top-level NASCAR race is "Handsome Harry" Gant, who was 52 years 218 days old when he was first past the chequered flag in the Champion Spark Plug 400 at Michigan Speedway in his Skoal Bandit Oldsmobile Cutlass in 1992.

⊙ THE SHORTEST-LIVED YOUNGEST FACE

Kyle Busch only had a short reign as the youngest ever race winner. He scored his first win at California Speedway in 2005 when aged just 20 years 125 days, just four days younger than the record that Donald Thomas set 53 years earlier. Within four years, his record had fallen, to someone more than a year younger, Joey Logano.

TOP 10 OLDEST WINNERS

1	Harry Gant	52 years 218 days
2	Morgan Shepherd	51 years 150 days
3	Mark Martin	50 years 193 days
4	Bobby Allison	50 years 63 days
5	Dale Earnhardt	49 years 169 days
6	Dale Jarrett	48 years 76 days
7	Bill Elliott	48 years 34 days
8	Rusty Wallace	47 years 248 days
9	Geoff Bodine	47 years 115 days
10	Richard Petty	47 years 2 days

RACE STARTS

⊙ CONTROLLED EXCELLENCE

The epitome of consistency and speed must surely be Dale Jarrett's run in 1999 when he and his Robert Yates Racing Ford Taurus scored the greatest number of top-10 race finishes in a championship – 29. This was achieved from 34 starts, so it's not surprising that he landed the title.

⊙ THEY CALL HIM "IRONMAN"

Ricky Rudd just kept going and going, continually extending his record for the most consecutive starts. This reached 788 races in a row when he retired from NASCAR's top flight at the end of the 2005 season. After a year away he returned for more, finally retiring for good after the 2007 season after not adding to his 23 wins. His final total was 906 races in a career lasting 32 years.

⊙ EXPERIENCE LEADS TO RECORD AVERAGES

Cale Yarborough produced some remarkably competitive seasons during his 31-year career, however, he made only 560 starts during that time, as he was selective about when he raced. Despite this fact, in 1977 he took his second straight title and he achieved a remarkable average finishing position of 4.5. Three years later, his average starting position was 3.1. These are both records.

⊙ CELEBRATING IN GREY

When Terry Labonte rolled out for the First Union 400 at North Wilkesboro in 1996, his Hendrick Motorsport Chevrolet looked unusual, for its regular red, yellow and white Kellogg's livery had been replaced by a grey colour scheme. This was to mark the day that he equalled Richard Petty's then record of 513 consecutive starts. He marked the day in style by winning the race and, later that year, won his second Winston Cup title.

⊙ SON OUTSTRIPS FATHER

Buck Baker was definitely a hard act to follow for his son Buddy, and he did not exceed his father's career tally of 46 wins, stopping at 19. However, the one table in which Buddy ranks higher is that of races started, ending his career 12th overall, with 700 race starts to his father's 682.

⊙ WHEN 1,000 JUST ISN'T NEARLY ENOUGH

It already seems a long time since Richard Petty was last a frontrunner – his last win was in 1984 – but it seems positively ages since he scored his first win. That was back in 1960 at the Southern State Fairgrounds. His career just went on and on, gathering seven titles as he went. In all, he made 1,184 starts before he quit in 1992.

⊙ CHASING THE DREAM

Ken Schrader advanced from Midgets and Sprint Cars to IndyCars, but decided a top-level NASCAR career was for him in 1984. He ranks ninth in most race starts, with 732, the last of which was in 2008. Despite this number of starts he took just five wins, the most recent of these coming in 1991. However, he earned fame for a barrel roll across the finish line in the 1987 Pepsi Firecracker 400 at Daytona.

⊙ ART OF GATHERING POINTS

Making every start count is imperative in top-level NASCAR racing. There may be 30 plus rounds, but failing to finish costs a driver – big time. An entire season can be a disaster unless a run of top-five finishes can be achieved, which is far from easy in a 43-car field. However, Jeff Gordon displayed remarkable form in his third title year – 1998 – as he racked up a record 26 top-five finishes from 33 starts.

⊙ THE ALLISONS LOVED TO RACE

Bobby Allison ranks 10th in the all-time starts list, with 718. Add to that his brother Donnie's 242 plus his son Davey's 191 and you reach a family total of 1,151 starts. Davey lost his life in a helicopter accident at Talladega in 1991 and Bobby's other son Cliff was killed in NASCAR's second division in 1992.

DRIVERS WITH MOST RACE STARTS

#	Driver	Starts	#	Driver	Starts
1	Richard Petty	1,184	9	Ken Schrader	733*
2	Ricky Rudd	906	10	Bobby Allison	718
3	Dave Marcis	883	11	Rusty Wallace	706
4	Terry Labonte	870*	12	Buddy Baker	700
5	Kyle Petty	846	13	Buck Baker	682
6	Bill Elliott	822*	14	Dale Earnhardt	677
7	Darrell Waltrip	809	15	Dale Jarrett	668
8	Mark Martin	795*	* = still racing.		

DRIVER RECORDS

⊙ SUCCESS ACROSS THE BOARD

Mario Andretti, Dan Gurney and Juan Pablo Montoya share an
unusual record. They have all won races in NASCAR, F1 and IndyCar.
Gurney was first to complete this triple, when he drove his Eagle
to victory at Riverside in 1967. Andretti did it when he won the
1971 South African GP for Ferrari. Montoya finished off his triple by
winning the NASCAR race at Mexico City in 2007. Gurney even threw
in victory in the Le Mans 24 Hours – in 1967 – for good measure.

⊙ FIRST IMPRESSIONS

Proving that you don't have to hang around to achieve glory,
IndyCar racer Johnny Rutherford hit the Grand National Series with a
considerable bang when he triumphed at his first attempt, driving a
Smokey Yunick-run Chevrolet Impala in a 100-mile qualifying race at
Daytona in 1963. This equalled the feat of Jim Roper and Jack White
(1949), Harold Kite and Leon Sales (1950) and Marvin Burke (1951).

⊙ IT'S ALL ABOUT PERCENTAGES

Herb Thomas has the best wins to starts percentage of any of the
drivers who have contested 100 races or more. From his 228 race
starts, the 1950s' ace from North Carolina won 48 times, including
the 1954 and 1955 Daytona 500s, for an average of 21.053 per
cent. He won the overall title in 1951 and 1953, and the second of
these title-winning series was his best, as he collected 12 wins from
37 starts in his Fabulous Hudson Hornet. Contemporary Tim Flock
managed a 20.856 per cent average.

⊙ FASTEST TO 50

Jeff Gordon made the strongest impression of any driver in
NASCAR's Winston Cup. Not only was he champion in his third year,
but he reached the landmark of 50 wins in fewer races than any
other driver, managing this feat in only 232 race starts. He was also
second fastest to 40 wins, with Herb Thomas hitting that target in
just 151 races.

◉ NORTH CAROLINANS' STREAK ENDS

In every season from the start of the top-level NASCAR series until 2007 a driver from North Carolina won at least one round, largely thanks to the Petty family from 1949–77. However, that run came to an end in 2007 when none of Dale Earnhardt Jr, Dale Jarrett, Kyle Petty, Scott Riggs or Brian Vickers, all from North Carolina, could claim a victory. In the final round – the Ford 400 at Homestead, Florida – the best placed of this quintet, Jarrett, finished 17th.

◉ MOST FAMOUS FIGHT

This isn't so much a record, more of a landmark. It's NASCAR's first punch-up on live TV. This came in the 1979 Daytona 500, the first time NASCAR's most prestigious race was screened live. Cale Yarborough was drafting Bobbie Allison when they clashed going into Turn 3. Richard Petty shot by to win, but the cameras stayed on Yarborough and Allison as they became embroiled in a fight, with Allison's brother Donnie stopping and joining in. NASCAR's popularity soared because of it.

◉ FOUR MAKES A FLOCK

The record number of siblings to start a race is four. This was in the one and only season of the NASCAR Strictly Stock Series in 1949, at the second race, on Daytona Beach. The siblings involved were the Flocks – Bob, Fonty, Tim and Ethel, their sister. Tim finished second behind Red Byron, Ethel 11th and red-faced Bob and Fonty were sidelined by engine problems, giving Ethel bragging rights for every family occasion thereafter.

◉ LEAD, LEAD, LEAD, LOSE

The record for the most laps led in a season is held by Bobby Allison. In 1972, he led an astounding 4,343 laps with his Junior Johnson Chevrolet Monte Carlo in the first ever Winston Cup. Not that it helped him outscore Richard Petty, though, as he ended the year as runner-up. Petty, incidentally, led only 2,093 laps.

◉ LAP AFTER LAP AFTER LAP

Bobby Hamilton won four races, and never won the Winston Cup. However, he did have an exceptional 2001 campaign when he set the record for the most laps completed in a season – 10,750 – from 36 starts with his Andy Petree Racing Chevrolet. However, he won just once that year, at Talladega, and finished in the top 10 only six times, to end the season ranked 18th overall.

⊚ CLEAR BY 20,000 LAPS

Richard Petty holds the overall record for laps led, having been in front for 52,194 laps. Cale Yarborough is next up, with 31,676, and Bobby Allison is third on 27,539. Of the current drivers, Jeff Gordon is highest ranked, seventh overall on 21,657 up to the end of 2010.

⊚ HE'S IN THE MONEY

NASCAR's streets have been paved with gold for Jimmie Johnson, as you would expect for a driver with ffive titles to his name. Indeed, with prize money growing by the decade, he is obviously earning more than Richard Petty did in his pomp. Johnson holds the record for the most money earned in a season, landing $7,764,405 in 2006.

⊚ WINNING BY MILES

Ned Jarrett holds the record for the largest winning margin in terms of distance in a race. This was in the Southern 500 at Darlington Raceway in 1965, when he crossed the finish line in his Ford Fairlane 14 laps (19.25 miles) clear of Buck Baker's Plymouth. "Gentleman Ned" won 13 races that year to secure his second Grand National title.

⊚ STARTING AND FINISHING

Bobby Labonte certainly knows his way around an oval, as he has been in the top level of NASCAR for 20 years since his debut in 1982. He was runner-up to Dale Jarrett in 1999, started from pole 20 times, won 17 races, led 151 races and for 3,413 laps. He also ranks second in the table for the number of laps completed in the modern era, with 129,912 to Jeff Gordon's 130,709.

⊚ WHAT'S IN A NICKNAME?

Dale Earnhardt was always a hard driver, but his on-track antics in 1986 as he raced to his second Winston Cup title raised a few eyebrows, starting with the second race of the year, the Miller High Life 400 at Richmond. Passed by Darrell Waltrip with three laps to go, he struck back and spun Waltrip out at the next corner, only to crash himself, also taking out Joe Ruttmann and Geoff Bodine who'd been running third and fourth. Thereafter, he was known as "Ironhead" or "The Intimidator".

⊙ KEEP AWAY FROM THE WALLS

It was said in the early 1960s that Herman Beam looked "more like a chemist" than a racer. He did look somewhat meek – he was dubbed "The Turtle" – and very different from his rivals who were chiefly country boys (Beam was born in Johnson City, Tennessee). However, Beam had the last laugh as he recorded a remarkable run of 84 consecutive race finishes from 1961–63, keeping his car away from the walls and from his rivals.

TOP 10 HIGHEST WINS TO STARTS PERCENTAGES*

1	Herb Thomas	21.053%
2	Tim Flock	20.856%
3	David Pearson	18.293%
4	Richard Petty	16.892%
5	Fred Lorenzen	16.456%
6	Fireball Roberts	16.019%
7	Junior Johnson	15.794%
8	Jimmie Johnson	16.151%
9	Cale Yarborough	14.821%
10	Jeff Gordon	13.290%

For drivers with 100 starts or more.

TEAMS

In this form of motor sport, manufacturer assistance has always been very much hush-hush. The teams remain rooted in individuals, whether headed by former racers who turn to team ownership when they have hung up their helmets or people in love with the sport who simply set up teams in a romantic pursuit of glory. These days, all teams are multimillion-dollar businesses.

TEAM WINS

⊙ REMARKABLE PETTYS

Father and son Lee and Richard Petty clocked up 10 top-level
NASCAR series drivers' titles between them, 1954–79, and scored
all 260 of their race victories for the family team. Richard's son Kyle
added eight further race victories to push Petty Enterprises' tally to
268 wins in all. The team merged with Gillett Evernham Motorsports
in 2009 and now races as Richard Petty Motorsports.

⊙ A TEAM IN A ROUSH

Jack Roush runs a mean team, always running Fords, that grew out
of his racing engine business in 1988. The team has grown and
grown to become one of the pre-eminent outfits operating out of
North Carolina. The 2009 Sprint Cup wasn't its greatest campaign,
with its highest-placed driver only seventh, but it has 116 wins to its
name and had back-to-back champions in Matt Kenseth (2003) and
Kurt Busch (2004).

⊙ WOOD BE WARRIORS

Wood Brothers Racing really is part of NASCAR's furniture, having
been around since 1950. Started by five brothers from Virginia –
Glen, Leonard, Delano, Clay and Ray Lee – the team has guided
drivers, including Curtis Turner, Fireball Roberts, Tiny Lund and Fred
Lorenzen to 96 top-level wins. Despite this good record, Wood
Brothers Racing has never won a drivers' title. The team's greatest
claim to fame is that it invented the modern pit stop in the 1960s
and it was called up to the Indianapolis 500 to help Jim Clark in
1965. He won.

⊙ HENDRICK KEEPS ON WINNING

Hendrick Motorsports has been the predominant team since
assuming control from Richard Childress Racing in 1995, when Jeff
Gordon scored the first of his titles. It's still very much the team of
the moment, but with a driver line-up of Gordon, reigning champion
Jimmie Johnson, Mark Martin and Dale Earnhardt Jr, it wasn't likely
to lose out in 2009. Its cars have won every year since 1986.
Penske Racing has a streak five years shorter, its cars having won in
each of the last 19 years.

⊙ HE KNEW WHAT IT TAKES

The inimitable Junior Johnson ran his own car in his final year of racing in 1965, taking 13 wins. He then quit to run cars for others, who added 119 further wins and six drivers' titles before the team shut up shop at the end of 1995. The team's best period was from 1976–78, when Cale Yarborough raced to three titles. Darrell Waltrip then bagged a pair in 1981 and 1982, before adding another in 1985.

⊙ POWERED BY EARNHARDT

Richard Childress Racing has one particularly impressive record – it is the only team to have entered every single round since the end of the first year of the modern era, 1972. In that time, the team's best victory tally came in 1987, when Dale Earnhardt won 11 of the 29 rounds as he raced to his second title with the team.

⊙ TAKING A DIFFERENT APPROACH

Better known for his team's successes in IndyCar racing, Roger Penske's NASCAR team has had a strong presence, but has never landed a drivers' title. It made an unusual start in 1972, running Mark Donohue in the unlikely-looking AMC Matador. Regular wins didn't come until it tried more mainstream machinery in the early 1990s

⊙ BUD STARTS STRONG

Bud Moore Engineering has had its ups and downs, but it ranks 10th on the list of teams with the most wins – 63 – and has two titles to its credit. These came in 1962 and 1963, both with Joe Weatherly driving. He had given the team a win on its debut in 1961, winning a qualifying race. However, success didn't last and Brett Bodine scored its last win in 1993 before the team was sold.

⊙ RICHARD AND DALE

Richard Childress Racing is a team linked inextricably with one driver – Dale Earnhardt. Together, they won six titles and 62 races. Following Dale's death in the opening race of 2001, the team has won a further 25 races to add to the two Ricky Rudd scored in 1983. It's still going today, but the wins don't flow as easily as they did in Dale's day.

⊙ START WITH A BANG

Bud Moore Engineering's first two years in top-level NASCAR, 1961 and 1962, were its greatest. With Joe Weatherly at the wheel of first its Pontiac Catalina then its Mercury in the second half of 1962, he won nine races each year and the title in the 1962. He was champion again in 1963, but with only three wins.

TOP 10 TEAMS WITH MOST RACE WINS

1	Petty Enterprises	268		6	Holman-Moody	92
2	Hendrick Motorsports	188		7	Richard Childress Racing	89
3	Junior Johnson & Associates	132		8	Joe Gibbs Racing	77
4	Roush Fenway Racing	116		9	Penske Racing	64
5	Wood Brothers Racing	96		10	Bud Moore Engineering	63

⊙ TRIAL BEFORE COMMITMENT

Penske Racing ranks ninth in the race wins table, with 67 by the end of 2010. It made its top-level NASCAR debut in 1972, but it was a far from constant presence until 1976, when Bobby Allison ranked fourth despite not winning. Penske broadened its focus from just IndyCar racing to re-enter NASCAR again in 1991, this after 11 years away. Then the team settled down and Rusty Wallace started winning. Kurt Busch claimed the three most recent wins in 2010 in Penske's lead Dodge Charger, including the Sprint All-Star Race.

⊙ RACING AND BUILDING

Formed by John Holman and racer Ralph Moody in 1957, the Holman-Moody team was at the top of its game in the 1960s when it built the cars that won 48 out of the 55 races in 1965, then claimed consecutive Grand National titles for David Pearson with a Ford Torino Talladega in 1968 and 1969. Running Ford machinery from the 1950s to the 1970s, its cars clocked up 92 wins, but its main business was building cars for other teams.

⊙ FOOTBALL GOES RACING

Former Washington Redskins football coach Joe Gibbs formed his eponymous NASCAR team in 1991, first to race himself and then to run others. Since then, it has landed three drivers' titles and 77 wins, with all of its drivers – Kyle Busch, Denny Hamlin and Joey Logano – winning races in its Toyota Camrys in 2009.

MANUFACTURERS WITH MOST TITLES

1	Chevrolet	29*	=	Dodge	2
2	Ford	15*	=	Plymouth	2
3	Oldsmobile	4	=	Pontiac	2
4	Hudson	3	10	Mercury	1
5	Buick	2			
=	Chrysler	2	* Including one shared title.		

⊙ JGR'S TITLES

Bobby Labonte's best season was in 2000. He drove his Joe Gibbs Racing Pontiac Grand Prix to four wins and won the team's first drivers' title. Tony Stewart added titles in 2002 and 2005. Labonte was never such a force again and the team replaced him with JJ Yeley for 2006.

⊙ TWO TITLES IN ONE YEAR

Vending-machine magnate Raymond Parks was the man running the most successful team when NASCAR was formed for 1948. His cars had won all of the five races run on the Daytona Beach Road Course in the preceding years. His driver, Red Byron, then won NASCAR's Strictly Stock title for Parks in 1949, with Fonty Flock landing that year's Modified title for the team.

⊙ BOW-TIE BRILLIANCE

The most manufacturer titles claimed by one manufacturer since NASCAR competition began in earnest in 1949 is Chevrolet's tally of 29 (one of which, in 1985, it shared with Ford). The General Motors' marque scored its first win in 1958, and its most recent one in 2009, largely through the efforts of Hendrick Motorsports and especially its lead driver Jimmie Johnson.

⊙ BEST OF THE REST

Ford has won the manufacturers' title 14 times, plus one shared with Chevrolet in 1985, but the blue oval has seldom enjoyed dominance. Indeed, its best ever run was winning the title three years in a row, from 1963–65, with two-year runs in 1968–69 and 2003–04. In comparison, Chevrolet's best run is nine in a row from 1983–91. Ford has been runner-up 21 times.

⊙ FADING FAME

The automobile manufacturer Hudson had a significant presence in NASCAR's early days, landing the manufacturers' title in 1952, 1953 and 1954. However, its name was dropped in 1957, three years after the company merged with Nash to form American Motors.

MANUFACTURERS WITH MOST TITLES IN MODERN ERA

1	Chevrolet	25*	=	Mercury	1
2	Ford	7*	=	Oldsmobile	1
3	Buick	2			
4	Dodge	1	* Including one shared title.		

TEAM POLE POSITIONS

⊙ DO AS I DO

Junior Johnson, who claimed 13 poles in 1965, brought all his driving experience to bear when his team sent its drivers out to qualify and the rewards were clear. His cars scorched to 115 pole positions between 1965 and 1995, most notably with Cale Yarborough in the late 1970s and Darrell Waltrip in the early 1980s. Waltrip's dozen in 1981 and then again in 1982 stand out.

⊙ WHEN 24 BECOMES 68

Jeff Gordon remains the most successful of Hendrick Motorsports' phalanx of drivers in many ways, and his record of 68 poles for the team certainly stands clear. This run started when he put the team's No. 24 Chevrolet Monte Carlo on pole at Charlotte just before the end of the 1993 season. His best year for poles was in 1998 when he took 13.

⊙ THE CHEVY CHASE

Chevrolet has been the leading manufacturer almost every year since the early 1980s and this form is evident in qualifying, with Chevrolets claiming pole for seven races in succession both in 1999 and 2007. Had it not been for Denny Hamlin and Greg Biffle qualifying their Toyota and Ford first and second at California Speedway in 2009, though, Chevrolet would have a 13-race pole streak.

⊙ ISAAC GIVES K&K 20

Set up by Nord Krauskopf to promote his insurance business, the K&K Insurance team ran its Dodges with remarkable success between 1966 and 1977, taking 68 poles to add to its 43 wins. Bobby Isaac gave the team its most stunning year in 1969 when he claimed a record 20 poles in one season in his winged Dodge Daytona. He went on to be champion the following year.

⊙ MEAN, BUT NOT MOODY

David Pearson was in scintillating form in qualifying for Holman-Moody Racing in 1968 and 1969, notching up 12 poles in the former and 14 in the latter in his Ford Torino Talladega. Unsurprisingly these were two championship-winning years. Fred Lorenzen was also effective for the team, adding 30 poles between 1961 and 1966.

⊙ THE KING IS ON THE THRONE AGAIN

Petty Enterprises had set an incredible 151 poles by the end of 2009, but the team's glory days came when Richard Petty really earned his nickname "The King". This was from the mid-1960s to the mid-70s, when he set 126 poles, peaking with 18 in 1967.

⊙ PENSKE POACHES POLES

Penske Racing has gathered 83 poles since its debut in 1972. Rusty Wallace claimed 27 of these for the team, up to 2002, by which time Ryan Newman had taken over as the team's attack tool and bagged 43 poles by the end of 2009, including 11 from 36 races in 2003 alone in his Dodge Intrepid.

⊙ MAKE WAY FOR THE CHAMPION

NASCAR looks after its former champions well, as there is a rule called the "champion's provisional". This regulation stipulates that the final spot on the grid is available for any reigning or former champion who has failed to make the cut during qualification. If two former champions have been too slow, the one who was champion more recently is given the place on the grid.

⊙ SILVER FOX FLIES

Wood Brothers Racing has taken 118 poles in its lengthy career and Cale Yaborough used the team's No. 21 Ford Fairlane to take his first superspeedway pole for the Atlanta 500 in 1967. He went on to dominate the race. However, it was when David Pearson joined in 1972 that the poles really flowed, with 51 added by 1979.

⊙ POLE FOR THE BIG ONE

Hendrick Motorsports has set a line of records as long as your arm, but one of its drivers, Ken Schrader, managed the impressive feat of qualifying on pole for the season's most prestigious race, the Daytona 500, three years in a row from 1988. However, he failed to win on any of these occasions.

TOP 10 TEAMS WITH MOST POLE POSITIONS

1	Hendrick Motorsports	167	6	Penske Racing	83
2	Petty Enterprises	151	7	K&K Insurance	68
3	Wood Brothers Racing	118	8	Roush Fenway Racing	65
4	Junior Johnson & Associates	115	9	Yates Racing	49
5	Holman-Moody	85	10	Joe Gibbs Racing	46

TEAM PRIZE MONEY

⊙ THE MAN WHO MADE IT ALL HAPPEN

NASCAR founder Bill France was the man who made it all happen in 1948 by organizing the races and the prize fund that put the NASCAR show on the road. He also created a points system and made sure that each year from then on had a champion driver, boosting the marketability of the series. He even created a benevolent fund for injured drivers.

⊙ HOW CAR OWNERS SCORE

The points systems for drivers and car owners are broadly similar, with 185 points awarded for each race winner. But car owners can even claim points for cars that fail to qualify, that's to say those that are 44th fastest in qualifying and below. There is a three-point increment between positions, from 31 points for 44th and so on down the order. Prize money varies from race to race, but it's always more than $4 million per round, rising to $6 million at the races with generous title sponsors.

⊙ JUMPING AROUND

Bud Moore Engineering didn't have the budget to run a full season in 1963, but Joe Weatherly was so desperate to win a second straight title that he "bummed a ride" in the races the team missed. He drove for eight other teams, in Chrysler, Plymouth, Dodge and Mercury cars in addition to his regular Pontiac, collecting prize money of $74,623.76 which would have helped run a car all year. Conversely, Wood Brothers Racing used six drivers to land that year's owners' title.

⊙ ONCE THE LEADERS

Richard Childress Racing and Dale Earnhardt racked up points upon points during Dale's remarkable run of success between 1986 and 1994 as he collected six titles. Yet his most lucrative season was in 2000 when he won just short of $5 million as the amount of prize money awarded continued to climb. Since his death in the first race of 2001 the team's position in the prize-money table has slid, and it's now third overall behind Hendrick and Roush.

⊙ BOBBY AND TONY SHOW

Joe Gibbs Racing, set up by the former head coach of the NFL's Washington Redskins, is a team that has built its name and achieved its glory largely through the running of two drivers: Bobby Labonte and Tony Stewart. They both won titles and a combined prize-money haul of $89,070,821 for the team based at Huntersville, North Carolina, although Kyle Busch and Denny Hamlin have since taken the wheel.

⊙ FAR FROM RUSTY

When Penske Racing decided to get serious about Cup Series NASCAR in 1990, Rusty Wallace was the driver who really put the team on the map. His 36 wins over the next 11 years put points and prize money aplenty into the team's coffers. Apart from Ryan Newman's great 2003 campaign, when he collected eight victories, the pickings haven't been as rich since, leaving Roger Penske's team ranking fifth for prize money earned.

⊙ LOSING ITS BLOOM

Robert Yates Racing is no longer the hot ticket it was when Davey Allison was at the wheel in the early 1990s and the wins flowed, as they did when Dale Jarrett replaced him. Since Jarrett's departure after 2006 the team's form has dropped away, leaving it ranked sixth overall in the prize-money table.

⊙BILL PAID THE BILLS

Bill Elliott was the first driver to put large amounts of prize money into the pot for Ray Evernham's team after the talented engineer left Hendrick Motorsports and set up his own team for the 2000 season. Evernham's team has since seen Kasey Kahne boost its position to ninth in the prize-money table, with strong seasons from 2004–07.

⊙ ROUSH CHASES HENDRICK

Roush Racing ranks second overall in the all-time points standings and prize-money tables after particular success in the first decade of the 21st century. However, the team's 2005 campaign was a strange one. Driver Kurt Busch was fired with two races to go as he had been cited for reckless driving on the road and he was replaced by Kenny Wallace.

⊙ SABCO'S THWARTED TITLE SHOT

Felix Sabates's team went into partnership with Chip Ganassi in 2001 when the former racer wanted to branch out from IndyCar racing. Their combined team, SABCO/Chip Ganassi Racing, led for 25 weeks of the 2002 season through Sterling Marlin, but he suffered a neck injury at Kansas and his season was over. He tumbled to 18th in the rankings, but still earned the team $4,228,889.

⊙ THE TOP THREE

Running four cars gives Hendrick Motorsports quite an advantage over the one-car and two-car teams, but it's the sheer calibre of its drivers that makes the difference. In 2009 its drivers Jimmie Johnson, Mark Martin, Jeff Gordon and Dale Earnhardt Jr finished first, second, third and 25th. The team has done the bulk of its winning in the past 20 years, so it tops the prize-money table with $327 million.

TOP 10 TEAMS WITH MOST PRIZE MONEY EARNED

1	Hendrick Motorsports	$327,679,678
2	Roush Racing	$320,005,436
3	Richard Childress Racing	$206,708,253
4	Joe Gibbs Racing	$186,997,736
5	Penske Racing	$132,499,668
6	Robert Yates Racing	$127,267,241
7	Dale Earnhardt Inc.	$125,415,271
8	Petty Enterprises	$87,393,504
9	Evernham Motorsports	$71,441,190
10	Wood Brothers Racing	$50,836,122

OTHER TEAM RECORDS

⊙ A MAN USED TO MAKING A SPLASH

Carl Kiekhaefer was an unmissable presence in NASCAR in the 1950s. Having made his fortune through his Mercury outboard motors company, he bought a car to run in NASCAR in 1955 and it won immediately. Not afraid to spend his fortune, he brought in tailor-made transporters and raised the bar for his rivals, sometimes running as many as six cars. He pulled out of the sport at the end of 1956.

⊙ BIG NAMES OF NASCAR

Eighteen manufacturers have entered top-level NASCAR races. This includes, of course, "The Big Three" – General Motors, Ford and Chrysler; including their derivatives – and Alfa Romeo, Aston Martin, MG and Porsche, who all made odd outings in the 1950s and early 1960s. GM's Chevrolet and Chrysler's Dodge have entered the most models – eight apiece, from Chevrolet's 1955 Bel Air to its 2009 Impala SS and from Dodge's 1953 Coronet to its 2008 Charger R/T. Ford trails behind on six models.

⊙ NO SMOKEY WITHOUT FIRE

Nicknamed "Smokey" after a motorbike he raced when he was 16, Henry Yunick holds the record for the second most wins achieved by a crew chief – 57. These came in NASCAR's earliest days. Usually dressed in white overalls and a battered cowboy hat, Yunick guided Herb Thomas to drivers' titles in 1951 and 1953, and helped the likes of Marvin Panch, Fireball Roberts and Bobby Isaac to numerous wins.

⊙ MASTER BREWER

Tim Brewer is third on the all-time list for crew chief wins with 53. He plied his trade at Junior Johnson's team in the 1970s and early 1980s after serving his apprenticeship at Richard Childress Racing. He helped Cale Yarborough and Darrell Waltrip to the drivers' title in 1978 and 1981 respectively, before joining Morgan-McClure Motorsports. Tim is now a TV analyst for ESPN.

⊙ YUNICK'S TRICKS

The wiliest crew chief of them all, Smokey Yunick, had an astute technical brain. He pushed for safer cars after his driver, Fireball Roberts, crashed at Charlotte in 1964 and died as a result of his burns. But most of his intellect was focused on finding an advantage, achieving such tricks as lowering and modifying the roof and windows and raising the floor of Curtis Turner's Chevrolet Chevelle in 1966, then fitting a thick tube for the fuel line, adding five gallons to its capacity. He retired in 1970.

⊙ MAIN MAN IN CHARGE

Dale Inman holds the record for not only the most titles won under his command, but also the most race victories. His charges won the top-level NASCAR title on no fewer than eight occasions. It was at Petty Enterprises that he plied his trade for three decades, so he was seen as his cousin Richard Petty's right-hand man through all of "The King's" seven titles, before running Terry Labonte's title-winning campaign for Billy Hagan's team in 1984. His tally of wins is a staggering 198.

⊙ KIEKHAEFER'S 16-RACE RUN

Carl Kiekhaefer's team achieved a record in 1956 that is unlikely ever to be beaten – a 16-race winning streak. The run started with Buck Baker's win in one of the team's Chrysler 300s at Atlanta and ran to Herb Thomas's at Merced. The streak came to an end at the West Memphis Speedway when Ralph Moody won the event in his de Paulo Engineering Ford.

⊙ THE ONE TO WIN

The race that all drivers and crew chiefs want to win above all others is the season-opening Daytona 500. When it comes to this race, Dale Inman is the most successful crew chief, having helped Richard Petty to win it five times. Next up is Leonard Wood who claimed four Daytona scalps with Tiny Lund, Cale Yarborough, AJ Foyt and David Pearson.

TOP 10 MOST CREW CHIEF WINS

1	Dale Inman	198
2	Smokey Yunick	57
3	Tim Brewer	53
4	Ray Evernham	49
5	Kirk Shelmerdine	46
6	Chad Knaus	45
7	Jeff Hammond	43
8	Greg Zippadelli	34
9	Todd Parrott	29
10	Jimmy Fenning	27

⊙ STILL MAKING HIS MARK

Chad "The Magician" Knaus is the most successful of the crew chiefs still operating, with his driver Jimmie Johnson adding win after win as he raced his Hendrick Motorsports Chevrolet Impala to the drivers' title every year from 2006–09. As a result of this Chad established a new record. He became the first crew chief to be responsible for four consecutive drivers' titles.

⊙ KEEPING THE FANS ON THEIR TOES

NASCAR's stock cars are among some of the most dramatically liveried cars in motor sport. The fans never feel that they know all the cars' colours, as it has long been a tradition for some cars to be given new liveries to mark special occasions. Jeff Gordon is a past master at this and his DuPont Chevrolet's livery for the 1998 Winston Cup at Charlotte was in ChromaLusion, a paint that changes colour depending on the movement, light and viewing angle.

TRACKS

Anyone who thinks that all NASCAR tracks are the same, all ovals, should think again. One glance at Daytona or Talladega and it's obvious that there is simply no comparison between these superspeedways and the half-mile ovals at Bristol and Martinsville. NASCAR also is contested on road courses, at Sears Point and Watkins Glen. These not only have right-hand turns as well as left-hand ones, but there are notable gradient changes too. So, there's variety aplenty on the NASCAR tour.

TRACK LENGTHS

⊙ RAIDING INDYCAR'S SPIRITUAL HOME

It was a special moment when top-level NASCAR raced at the Indianapolis Motor Speedway, home of IndyCar racing, for the very first time. This occurred in 1994, when local resident Jeff Gordon won the inaugural Brickyard 400 (so named because the circuit used to be brick paved) on the famous 2.5-mile quad-oval in his Hendrick Motorsports Chevrolet.

⊙ NO TWO THE SAME

The 22 circuits used by the Sprint Cup in 2010 are not all the same. The road courses at Sears Point and Watkins Glen are obviously different to the 20 oval circuits, but the ovals can be divided into: ovals – Bristol, Dover and Martinsville; tri-ovals – Daytona, Kansas City and Pocono; quad-ovals – Atlanta, Charlotte, Homestead, Indianapolis, New Hampshire International Speedway and Texas Speedway; those with unequal ends – Darlington; and D-shaped ovals – California Speedway, Chicagoland, Las Vegas, Michigan, Phoenix, Richmond and Talladega.

⊙ IT COULDN'T BE MORE DIFFERENT

Clocking in at 4.1 miles in length, Road America at Elkhart Lake in Wisconsin was off NASCAR's regular (southern) patch, so its twists and turns were alien to most of the drivers. The Grand National series went there just once, in 1956, with Tim Flock taking the laurels in one of Carl Kiekhaefer's Mercury Montereys.

⊙ LONG LAP ON LONG ISLAND

NASCAR visited the Bridgehampton Race Circuit on New York's Long Island in 1958, 1963, 1964 and 1966. The 2.85-mile clockwise road course was an extremely challenging one, with high-speed legs up and over the sand dunes. Jack Smith was the first to win there in his Chevrolet in 1958. The circuit is now under a golf course.

⊙ WHAT'S IN A NAME?

Neat and tidy in shape, with four equal-shaped corners, Martinsville Speedway's 0.526-mile oval is the shortest used by the Sprint Cup. Nicknamed "The Paperclip" due to its compact shape, its low banking (just 12 degrees) keeps speeds down. Its annual Sprint Cup races are run over 500 laps.

⊙ THE GREAT AMERICAN RACE

Daytona International Speedway is one of the longer circuits used in the Sprint Cup Series. At 2.5 miles, the ever-popular Florida venue owes its high average speeds not so much to lap length as to its turns being banked at 31 degrees. When the circuit was built in the late 1950s this was the steepest that asphalt could be laid.

⊙ NO SIDE THE SAME

Pocono Raceway in Pennsylvania is a triangular and tricky circuit, with each of its three corners appreciably different in angle and degree of banking. So it comes as no surprise that its 2.5-mile lap is dubbed "The Tricky Triangle" and it certainly gives the engineers a headache as they try to set up the cars.

⊙ ARE WE THERE YET?

In the case of the Islip Speedway used by the Grand National Series between 1964 and 1971, the answer is "yes", as the New York circuit was only 0.2 miles long, making the 10 quarter-mile circuits used – Bowman Gray Stadium, Buffalo Civic Stadium, Dixie Speedway, Gamecock Speedway, Heidelberg Raceway, Huntsville Speedway, McCormick Field, Norwood Arena, Starkey Speedway and Tar Heel Speedway – seem lengthy.

⊙ GEORGIA'S VERY OWN ROAD CIRCUIT

There were two very different circuits that NASCAR used at the Augusta International Raceway in the 1960s. One was a 0.5-mile oval, the other a 3-mile road course that was used for the second round of the 1964 season only. Fireball Roberts was the winner, but strangely he and five other drivers out of the first seven finishers here died before the following racing season.

⊙ SHORT BUT NOT SWEET

Bristol Motor Speedway is known as "Thunder Valley" and bills itself as "The World's Fastest Half Mile". Actually, it's slightly longer than that, at 0.533 miles. What isn't open for debate is that its all-enclosing grandstands make it a real bullring, with spectators able to see the entire circuit from any vantage point.

⊙ REASONS TO BE FEARFUL

Talladega Superspeedway in Alabama, also known as "The Big One", is the longest circuit on the Sprint Cup schedule at 2.66 miles. Its length, steep banking and potential speeds concerned even the toughest drivers from the outset and there was a driver boycott at its debut race in 1969, leaving stand-in Richard Brickhouse to take his only win. However, it has been a firm fixture ever since.

LONGEST TRACKS

1	Daytona Beach Course*	4.17 miles
2	Road America*	4.1 miles
3	Augusta*	3 miles
4	Bridgehampton*	2.85 miles
5	Talladega	2.66 miles
6	Riverside*	2.631 miles
7	Daytona	2.5 miles
=	Indianapolis	2.5 miles
=	Ontario*	2.5 miles
=	Pocono	2.5 miles
=	Willow Springs*	2.5 miles
12	Watkins Glen	2.45 miles
13	California	2 miles
=	Linden	2 miles
=	Michigan	2 miles
=	Montgomery*	2 miles
=	Texas*	2 miles

No longer used.

LOCATIONS

⊙ ROOMS WITH A VIEW

Charlotte Motor Speedway, now known as Lowe's Motor Speedway, goes by the nickname of "The Beast of the South East" because it's so tricky. Alternatively, perhaps it was dubbed this as a spectator threw a bottle into the path of Junior Johnson when he was leading the 1963 Southern 500 by two laps, costing him the race. Fifty-two apartments were built over the banking at Turn 1 in the mid-1980s so fans can watch the racing from the comfort of their own homes.

⊙ MONSTER BY NAME, MONSTER BY NATURE

Dover International Speedway probably has the most evocative nickname of any current Sprint Cup track. The circuit in Dover Downs, Delaware, is known as "The Monster Mile", with its steep (24-degree) banking and tight exits to its corners providing an extremely testing challenge. Multicar accidents have long been a feature of races at Dover. Richard Petty was the first NASCAR winner here, in 1969, unusually in a Ford Torino Talladega.

⊙ ON THE BEACH

The Daytona International Speedway of today is unrecognizable from the track that was used until 1959, as this was simply a bumpy blast along the beach. Actually, it can't have been that bumpy because Malcolm Campbell attempted a world land speed record here in 1935. Long before NASCAR was formed, the first car race at Daytona was held in 1936, with drivers racing up the beach, then back down a two-lane highway.

⊙ CLOSE TO HOME

Charlotte Motor Speedway is home from home for the majority of the NASCAR teams, as their team headquarters are clustered together around the North Carolinan city. They can reap the benefits of being part of a centre of excellence, not just in terms of qualified technicians but also specialist parts suppliers.

⊙ DEFINITELY NOT SOUTHERN

NASCAR has long been associated with the Deep South, but Watkins Glen in upper New York State has been on the NASCAR roll-call since 1986. It's a dipping, twisting road course rather than an oval or superspeedway and its differences are a welcome change within the Sprint Cup Series campaign.

⊙ DEEP IN THE DEEPEST SOUTH

Homestead-Miami Speedway is NASCAR's most southern outpost. This Floridian quad-oval was built by race promoter Ralph Sanchez for IndyCar races for 1995, but the crowds didn't come, so he welcomed the Indy Racing League instead. The venue has hosted NASCAR events since 1999, with Tony Stewart winning the first race in his Joe Gibbs Racing Pontiac Grand Prix.

⊙ A MOVE FOR GREATER SAFETY

There was much concern about rising lap speeds when four deaths occurred within nine months. The last of these was that of Dale Earnhardt, who crashed on the final lap of the 2001 Daytona 500. This led to NASCAR improving driver safety. Drivers have to wear head and neck restraint collars, while a new range of larger and safer cars was introduced in 2007. The oval tracks were modified too. SAFER (steel and foam energy reduction) barriers were installed to absorb errant cars' energy.

⊙ ONTARIO, BUT NOT IN CANADA

The Ontario Motor Speedway was actually in California, to the east of Los Angeles, rather than in the Canadian province of the same name. This 2.5-mile speedway hosted races from 1971–80, latterly under the title of the Los Angeles Times 500. The circuit even hosted a non-championship F1 race, the Questor GP, in 1971. The bulldozers arrived in 1980 and the track was demolished to make way for housing.

⊙ FIFTY YEARS OF FUN

North Wilkesboro Speedway in North Carolina opened in 1947 and was on the championship calendar from 1949–96 (it was a dirt track through to 1957). It hosted two rounds per season, most recently the Holly Farms 400 and the First Union 400. This short oval was then closed but was due to reopen in 2010.

FASTEST AVERAGE RACE SPEEDS

	Track	Year	Driver/Car	Speed
1	Talladega	1997	Mark Martin/Ford	188.354mph
2	Talladega	1988	Bill Elliott/Ford	186.288mph
3	Talladega	2001	Bobby Hamilton/Chevrolet	184.003mph
4	Talladega	2002	Dale Earnhardt Jr/Chevrolet	183.665mph
5	Talladega	1995	Mark Martin/Ford	178.902mph
6	Daytona	1980	Buddy Baker/Oldsmobile	177.602mph
7	Talladega	1992	Ernie Irvan/Chevrolet	176.309mph
8	Daytona	1987	Bill Elliott/Ford	176.263mph
9	Talladega	1978	Lennie Pond/Oldsmobile	174.734mph
10	Talladega	1990	Dale Earnhardt/Chevrolet	174.430mph
11	Michigan	1999	Dale Jarrett/Ford	173.997mph
12	Daytona	1980	Bobby Allison/Mercury	173.473mph
13	Michigan	2001	Sterling Marlin/Dodge	173.473mph
14	Talladega	1995	Sterling Marlin/Chevrolet	173.188mph
15	Talladega	1984	Cale Yarborough/Chevrolet	172.988mph
16	Daytona	1979	Neil Bonnett/Mercury	172.890mph
17	Daytona	1998	Dale Earnhardt/Chevrolet	172.712mph
18	Daytona	1985	Bill Elliott/Ford	172.265mph
19	Daytona	1984	Richard Petty/Pontiac	171.449mph
20	Talladega	1987	Bill Elliott/Ford	171.293mph

⊙ RACING IN THE DESERT

It's not difficult to see why Phoenix International Raceway is an extremely different location to that for most NASCAR events. Not only is it on the western side of the USA, it's also in the desert. This race in Arizona, first run in 1988, is slotted into the end of the calendar (usually it's the penultimate race). Ford driver Alan Kulwicki was the first winner.

⊙ CROSSING THE CONTINENT

Although the vast majority of rounds are held on circuits on the eastern side of the USA, there are always one or two races every season on the West Coast. Sears Point, or Infineon Raceway as it's also known, is just to the north-east of San Francisco, and it's a road circuit too, making the difference from the norm all the greater. It's not exactly a short hop for the teams either, as it's 2,300 miles from their headquarters in Charlotte.

LAP RECORDS

⊙ FASTEST OF THE FAST

Talladega holds the record as the fastest venue, with Bill Elliott's Coors Ford Thunderbird lapping the superspeedway in Alabama during qualifying at 212.809mph in 1987. This was back in the days before a restrictor plate was fitted to each car to keep their speeds in check at the fastest tracks. Daytona is next fastest, with Elliott also setting the record lap there in 1987 of 210.364mph.

⊙ THINKING BIG IN TEXAS

Circuit owner Bruton Smith wanted a track capable of producing high lap speeds when he built the Texas Motor Speedway near Fort Worth and Dallas, as Texans are famed for thinking big. And fast he got when it opened in 1997, with Terry Labonte increasing the D-shaped circuit's record to 192.137mph in 2000 in his Hendrick Motorsports Chevrolet.

⊙ HIGHEST RACE AVERAGE

Mark Martin and his Roush Racing Ford Thunderbird proved to be the ultimate combination on superspeedways when his victory in the 1997 Winston 500 at Talladega Superspeedway became the victory with the highest average race speed, 188.354mph. This eclipsed Bill Elliott's 186.288mph set at the same circuit in 1988.

⊙ PURE SPEED

The fame of Daytona International Speedway is global and to many fans this track is all about speed. Many think of Bill Elliott when he lapped at 210.364mph in qualifying in 1987, but older fans think of the dramatic, droop-snooted and high-winged Plymouth Superbirds, like the one Pete Hamilton used to win here in 1970.

⊙ GEOFF'S GEORGIA GOLD

Atlanta Motor Speedway, a high-banked superspeedway, boasts the third-fastest lap of any track visited currently by NASCAR's Sprint Cup, with the Georgia circuit being lapped at 197.478mph by Geoff Bodine in his self-run Ford Thunderbird during his pole position-claiming qualifying run in 1997.

TOP 10 LAP RECORDS OF CURRENT CIRCUITS*

	Track	Year	Driver	Speed
1	Talladega	1987	Bill Elliott	212.809mph
2	Daytona	1987	Bill Elliott	210.364mph
3	Atlanta	1997	Geoff Bodine	197.478mph
4	Michigan	2005	Ryan Newman	194.232mph
5	Texas	2000	Terry Labonte	192.137mph
6	Chicagoland	2005	Jimmie Johnson	188.147mph
7	Fontana	2002	Ryan Newman	187.432mph
8	Indianapolis	2004	Casey Mears	186.293mph
9	Charlotte	2000	Dale Earnhardt Jr	186.034mph
10	Homestead	2003	Jamie McMurray	181.111mph

These are qualifying lap records.

⊙ GREAT VIEWS, GREAT SPEEDS

Michigan International Speedway stands as the fourth-fastest circuit used by the Sprint Cup, behind only Talladega, Daytona and Atlanta. High speeds are maintained by the 18-degree banking around the 2-mile speedbowl. Ryan Newman has qualified at 194.232mph here, but the fastest race average of 173.997mph was achieved in 1999 when Dale Jarrett won in a Robert Yates Racing Ford Taurus.

⊙ NOT ALL OVALS ARE FAST

When you think of a NASCAR oval you tend to think of steeply banked corners and high speeds. However, Martinsville doesn't fit this description and is NASCAR's slowest oval, the only one not yet lapped at 100mph. The 0.526-mile track has a qualifying best of just 95.371mph, set by Tony Stewart in his Pontiac in 2000, and the fastest average speed in a race was Jeff Gordon's 82.223mph in 1996.

⊙ THE SLOWEST OF ALL

The Sears Point road course – also known as Infineon Raceway – in northern California is the slowest circuit used by the Sprint Cup. The fastest ever qualifying lap around this 12-turn twister is just 94.303mph, set by Jeff Gordon in his Hendrick Motorsports Chevrolet Monte Carlo in 2004.

⊙ FROM STORM TO STORMING

Homestead-Miami Speedway started life as a project to help Dade County to recover from being hit by the devastating Hurricane Andrew in 1992, but it has grown into a regular venue for the Sprint Cup. Jamie McMurray proved just how quick it could be when he lapped the Florida circuit at more than 181mph when qualifying in 2003 in his SABCO/Chip Ganassi Dodge.

⊙ WAY OUT WEST

California Speedway, also known as Fontana, is a prodigiously fast circuit, with Gil de Ferran lapping it at 241.426mph (a world record for a circuit) in qualifying for the 2000 IndyCar race. If its banked turns weren't as low-angled, then speeds would be higher still. In NASCAR's visits, the highest qualifying speed is 187.432mph.

⊙ TRIANGULAR AND TRICKY

The tri-oval Pocono Raceway in Pennsylvania is a tricky drive due to the fact that each of its turns is very different and the degree of banking drops from 14 degrees at Turn 1 to 8 degrees at Turn 2 and just 6 degrees at Turn 3. If the banking was uniformly at 14 degrees the lap record would be higher than the current 172.391mph.

NUMBER OF RACES HELD

⊙ DAYTONA'S DOUBLE

Daytona International Speedway has been on NASCAR'S rota ever since it opened in 1959, taking over from the Daytona Beach Course. The track has hosted two top-level NASCAR races every year since. The Daytona 500 is traditionally right at the start of the season and the second race is held as close as possible to Independence Day on 4 July. This Florida venue has hosted 125 races.

⊙ PETTY PLEASURES

Richmond International Raceway has been on the calendar since 1953, when Lee Petty won the Richmond 200 in his Dodge Coronet. Since then, the Virginia circuit has hosted a further 106 races, to put it third on the list of the most races held. Richard Petty showed how much his family liked this circuit by winning seven Richmond races from 1970 to 1973.

⊙ FIREBALL WINS FOR SMOKEY

Fireball Roberts was the first NASCAR racer to win at Atlanta Motor Speedway back in 1960, crossing the finish line in front in his Smokey Yunick Pontiac Catalina. Dodge drivers Kurt Busch and Kasey Kahne were the winners of the two races held in 2009 at this circuit at Hampton, just outside the Georgia state capital, when it became the sixth track to host its 100th top-level NASCAR race.

NUMBER OF RACES HELD

1	Daytona	125	6	Atlanta	101
2	Martinsville	122	7	Bristol	98
3	Richmond	107	8	North Wilkesboro	93
4	Darlington	106	9	Michigan	81
5	Charlotte	102	=	Talladega	81

⊙ HOME FROM HOME

Promoter Bruton Smith's Charlotte Motor Speedway first appeared on the NASCAR calendar in 1960, when Joe Lee Johnson won the World 600 in his Chevrolet. The track has featured every year since. Jimmie Johnson was the most recent winner in the circuit's 102nd top-level NASCAR race.

⊙ GREAT RICHES

The Indianapolis Motor Speedway, long the jewel in the IndyCar crown, finally joined the NASCAR roster in 1994 with its Brickyard 400 and came in with the then record $3.2 million purse. Indiana resident Jeff Gordon pocketed much of that for winning in his Hendrick Motorsports Chevrolet. The circuit had hosted just 16 NASCAR races by the end of 2009, but it's very much established on the calendar.

⊙ SOMETHING A LITTLE DIFFERENT

Riverside International Raceway, the track in the desert near San Bernardino, was one of NASCAR's rare road circuits and it was notable for its uphill S-bends. Traditionally used at the start of the season, usually before the Daytona 500 until 1982, it hosted 48 races and was the scene of a famous end-over-end accident for AJ Foyt in 1965. F1 racer Dan Gurney was the most successful here, winning five times. It was last visited by NASCAR in 1988 and was closed in 1989 to make way for a shopping mall.

⊙ VICTORY OF VIRGINIA

Martinsville Speedway in Virginia has hosted the second most top-level NASCAR races, with 122 by the end of 2009. Like Daytona, it was there from the beginning in 1949. Unlike Daytona, it's the same track today. Inaugural NASCAR champion Red Byron was the winner of the 1949 race in his Oldsmobile. Joe Gibbs's Toyota driver Denny Hamlin was the winner of the most recent race held here, the second of Martinsville's 2009 races.

⊙ IGNORE ITS REPUTATION

The nickname for Darlington Raceway – "The Lady in Black" – emphasizes its reputation as a widow-maker, with drivers knowing that they need to clip the wall at Turn 4 for a fast lap. Not that this stopped Darrell Waltrip and Richard Petty risking all on the final lap of the 1979 Rebel 500 as they swapped the lead four times. Waltrip made the winning move in his DiGard Chevrolet by diving low through Turn 3. Darlington has hosted 106 races.

⊙ DOVER AND OVER AND OVER

Dover International Speedway in Delaware stands 11th on the list of most top-level NASCAR races held. Its 80 races span from Richard Petty's victory here in his Ford Torino Talladega in the Mason-Dixon 300 in 1969 to Chevrolet driver Jimmie Johnson's in the circuit's AAA 400 in 2009.

OTHER TRACK RECORDS

⊙ BREAKING THE 200MPH BARRIER

The first 200mph qualifying lap was set at Talladega Superspeedway in 1982 by Benny Parsons. Driving a Ranier Racing Pontiac Grand Prix, he broke the mark with a lap in 200.175mph to take pole for the Winston 500. However, this didn't result in victory in the race, which went to Darrell Waltrip in a Junior Johnson Buick Regal, at an average speed of 156.597mph. Waltrip passed Parsons on the final lap.

⊙ NASCAR GOES BOWLING

The steepest banking of any circuit used by NASCAR is at Bristol Motor Speedway. The banks are at 36 degrees, making it incredibly bowl-like. This 0.533-mile oval is also unusual as it has a concrete surface and two pit lanes, one on either side of the circuit as it's too short to fit all the cars on one side. Racing here has been described as "like flying fighter jets in a gymnasium".

⊙ LET THERE BE LIGHT

There has been night racing at short ovals for years, but Charlotte Motor Speedway became the first longer circuit – 1.5 miles – to instal floodlights and this gave The Winston (a non-championship race) in 1992 an exciting new appearance. Dale Earnhardt led Kyle Petty and Davey Allison into the final lap, but Petty spun him out at Turn 3. Petty was then outdragged by Allison out of the final corner, but they clashed after the finish line, Allison hit the wall and spent the night in hospital.

⊙ WHO'S IN THE LEAD?

The record number of changes of lead (this is counted only according to who is leading at the end of the lap) came during the 1984 Winston 500 at Talladega when there were 75 changes of the lead. As the lap at the Florida track is 2.66 miles long, that number was, in reality, way short of the true mark because of the multiple changes of lead during the laps. However, it was Cale Yarborough's Harry Ranier team Chevrolet which was in front when it counted.

⊙ CIRCUIT EXPERT

There have been 10 examples of drivers winning at a particular race circuit on four consecutive occasions, with Richard Petty leading the way by having achieved this incredible feat at four circuits: the Nashville 400 (1964–67); the Old Dominion 500 at Martinsville (1967–70); the Gwyn Staley 400 at North Wilkesboro (1970–75); and the Capitol City 500 at Richmond (1970–74).

⊙ WHAT A PLACE TO START

Charlotte Motor Speedway – now known as Lowe's Motor Speedway – is quite a place for a driver to score a first top-level NASCAR win, yet six drivers have done just that at the circuit's spring meeting. They are David Pearson in 1961, Jeff Gordon in 1994, Bobby Labonte in 1995, Matt Kenseth in 2000, Casey Mears in 2007 and David Reutimann in 2009.

⊙ SIX TO GO

Dominant Sprint Cup racer Jimmie Johnson isn't perfect as he hasn't won at each of the championship venues. The six tracks that have eluded him up to the end of the 2009 season are Bristol, Chicagoland, Homestead-Miami and Michigan, plus the two road circuits, Sears Point and Watkins Glen.

⊙ ROOM FOR MORE

Indianapolis Motor Speedway is the current NASCAR Sprint Cup Series-hosting circuit that can accommodate the largest number of spectators. Its massive grandstands, which wrap from Turn 2 back through Turn 1, down the main straight, through Turn 4 and on to Turn 3, can hold more than a quarter of a million spectators.

⊙ GURNEY'S CALIFORNIAN GOLD

F1 grand-prix winner Dan Gurney was the ultimate circuit specialist. He won NASCAR's race at Riverside in his native southern California four years in a row between 1963 and 1966, then added another win here in 1968, all in Fords. He also won two IndyCar races here, in 1967 and 1968.

⊙ LOVE OF ROAD COURSES

Jeff Gordon reigns supreme as the NASCAR driver who has scored the most victories on road courses. He has taken nine, which is two more than contemporary Tony Stewart. Gordon gathered these wins at Sears Point and Watkins Glen, showing a mastery of tracks that are markedly different to NASCAR's regular ovals and superspeedways. He also qualified on pole seven times on these two road courses.

⊙ POPULARITY STATISTIC

The largest crowd ever to attend a top-level NASCAR event was 314,980 at the Indianapolis Motor Speedway in 1995. This marked the Winston Cup's second visit to the home of the Indianapolis 500 IndyCar race for its stock car equivalent, the Brickyard 400. Dale Earnhardt rewarded his legions of fans with victory.

CIRCUIT CAPACITY

1	Indianapolis	315,000
2	Texas	191,122
3	Daytona	168,000
4	Bristol	160,000
5	Talladega	143,231
6	Las Vegas	142,000
7	Charlotte	140,000
=	Dover	140,000
9	Michigan	137,243
10	Atlanta	124,000
11	Fontana	122,000
12	Richmond	112,029
13	Sears Point	102,000
14	New Hampshire	91,000
15	Kansas	81,687

PART 3: RALLYING

The World Rally Championship is the most testing form of motor sport, with competitors having to tackle stages on every sort of surface imaginable, from gravel to snow, ice, mud, dust and, occasionally, asphalt, with cars being pushed right to the edge of precipices and high over jumps, flat-out. The test is as much about machine as man, and the cars often limp to the end of a stage after hitting a boulder or coming down to earth from a mighty jump.

WORLD RALLY CHAMPIONSHIP

Rally drivers are heroes, as they take their craft right to the ragged edge, pushing on at superhuman speeds with seemingly little regard for their own safety. Images of Sandro Munari in a Lancia Stratos, Ari Vatanen in a Ford Escort, Stig Blomqvist in an Audi Quattro, Colin McRae in a Subaru or Sébastien Loeb in a Citroën all fit the bill precisely.

CHAMPIONS

⊙ STARTING A TREND
The WRC has been running since 1973, but the Drivers'
Championship was not introduced until the end of the 1979 season.
The first champion was Sweden's Björn Waldegård, who won for
Ford in Greece and Canada and finished second in four other events
to pip Hannu Mikkola to the title by a point.

⊙ ROCK AND ROHRL
Walter Rohrl's talent was obvious from the outset, but he was to be
crowned champion driver just twice, despite winning 14 times. The
tall German had his early WRC outings in Opels, but he really hit the
winning trail when he got his hands on a Fiat 131 Abarth, scooping
the 1980 title. His second title was won for Opel in 1982 and he
then moved to Lancia and subsequently to Audi.

⊙ THE FIRST TO FOUR
Juha Kankkunen showed his talent when he landed the WRC drivers'
title in his first full season in the series in 1986 for Peugeot. He
repeated this success in 1987, albeit with Lancia, then added
another title in 1991 before claiming his fourth in 1993, with a third
manufacturer, Toyota.

⊙ MAKINEN STARTS A RUN
Juha Kankkunen won consecutive titles in 1986 and 1987. This
was matched by Miki Biasion in 1988 and 1989. However, Tommi
Mäkinen took domination of the title to a new level with a run that
started in 1996 and ended in 1999. He took the four titles in a row
with Mitsubishi, albeit winning in 1997 by only one point from Colin
McRae and two from Carlos Sainz the following year.

⊙ MR SPECTACULAR SCORES
Colin McRae was a driver who appeared to know no fear, taking
risks that most of his rivals wouldn't even have considered. He
jumped higher, flew further and crashed in a more spectacular
fashion. But, once that first win was in the bag in 1993, the wins
flowed and in 1995 he became Britain's first WRC champion after
winning in New Zealand and Britain for Subaru. Sadly, he died in a
helicopter crash in 2007.

⊙ AN ITALIAN IN AN ITALIAN

Miki Biasion started his competition career in motocross, but his friend and future co-driver Tiziano Siviero convinced him to have a go at rallying. Lancia in particular was delighted by this decision. He took over from Juha Kankkunen as its standard bearer, winning the title in 1988 and 1989, to give Lancia the publicity of an Italian driver winning the championship in an Italian car.

⊙ LOOK BEYOND THE RECORDS

Carlos Sainz dabbled in racing before concentrating on rallying and he is a driver whose presence was greater than the record books show. Sure, there are 26 wins against his name, but there should have been more than two drivers' titles. He took his first, for Toyota, in 1990. A close runner-up to Juha Kankkunen in 1991, he was champion for a second time with Toyota in 1992, then was runner-up three times. His nearest miss was in 1998 when he finished just two points down on Tommi Mäkinen after his Toyota's engine failed with just 500 yards to go.

⊙ A TWO-PART CAREER

Think Marcus Grönholm and you tend to think of him in a Peugeot 206 World Rally Car. This isn't surprising since he was world champion in it twice, in 2000 and 2002, claiming nine wins in those two campaigns and three in the year in between. He switched to Ford in 2006 and, but for a couple of accidents, could have beaten Sébastien Loeb to the 2007 crown before retiring from the sport.

⊙ MIND OVER MATTER

Richard Burns spent his entire career being compared to fellow British star Colin McRae. Burns was English, McRae was Scottish; Burns was smooth, McRae was ragged. However, they both became world champion. Burns achieved this accolade in 2001, when he won only in New Zealand, but was second in four other events in his works Subaru Impreza, showing his considered approach.

⊙ SIX IN SUCCESSION

Sébastien Loeb was nearly toppled in 2009, but he held off the challenge of Ford's Mikko Hirvonen to win by a point. This was not only his record sixth WRC title, but his sixth in a row, the Citroën ace blocking the others out every year from 2004 to 2009, to make him rallying's equivalent of Michael Schumacher at the start of the decade.

DRIVERS WITH MOST WRC TITLES

1	Sébastien Loeb	6
2	Juha Kankkunen	4
=	Tommi Mäkinen	4
4	Miki Biasion	2
=	Marcus Grönholm	2
=	Walter Rohrl	2
=	Carlos Sainz	2
8	Didier Auriol	1
=	Stig Blomqvist	1
=	Richard Burns	1
=	Colin McRae	1
=	Hannu Mikkola	1
=	Timo Salonen	1
=	Petter Solberg	1
=	Ari Vatanen	1
=	Björn Waldegård	1

⊙ ALL FLAIR AND GRIT

Ari Vatanen and the late Ferrari F1 driver Gilles Villeneuve were pure box office for TV directors. Their style was so spectacular and their spirit never-say-die. They also left the sport with less than their due; Villeneuve sadly after a fatal accident. Vatanen's best seasons were with a privately entered Ford Escort and he claimed the crown in 1981. He rediscovered his winning ways with Peugeot in 1984, but was never champion again, despite setting a then record five wins in a row.

WINS

⊙ GREAT IN ANY CAR

Hannu Mikkola proved his speed and adaptability by scoring his first three WRC event wins in three different makes of car. The first, the 1974 1000 Lakes Rally, was won in a Ford Escort RS1600. The second, the 1975 Rally of Morocco, was won in a Peugeot 504. And in the third, the 1975 1000 Lakes Rally, he was driving a Toyota Corolla. He didn't win again until 1978, when he won the Lombard RAC Rally, again in a different model of car, this time a Mk2 Escort RS.

⊙ A FINN CON BRIO

Markku Alén was Finnish by birth, but was always thought to have a Mediterranean temperament, so he fitted in extremely well with Fiat and Lancia, driving for the sister Italian manufacturers for 16 years. He scored 20 WRC wins, starting with the 1975 Rally of Portugal in a Fiat 124 Abarth and finishing in 1998 with victory in the Rally of Great Britain (which was then known as the RAC Rally) in a Lancia Delta Integrale.

⊙ 1000 LAKES, 100,000 FANS

It's only fitting that Finnish ace Ari Vatanen's only drivers' title-winning year – 1981 – should include victory in his home event, the 1000 Lakes Rally. He and his co-driver, David Richards, guided their Rothmans-liveried Ford Escort RS1800 to victory on this fast summer gravel rally a fraction under a minute clear of Vatenen's compatriot, Markku Alén, who was driving a Fiat 131 Abarth.

⊙ SHONE ON HOME GROUND

Didier Auriol clearly found strength from within to deliver more at home. As a Frenchman, that meant France's big rally, the Tour de Corse. He won the tarmac rally on the island of Corsica no fewer than six times between 1988 – when he triumphed in a Ford Sierra RS Cosworth – and 1995 – in a Toyota Celia GT-Four. For good measure, he won the Monte Carlo Rally, most of which is held in France, three times.

⊙ SEE IT, WIN IT

Clearly, nobody had told Juha Kankkunen that the Safari Rally is a tough one, as he turned up in 1985 to try it for the first time and won it. He drove a Toyota Celica Twin Cam Turbo with co-driver Fred Gallagher and beat his far more experienced teammate Björn Waldegård by 34 mins.

⊙ AS CLOSE AS IT GETS

Drivers are often separated by fractions of a second at the end of a special stage, but the almost unbelievable nearly happened in the Rally New Zealand in 2007 when Marcus Grönholm beat Sébastien Loeb by the blink of an eye over the entire rally. The gap between his Ford Focus RS WRC and Loeb's Citroën C4 WRC was just 0.3 secs. This beat the previous closest rally result of 2.1 secs, when Colin McRae beat Carlos Sainz in Portugal in 1998.

⊙ FROM ESCORTS TO QUATTROS

Many rally fans think of Ford Escorts when they think of Hannu Mikkola, as he won five times in this make of car in the 1970s. However, he won his only drivers' title, in 1983, in the much more powerful Audi Quattros A1. His final rally win was in 1987, when he won the Safari Rally in the bulky, four-door Audi 200 Quattro.

⊙ BUILDING TO A CLIMAX

Petter Solberg is a born entertainer, whether he is at the wheel of a car or in his earlier incarnation as Norway's disco-dancing champion. The way that he developed for Subaru in 2003 showed how he built on his first win in the last round of 2002. He began the season slowly in his 555-liveried Impreza, started winning mid-season in Cyprus, then ended with a bang to become champion. He achieved victory in the final round, the Rally of Great Britain, to pip Sébastien Loeb to the title by a single point.

⊙ NO PAIN IN SPAIN

Carlos Sainz has the third most WRC wins to his name: 26. They started flowing from midway through his first title-winning year, 1990, when he won the Acropolis Rally in Greece for Toyota. He was champion again in 1992, and one result that really pleased him was on home ground in Spain, in the Rallye Catalunya. He won the event again three years later, having moved on to join Subaru.

⊙ STAND AND DELIVER

Miki by name but certainly not Mickey Mouse by nature, Biasion was a driver who delivered when the pressure was on. His long-time employer Lancia had every reason to praise him for the way he handled himself in 1988 and 1989 in particular, when he won the drivers' title, reeling off a run of four wins in succession in each of those campaigns.

TOP 10 DRIVERS WITH MOST WRC RALLY WINS

1	Sébastien Loeb	54
2	Marcus Grönholm	30
3	Carlos Sainz	26
4	Colin McRae	25
5	Tommi Mäkinen	24
6	Juha Kankkunen	23
7	Markku Alén	20
=	Didier Auriol	20
9	Hannu Mikkola	18
10	Miki Biasion	17

⊙ WINNER, BUT NOT AT ALL COSTS

Richard Burns worked his way through rallying's ranks to reach the WRC and scored his first win in 1998, for Mitsubishi. However, he's more usually associated with Subaru, for whom he became world champion in 2001, and later Peugeot, with whom he ended his career. He might have been champion again in 2003, but illness interceded before the final-round decider and he died two years later from a brain tumour.

POINTS

⊙ TWO SYSTEMS, YET THE SAME SCORE

Timo Salonen's 1985 drivers' title-winning campaign yielded 127 points, the seventh highest in WRC history. He drove his Peugeot 205 Turbo 16 to victory in Portugal, Greece, New Zealand, Argentina and Finland. This points tally was equalled in 2005 by Sébastien Loeb, who recorded a remarkable 11 wins and reached this total despite a less generous scoring system.

⊙ A FINN AND A SWEDE

Two world champions hold joint ninth place in the table for the most points scored by a driver in one WRC season. Finnish ace Hannu Mikkola scored 125 points for Audi in 1983, and that tally was matched by Sweden's Stig Blomqvist the following year, in a super-powerful Audi Quattro A2 Group B car.

⊙ THE END OF THE BONANZA

The FIA amended its WRC scoring scheme for 1997. Wins were no longer worth 20 points; the first eight finishers were awarded points in descending order from 10. So the winner received 10 points, then eight, six, five, four, three, two and one, down to eighth place. This signalled the end of the three-figure seasonal hauls.

⊙ HURT BY RETIREMENTS

Colin McRae ranks eighth on the list of all-time point scorers. But, had he not attacked quite so hard, risking all for victory, he would surely have ranked several places higher. In 1999 and 2000, though, it was persistent car failure from the new Ford Focus World Rally Car that stopped the points flowing. He retired from the final eight rounds in 1999.

TOP 10 DRIVERS WITH MOST WRC POINTS

#	Driver	Points	#	Driver	Points
1	Carlos Sainz	1,242	6	Didier Auriol	747
2	Juha Kankkunen	1,136	7	Hannu Mikkola	655
3	Markku Alén	840	8	Colin McRae	626
4	Sébastien Loeb	783	9	Marcus Grönholm	615
5	Miki Biasion	768	10	Stig Blomqvist	573

⊙ CLOSE IT OUT

Sébastien Loeb's nose for a World Rally Championship title is unfailing, as his record of six drivers' crowns in succession from 2004 to 2009 demonstrates. However, it is his ability to close out the very tight battles as much as his form that proves what a true champion he is. Average out his winning margins from 2006, 2007 and 2009 and it comes out to just two points each year, or, to put it another way, the difference between first and second place finishes in a single rally.

⊙ ROHRL RACES CLEAR

The largest points margin between the drivers' champion and the driver in second place until the change in the points system in 1977 came in 1980, when Fiat's Walter Rohrl beat Ford driver Hannu Mikkola by 54 points. Five years later, Peugeot's Timo Salonen beat the runner-up, Audi's Stig Blomqvist, by 52 points.

⊙ HARDER TO BREAK CLEAR

Marcus Grönholm's 40-point advantage over 2002 runner-up Petter Solberg was all the more impressive as a win was now worth just 10 points, having previously been 20. However, this margin was exceeded by Sébastien Loeb during his remarkable 2005 campaign, when he won the drivers' title by 56 points over Solberg and Grönholm.

⊙ MOST POINTS IN A SEASON

The record for the most points scored by a driver in a season is 150, collected by Juha Kankkunen in 1991. In this season he won the Safari Rally, Acropolis Rally, 1000 Lakes Rally, Rally Australia and Britain's RAC Rally in his Lancia Delta Integrale 16V. These victories led to him claiming the third of his four world titles. He also ranks fifth and sixth for his tallies of 135 in 1993 and 134 in 1992.

⊙ YOU DON'T NEED TO WIN BY MANY

The narrowest winning margin in the history of the WRC is just one point, and this has happened three times. This was the margin by which Björn Waldegård beat Hannu Mikkola as he followed him home in the Ivory Coast Rally in 1979, when all the frontrunners changed to Mercedes for this unusual rally. It was also the difference as Sébastien Loeb beat Marcus Grönholm to win the 2006 title with Citroën and the margin by which he had lost to Petter Solberg three years earlier.

CAREER DURATION

⊙ PATIENCE OF A SAINZ

Carlos Sainz deserved more than two WRC titles for the excellence shown throughout his lengthy career. He still racked up records aplenty, although some have since been blitzed by Sébastien Loeb. However, one that stands is that he made the most WRC starts – 196. Juha Kankkunen is second on 161, with Didier Auriol on 152, Marcus Grönholm on 151 and Petter Solberg on 149.

⊙ FROM 73–03

One feature of the WRC is the exceptional length of the top drivers' careers. Stig Blomqvist shares the record for career longevity with Pentti Airikkala, at 31 years, but he has the distinction of his career being all but continuous, as he competed in the WRC from its first year, 1973, through until 2003, missing only the 1990 season. To make his career even more impressive, Stig drove his first international rally back in 1967.

⊙ NEVER SLOW DOWN

Some drivers have lengthy careers built in pursuit of a win that may or may not come, others continue to compete but are past their competitive best. But Markku Alén was a threat from the outset of his international career at the start of the 1970s through to his final part-season in 1993 when he was still able to finish second in the Safari Rally. A one-off in the 1000 Lakes Rally in 2001 was only for fun and he finished 16th.

⊙ FROM 51ST TO 1ST

Kenneth Eriksson spread his six wins fairly evenly across his 23-year WRC career that started in 1980 with an outing in the Swedish Rally, his home event. Driving an ancient Saab 96, he finished only 51st, but that didn't put him off and his break came with VW in 1986, for whom he scored his first win in 1987. He also won for Mitsubishi in 1991 and 1995, and then twice for Subaru in 1997.

⊙ A CAREER WITH AN EXTENSION

Pentti Airikkala had a WRC career that stretched to 31 years, like Stig Blomqvist, and his international rally career stretched back even two years before the WRC started in 1973. However, his WRC career was stretched by the fact that Pentti had a 13-year hiatus between contesting three rounds in 1990 and a one-off outing in the 2003 Rally of Great Britain.

⊙ CAREER BREAKS

A large number of drivers who went on to great things in the WRC gained their first WRC experience in their home rally and then took years to find the money for a full-season attack. However, the longest gaps have tended to come at the end of a driver's top-line career. Achim Warmbold had a 14-year gap between his penultimate WRC event, the 1986 Monte Carlo Rally, and his final one, the 2000 Rally of Great Britain, in which he competed with his son Anthony.

⊙ ALWAYS THE BRIDESMAID

Manfred Stohl ranks 10th in the table for the most career starts in the World Rally Championship, with 126, but he is the only driver on that list never to have won a round. The privateer from Austria has achieved a podium finish six times, but never finished higher than second, which he first achieved in Cyprus in 2005. He came third in the same year's season-ending Rally Australia. He followed this with a trio of third places in 2006 at Mexico, Australia and New Zealand, then rounded out the season with second place in the Rally of Great Britain to end the year a career-best fourth overall.

⊙ FOR EKLUND READ SAAB

Per Eklund started rallying in the late 1960s, making his name driving a Saab, so it was fitting that he took his one and only WRC win in one, in the 1976 Swedish Rally. He brought his WRC career to a close in a Saab too, a 900 Turbo, in the Rally of Great Britain in 1997. Two years later, he won the FIA Rallycross title, in a Saab, of course.

⊙ EVEN THE GREATS RETIRE

Hannu Mikkola started a lot of rallies – 123 – but he also failed to finish as many as he would have liked. During his WRC career he retired a record 61 times, many of which came in his winding-down years with Mazda between 1988 and 1991. Had he not retired so many times in 1980, when with Ford, he might have stood a chance of taking the title battle to Fiat's Walter Rohrl.

DRIVERS WITH MOST YEARS IN WRC

1	Pentti Airikkala	31*
=	Stig Blomqvist	31*
3	Ari Vatanen	30*
4	Markku Alén	29*
=	Timo Salonen	29*
6	Achim Warmbold	28*
7	Per Eklund	25*
8	Jean-Claude Andruet	23*
=	Kenneth Eriksson	23
=	Mats Jonsson	23*
=	Juha Kankkunen	23*
=	Jean Ragnotti	23*
13	Didier Auriol	22
14	Hannu Mikkola	21*
=	Jorge Recalde	21*

* Not continuous.

⊙ RALLYING'S TOP WOMAN

Michèle Mouton – the only woman ever to win a WRC round – was no flash in the pan. After dabbling with outings in her two local events – the Monte Carlo Rally and the Tour de Corse – in the 1970s, she got serious with Audi in 1981 and scored the first of her four WRC wins, in the Sanremo Rally. She added three more in 1992, in Portugal, Greece and Brazil. Her WRC career stretched to 13 years.

MISCELLANEOUS
DRIVER RECORDS

⊙ FLYING IN FINLAND

The 1000 Lakes Rally in Finland has always been acknowledged as an event in which the drivers have to balance speed against potential danger. This is shown by the fact that Marcus Grönholm's winning average speed in this gravel event in 2005 was the fastest for any rally in WRC history. His Peugeot 307 World Rally Car averaged 76.342mph. This pipped Richard Burns's average of 76.074mph in his Subaru Impreza World Rally Car in the 2000 Safari Rally.

⊙ QUICKEST FROM A TO B

If a footballer takes "one game at a time", then rally drivers could be said to break each rally down into individual stages and try to pick them off one after another. Best at this is Markku Alén, with a record 793 stage wins to his name. Carlos Sainz has 756 and Juha Kankkunen 700. Catching them all up, and fast, is six-time WRC champion Sébastien Loeb, whose tally at the end of 2009 was 647. *(All of these figures are from 1978 onwards.)*

⊙ SAINZ TOPS LOEB

Carlos Sainz may have won just two world drivers' titles compared to Sébastien Loeb's six, but he has finished in a podium position (top three) on many more occasions. The Spaniard has 97 podiums, 16 more than Loeb has achieved in his far shorter but more garlanded career. Four-time champion Juha Kankkunen has finished in the top three 75 times and fellow Finn Marcus Grönholm 61.

⊙ WHEN YOUTH COMES FIRST

Jari-Matti Latvala had every reason to be pleased when he won the Swedish Rally for Ford in 2008. It was his first win, but it also made him the youngest winner of a WRC round ever, at just 22 years and 313 days. He took the record from fellow Finn Henri Toivonen, who was 24 years and 86 days when he won the RAC Rally of Great Britain in 1980.

⊙ LAKES, TREES AND CHAMPIONS

Finland leads the way when creating WRC champions. Whether it's because Finland offers thousands of miles of gravel roads on which to practise one can only surmise, but the record is plain to see. This sparsely populated country has produced six champions: Marcus Grönholm, Juha Kankkunen, Tommi Mäkkinen, Hannu Mikkola, Timo Salonen and Ari Vatanen. They have won 13 titles between them. France, Great Britain and Sweden are next up with two champions each.

⊙ THOSE FINNS DO FLY

Finland, France and Sweden are the three countries at the top of the table for the number of WRC round wins achieved by drivers from their nation. Finland had 157 wins to its name by the end of the 2009 season, with Sébastien Loeb boosting France's tally to 121. Sweden, though, is a long way behind, on 43, seven ahead of Great Britain.

⊙ THE WEALTH OF ONLY A FEW NATIONS

The spread of nationalities that have experienced victory in a round of the WRC remains narrow, with drivers from only 16 countries having done so, as Scandinavian and Northern European drivers have dominated. Argentina, Belgium, Canada, Japan and Portugal have won one apiece and Austria only two.

⊙ GETTING IN THE GROOVE

The record for the most wins in succession is held by French multiple WRC champion Sébastien Loeb. He won six rallies in a row in 2005, when he triumphed in New Zealand, Italy, Cyprus, Turkey, Greece and Argentina for Citroën. Peugeot's Marcus Grönholm restricted him to second place in the next event in Finland.

⊙ FIRST HAT-TRICK

Winning consecutive rallies was a real problem for drivers in the WRC up to the 1980s, and few even won two rallies in a row. Stig Blomqvist was the first to score three in succession when he won in Greece, New Zealand and Argentina in his Audi Quattro A2 in 1984.

⊙ FOUR AND RISING

Within a year of the first three-in-a-row winning streak in 1984, Timo Salonen became the first driver to make it four consecutive WRC wins. He had a great run through the same rallies that Blomqvist won in 1984, then he added the 1000 Lakes Rally in his native Finland in his works Peugeot 205 Turbo 16.

⊙ USING HIS EXPERIENCE

Björn Waldegård, the first WRC champion, holds the record as the oldest driver to win a WRC round. This was the Safari Rally in Kenya in 1990, which he won in a Toyota Celica GT-Four with co-driver Fred Gallagher, when he was 46 years and 155 days. He was a year and a half older than Hannu Mikkola, who had set the record at the same event three years earlier.

DRIVERS WITH MOST SUCCESSIVE ROUND WINS

1	Sébastien Loeb	6 (twice)
2	Sébastien Loeb	5 (twice)
3	Mikko Hirvonen	4
=	Timo Salonen	4
5	Didier Auriol	3
=	Miki Biasion	3
=	Stig Blomqvist	3
=	Marcus Grönholm	3
=	Sébastien Loeb	3
=	Tommi Mäkinen	3 (twice)
=	Colin McRae	3 (twice)
=	Petter Solberg	3

MANUFACTURER RECORDS

⊙ THE FIRST XI

The most successful year that any manufacturer has enjoyed since the creation of the WRC in 1973 is Citroën's 2005 campaign in which it won 11 of the 16 rounds with its Xsara World Rally Car. Wins in Monte Carlo, New Zealand, Italy, Cyprus, Turkey, Greece, Argentina, Germany, France, Spain and Australia meant the team ended the year as the clear champion. Sébastien Loeb took the first 10 of these to win the Drivers' Championship, François Duval won the last.

⊙ LANCIA MILES AHEAD

When it comes to winning titles, Lancia leads the way with 10 crowns since the WRC began in 1973. Citroën moved to equal second with fellow French manufacturer Peugeot in 2009 on five titles apiece, with Fiat, Ford, Subaru and Toyota claiming three titles each. Audi has two and Mitsubishi, Renault-Alpine and Talbot have all won one.

⊙ FORD'S WORLD DOMINANCE

Some manufacturers are associated mainly with racing, others with rallying, some with both. Ford is very much from this third group, as it has been a hit on the rally stages since the Ford Escort made its mark in the 1970s. It bounced back with the Escort RS Cosworth in the 1990s and has blazed a trail with its Focus RS World Rally Cars through the 2000s. However, the marque bearing the blue oval has also won the Le Mans 24 Hours and its engines have won the F1 World Championship and the Indy 500, demonstrating a remarkable spread of influence.

⊙ WHEN CARS WERE ROCKETS

The Group B years between 1983 and 1986 were when the cars contesting the WRC were in their ultimate form. They had lightweight bodies powered by 400bhp engines. It was in this era that Audi built on the form that it had shown with its early Quattros, with its 1985 Quattro Sport S1 famed as the most powerful rally car ever, pushing out up to 550bhp.

⊙ SPEED EQUALS SALES

Subaru was known for little other than utilitarian four-wheel-drive cars and pick-ups. Then it went rallying, and there has never been a clearer example of a brand having its image transformed. After finding form with the Legacy, the introduction of the Impreza pushed it to the front and manufacturers' titles followed in 1995, 1996 and 1997, plus wins every year after that up to 2005. Many of Subaru's road cars are sold with mock rally livery.

⊙ HANG ON IN THE BACK

The vast majority of WRC event-winning cars have been two-door models, but there have been some four-door winners too. They are: the Audi 200 Quattro; the Violet 160J and Violet GT made by Datsun; every one of Mitsubishi's WRC entries, from the Colt Lancer and Galant VR-4 to its Lancer Evolution range; the Peugeot 504; and the Legacy and the Impreza ranges manufactured by Subaru.

⊙ MERCEDES'S AFRICAN STEAMROLLER

Mercedes-Benz has won only two WRC events: the Ivory Coast Rally in 1979 and 1980. The first of these was actually a remarkable one-two-three-four finish, headed by Hannu Mikkola in the first of its four 450 SLCs. However, this result was largely due to the fact that the other teams stayed away from what they considered to be a poorly organized event, allowing the heavy but strong grand tourer to become a winning machine.

⊙ FROM BIG TO SMALL

Peugeot's first foray into the WRC was rewarded by the toughness of its 504 model that suited the African events perfectly. They weren't the fastest cars out there, but they were rugged and so came away with two wins in 1975, with Ove Andersson winning the Safari Rally and Jean-Pierre Nicolas the Morocco Rally.

⊙ THE CAR IN FRONT WAS A TOYOTA

Toyota owes its successes in the WRC not just to an ample budget but also to the rallying nous of former competitor Ove Andersson. Andersson set up a European base from which Toyota sent out its four-wheel-drive Celica Turbo for Carlos Sainz, Juha Kankkunen and Didier Auriol to win the drivers' titles from 1992 to 1994. Toyota took the manufacturers' spoils in 1993 and 1994 for good measure.

⊙ GLORY WITH EVOLUTION

Being clear about which car won the most rallies comes down to defining when a model began and finished its life, as they were always being updated. Take the Lancia Delta, which shares the record as the most successful car of all with 46 wins – a tally it shares with Subaru's Impreza. The Delta's wins between 1987 and 1992 can be broken down into 11 for the Delta HF 4WD, 14 for the HF Integrale, 13 for the HF Integrale 16V and eight for the Super Delta HF Integrale.

MANUFACTURER WITH MOST WRC ROUND WINS

1	Ford	73
=	Lancia	73
3	Citroën	60
4	Peugeot	48
5	Subaru	47
6	Toyota	43
7	Mitsubishi	34
8	Audi	24
9	Fiat	21
10	Datsun/Nissan	9
11	Opel	6
=	Renault	6
=	Renault-Alpine	6
14	Saab	4
15	Mazda	3
16	BMW	2
=	Mercedes-Benz	2
=	Porsche	2
=	Talbot	2
20	VW	1

RALLY VENUES

◉ SWEDE SMELL OF SUCCESS

Held early in the season, usually straight after the Monte Carlo Rally, the Swedish Rally is supposed to mean one thing, snow, and lots of it. This is very much part of the variety built into the WRC, to be balanced against the gravel, asphalt, dust and dirt roads used in the other events. Home drivers won each of the first seven times it was part of the WRC: Stig Blomqvist (1973, 1977 and 1979), Björn Waldegård (1975 and 1978), Per Eklund (1976) and Anders Kullang (1980).

◉ AFTER JUHA

Any Australian who became a rally fan when Rally Australia joined the WRC in 1989 could have been excused for thinking that you had to be called "Juha" to win the Perth-based event, as Juha Kankkunen won it four times out of the first five.

◉ THE FINNS KNOW BEST

Scandinavia is the land of the midnight sun in high summer, and this is when Finland hosts its 1000 Lakes Rally. This epic rally is a high-speed blast along endless gravel tracks past lakes and through forests. The Finnish drivers, having been reared on these roads, showed that they knew best how to attack them. A home driver won from 1973 to 1988: Tommi Mäkinen, Hannu Mikkola, Markku Alén, Kyösti Hämäläinen, Ari Vatanen and Timo Salonen.

◉ SPREADING THE MESSAGE

Thirty countries in six continents have hosted rounds of the WRC. Great Britain leads the way, having staged 37 events, with Finland and France (chiefly its Tour de Corse) right behind on 36, then Greece (Acropolis Rally) and Italy (the Sanremo Rally until 2003 and the Sardinian Rally from 2004) are both on 35, while the Monte Carlo Rally has been held 34 times.

⊙ LET'S TWIST AGAIN

France's most senior rally, the Tour de Corse, has been held on the island of Corsica since 1956. It features fast, asphalt roads on which the drivers do well not to look over the numerous precipitous drops. French drivers have a great record here and perhaps Jean Ragnotti's win in 1982 stands out as his stubby Renault 5 Maxi Turbo looked so well suited to the ever-twisting route.

⊙ ONE-HIT WONDERS

Over the years the FIA has experimented with the World Rally Championship. New venues have been tried and several countries have been featured and then dropped. By the end of 2009, three countries had been used just once. These are Austria (used in the WRC's first season, 1973), China (1999) and Jordan (2008). Poland escaped this ignominy in 2009, when it added a second WRC event to the one it hosted back in 1973.

⊙ A CHANGE OF NAME BUT NOT IDENTITY

Rallies can assume the identity of a long-time event sponsor, and this is the case with Great Britain's long-running rally. It was known as the RAC Rally from 1933 to 1998 and still gets called this even though its name changed to the Rally of Great Britain in 1998. It's usually held at the end of the year, often in foul weather, making it far from easy to win. Hannu Mikkola and Petter Solberg have enjoyed the most success with four wins apiece.

⊙ BY JORGE!

Rally Argentina is tough. Its roads are as rough as those experienced in Greece's Acropolis Rally, but the one advantage is that it's held in winter temperatures, so the sun is not scorching the drivers as they attack. The Rally always draws a huge crowd as it snakes around the upcountry area around Cordoba. Jorge Recalde became a national hero when he recorded a home victory in the event in a works Lancia Delta Integrale in 1988.

⊙ A PARTICULAR TYPE OF DIRT ROAD

Kenya's Safari Rally was an event apart from the European norm. Local knowledge of the roads and the way to drive on the unique surfaces was worth a great deal. Shekhar Mehta showed this as he won his home event five times between 1973 and 1982. Fellow Kenyan Joginder Singh took the garland in Nairobi twice in the early 1970s and Ian Duncan raced to victory in 1994.

⊙ NICE VIEW, NO TIME TO STOP

Some of the most spectacular scenery of any rally in the WRC is in New Zealand. The drivers have little time to enjoy it though, as since 1977 they have been fully occupied keeping their cars on the twisting and undulating dirt roads. Carlos Sainz and Colin McRae both won the event three times in a row, from 1990–92 and from 1993–95, respectively.

⊙ THE USA STAYS AWAY

The USA has some magnificent terrain for rallying, but it has yet to make much of an impact on the WRC. The championship did make two visits in the mid-1970s, then three more in the late 1980s, but the event failed to cement its place on the calendar. Its lowest moment was in 1974 when a local sheriff crashed as a result of giving chase to Sandro Munari in his Lancia Stratos for driving too fast through a village.

COUNTRIES THAT HAVE HOSTED MOST WRC RALLIES		
1	Great Britain	37
2	Finland	36
=	France	36
4	Greece	35
=	Italy	35
6	Monte Carlo	34
7	Sweden	33
8	Portugal	30
9	Kenya	29
=	New Zealand	29
11	Argentina	28
12	Spain	19
13	Australia	18
14	Ivory Coast	15
15	Cyprus	8

⊙ HELAS HELLAS

Searing heat, dust, ruts, rocks and retirements are features of the Acropolis Rally, Greece's annual event. This rally is acknowledged as a car breaker and is so tough that no manufacturer has achieved dominance in it, although Ford comes out best thanks to a four-year run from 2000 to 2003. The first three wins were taken by Colin McRae.

MONTE CARLO RALLY

Just as the Monaco Grand Prix is a special event on the
Formula One calendar, the Monte Carlo Rally remains
a jewel in the World Rally Championship's crown.
No longer do cars head there from assorted cities
around Europe as they did until the 1960s, but the
magic is still there, especially if there is snow lining
the precipitous Col du Turini.

DRIVER RECORDS

⊙ JUST TOO FAST

The 1986 season should have been the zenith of the Group B class. Henri Toivonen, driving a Lancia Delta S4, set the ball rolling by winning the Monte Carlo Rally from Timo Salonen, and by more than four minutes at that. However, four rounds later the Finnish ace was killed, along with his co-driver Sergio Cresto, in the Tour de Corse. This triggered the end for Group B, its cars considered too fast to be safe for drivers and spectators alike.

⊙ A CHAMPION'S PERFORMANCE

Sébastien Loeb's most recent win in the Monte Carlo Rally – his fifth – came in 2008 in his Citroën C4 World Rally Car, when he won by more than 2.5 minutes from Mikko Hirvonen in his Ford Focus. This proved to all that the former champion gymnast was a driver on top of his game as he set off towards his fifth drivers' title.

⊙ THE ONE THAT COUNTS

If you're going to win only one WRC round, you might as well make it the most famous one. This is what Piero Liatti did. He had his greatest day when he won the Monte Carlo Rally in 1997 for Subaru, emphasizing his prowess on asphalt events. Well, asphalt coated in parts by snow.

⊙ THE OTHER STRATOS WINNER

Three-time winner Sandro Munari wasn't the only driver to win the Monte Carlo Rally in a Lancia Stratos. Bernard Darniche did so as well in 1979, albeit in a much less flamboyant manner, in his French blue Team Chardonnet Lancia Stratos. He won again in the car in 1981, this time on the Tour de Corse.

⊙ SEIZING THE MOMENT

Bruno Saby had a lengthy rally career, but seldom drove in many WRC rounds in the course of a season. Despite this, he was able to win two events, one of which was on home ground in the Monte Carlo Rally (all Frenchmen class it as a French event). His Monte win came in 1988 when he campaigned a Delta HF 4WD for the works Lancia team, as the top names stumbled.

⊙ DIFFERENT CAR, SAME RESULT

Frenchman Didier Auriol won the Monte Carlo Rally on three occasions. He was driving a Lancia in 1990 and again in 1992. However, in 1993, after Lancia had pulled out, he was behind the wheel of a Toyota Celica Turbo 4WD. This was a tight event, though, as he beat his compatriot François Delecour, in a Ford Escort RS Cosworth, by only 15 seconds in an event that was unusually light on snow.

⊙ GRÖNHOLM BUTTS IN

Marcus Grönholm is the driver who "broke" Sébastien Loeb's recent winning run in the Monte Carlo Rally, or perhaps that should say "interrupted" it. The Finn put his name on the trophy in 2006 when he brought his works Ford Focus RS World Rally Car home just over a minute clear of Loeb.

⊙ THAT MONTE MAGIC

French drivers have won the Monte Carlo Rally a remarkable 14 times since the World Rally Championship began in 1973: Jean-Claude Andruet (1973), Jean-Pierre Nicolas (1978), Bernard Darniche (1979), Jean Ragnotti (1981), Bruno Saby (1988), Didier Auriol (1990, 1992 and 1993), François Delecour (1994) and Sébastien Loeb (2003, 2004, 2005, 2007 and 2008). This success is way in excess of their winning average in other events.

⊙ THREADING THE NEEDLE

The Monte Carlo Rally wasn't a natural hunting ground for Ari Vatanen, because he was a driver who liked to use all of the road and more. There is seldom "more" on an Alpine pass, just a rock face on one side and a stone wall or snow bank on the other, so it's no surprise that he often retired there. However, he triumphed in 1985, and in some style, too, taking his Peugeot 205 T16 to a clear win over Walter Rohrl's Audi.

⊙ ROHRL LEADS AUDI'S WAY

The Audi Quattro A2 was the car to have in 1984 as Group B entered its second year. Walter Rohrl laid down a marker when he won the opening round, the Monte Carlo Rally, leading homean Audi one-two-three ahead of teammates Stig Blomqvist and Hannu Mikkola. It was his fourth win in this rally and his third in a row.

DRIVERS WITH MOST MONTE CARLO RALLY WINS

1	Sébastien Loeb	5
2	Tommi Mäkinen	4
=	Walter Rohrl	4
4	Didier Auriol	3
=	Sandro Munari	3
=	Carlos Sainz	3
7	Miki Biasion	2
8	Jean-Claude Andruet	1
=	Bernard Darniche	1
=	François Delecour	1
=	Marcus Grönholm	1
=	Piero Liatti	1
=	Jean-Pierre Nicolas	1
=	Jean Ragnotti	1
=	Bruno Saby	1
=	Henri Toivonen	1
=	Ari Vatanen	1

⊙ A MAN, A CAR, A PLACE

People who were fans of rallying in the 1970s will associate only one car and driver combination with the Monte Carlo Rally: Sandro Munari and his white, green and red Alitalia-liveried Lancia Stratos. They won together in 1975, 1976 and 1977. The Italian was particularly spectacular in the mountain stages, hurling the stubby sports car uphill, its Dino V6 engine barking away behind his shoulders.

MANUFACTURER RECORDS

⊙ NO PREPARATION, TOP RESULT

Porsche's long-living and iconic 911 sports car is far more readily associated with glory on the racetrack, but Jean-Pierre Nicolas used one to win the Monte Carlo Rally in 1978. He used its power to overcome Jean Ragnotti's far nimbler Renault 5 Alpine up and over the mountain stages despite having only just done the deal to rally the car.

⊙ LANCIA LORDS IT

Lancia has been by far the most successful manufacturer in the Monte Carlo rally since the WRC kicked off in 1973, taking 11 wins. Among these, Sandro Munari become synonymous with the marque's success in the 1970s, winning three times in a row in a Stratos. Its most spectacular win came in 1986, though, with Henri Toivonen wrestling its Group B Delta S4 around for a clear win.

⊙ ENDING THE LONG WAIT

Citroën tasted glory in the Monte Carlo Rally in the pre-WRC days, with Pauli Toivonen (father of Henri), who won in 1966. The French manufacturer then had to wait until 2003 to spray champagne in the principality again, doing so when Sébastien Loeb led home Carlos Sainz and Colin McRae in a Citroën one-two-three. Citroën and Loeb then won again in 2004, 2005, 2007 and 2008.

⊙ 40 YEARS ON

Ford tried for years to win the Monte Carlo Rally following its success there in pre-WRC days in 1953 when Maurice Gatsonides triumphed in his Zephyr. Its luck finally changed in 1994 when François Delecour beat the Toyota Celica Turbo 4WD of reigning champion Juha Kankkunen with his duck-tailed Escort RS Cosworth.

⊙ MITSUBISHI'S MONTE MAGIC

Mitsubishi and Tommi Mäkinen enjoyed an incredible run in the WRC from 1996 to 1999, winning the drivers' title each year. However, Mäkinen's four-year streak in the Monte Carlo Rally was out of kilter with that as he won the famous season-opening event each year from 1999 to 2001 in Mitsubishi Evo 6s. (Mäkinen won again in 2002 in a Subaru.)

⊙ MAKING AN IMPREZAION

Subaru has three Monte Carlo Rally wins to its name, starting with Carlos Sainz's victory in 1995, when the Spaniard kept his dark blue and yellow Impreza 555 clear of local expert François Delecour's Ford. The Japanese manufacturer's other wins came in 1997 and 2002 through Piero Liatti and Tommi Mäkinen respectively.

⊙ TOYOTA COMES BACK FOR MORE

Victory in the Monte Carlo Rally isn't always a sign that further success will follow, but Carlos Sainz's win for Toyota in the 1998 season opener heralded a strong season for the Japanese manufacturer. It re-established itself in the WRC with its Corolla model after its successes earlier in the decade with derivations of its Celica coupé.

⊙ ROHRL'S THE MAN FOR MONTE

Walter Rohrl won the Monte Carlo Rally four times out of five between 1980 and 1984, each time in a different car. He gave both Fiat and Opel their only wins in this world-famous event, driving a 131 Abarth and then an Ascona 400 in 1980 and 1982. His other Monte wins were for Lancia and Audi.

⊙ 5 GOES WILD IN THE COUNTRY

Success on home ground is always worth double that of a win anywhere else for a motor manufacturer. Renault was ecstatic when Jean Ragnotti gave its little, wide-tailed 5 Turbo victory in the Monte in 1981. The previous Monte win for a Renault came back in pre-WRC days in 1958, when Guy Monraisse won in a Dauphine.

⊙ ALPINES FOR THE ALPINE PASSES

The first time that the Monte Carlo Rally was contested as a round of the WRC, in 1973, it was won by Jean-Claude Andruet in one of the tiny, Renault-engined Alpine-Renault A110s. In fact, these low-lying French sports cars filled five of the first six places. The non Alpine-Renault A110 was a Ford Escort RS1600, driven by Hannu Mikkola into fourth place.

MANUFACTURERS WITH MOST MONTE CARLO RALLY WINS

#	Manufacturer	Wins
1	Lancia	11
2	Citroën	5
3	Mitsubishi	3
=	Subaru	3
=	Toyota	3
6	Ford	2
7	Alpine-Renault	1
=	Audi	1
=	Fiat	1
=	Opel	1
=	Peugeot	1
=	Porsche	1
=	Renault	1

⊙ PEUGEOT'S SLIM PICKINGS

For all its years of rallying dominance, Peugeot has won the Monte Carlo rally only once in the WRC era. This was in 1985 when Ari Vatanen won the battle of the Group B bruisers in a 205 Turbo 16. Most recently, Peugeot won the Monte through Sébastien Ogier in 2009, but in a round of the International Rally Challenge rather than the WRC, as it was the Monte's turn to stand down from the WRC for a year.

PARIS–DAKAR RALLY

The Paris–Dakar Rally was an event like no other.
Trucks, buggies and motorbikes hurtled over massive
sand dunes, past villages and then arrived, bedraggled,
on the West African beach at Dakar to reach the finish.
Every competitor would have a tale to tell.
It lives on today, known as the Dakar Rally, even
though since 2009 (due to security reasons) it has
been held in South America.

DRIVER RECORDS

⊙ MASTER OF ALL TRADES

Jacky Ickx is a competitor who has displayed a remarkable array of skills in his ultra-successful career. An F1 grand prix winner (he was runner-up in the 1970 Drivers' Championship), he was long the driver with the most wins in the Le Mans 24 Hours and then he demonstrated in 1983 that he could hack it on an entirely tougher and less predictable terrain as he won the Paris–Dakar Rally in a Mercedes 280G.

⊙ WINNING IN HIS OWN CAR

Jean-Louis Schlesser, World Sports-Prototype champion for Mercedes in 1989, is one of many, mainly French, racers who have spent the twilight years of their careers competing in this event. In fact, he has turned it into a business, building Schlesser buggies – lightweight vehicles with high ground clearance made especially for such events. It was in one of these that he won in 1999 and 2000.

⊙ FIRST OF A LONG LINE

Alain Génestier, the winner of the first Paris–Dakar Rally in 1979, would have had no idea that it would grow into a world-famous event. When he reached Dakar, the Senegalese capital, in his Range Rover he couldn't have imagined that his name would be joined by a host of the great and good from racing and rallying. He was probably simply relieved that he had finished the 6,000-mile journey into the unknown.

⊙ ARI'S HAT-TRICK

Ari Vatanen had a three-year winning streak in the Paris–Dakar Rally from 1989 to 1991. He scored the first two of these with Peugeot and then transferred with winning effect to Citroën for his 1991 victory. Bruno Berglund was his co-driver on all three occasions. The flying Finn had already won the event in 1987, also with Peugeot.

⊙ DOWNHILL AND UPHILL

Luc Alphand made his name in World Cup skiing events (he was world champion in 1997), but he loved the adventure of the Dakar and added victory in it in 2006 to his packed career history. He won the event in a Mitsubishi Pajero when the rally's route ran from Lisbon in Portugal to Dakar. To keep up his kicks, he also races sports cars in the Le Mans 24 Hours.

⊙ METGE MAKES HIS MARK

The first driver to stamp his authority on the Paris–Dakar Rally was former touring car racer René Metge – the French champion in 1975 – when he followed up his victory in a Range Rover in 1981. He scored two more wins, in 1984 and then in 1986, both times driving Porsches as the German manufacturer started to take the Paris–Dakar Rally as seriously as the Le Mans 24 Hours, in which it has had so much success.

⊙ THE LONGER THE BETTER

Pierre Lartigue matched Ari Vatanen's feat of taking three Paris–Dakar Rally victories in a row when he was triumphant in 1994, 1995 and 1996, for Citroën. Having already won the Paris–Moscow–Peking Enduro for Citroën in 2002, this former rally driver really found his niche in these long-distance, rough-terrain events and was World Rally Raid champion every year from 1993 to 1996.

⊙ FOUR WHEELS GOOD, TWO WHEELS MAD

After Stéphane Peterhansel, the second most successful motorbike rider in the history of the Dakar Rally is Cyril Neveu. He won in the inaugural year, then again in 1980, 1982, 1986 and 1987.

⊙ KEEP ON TRUCKING

Two drivers have won the truck section six times. They are Vladimir Chagin, between 2000 and 2010, all in Russian Kamaz trucks, and Karel Loprais, who won first in 1988 and most recently in 1999. He too showed brand loyalty, doing all his winning in Tatra trucks from the Czech Republic.

⊙ SAINZ JOINS THE GANG

Carlos Sainz is the third World Rally champion to have won the Dakar Rally, after Ari Vatanen and Juha Kankkunen. He claimed his victory for Volkswagen at the start of 2010, resisting a late charge by his teammate Nasser Al-Attiyah as they approached the finish in Buenos Aires. He brought his VW Race Touareg home just 2 mins and 12 sesc ahead after 5,778 miles. It was the first win for a Spaniard on four wheels in this event.

DRIVER WITH MOST DAKAR RALLY WINS – CARS

1	Ari Vatanen	4
2	Pierre Lartigue	3
=	René Metge	3
=	Stéphane Peterhansel	3
5	Hiroshi Masuoka	2
=	Jean-Louis Schlesser	2

Fourteen drivers have won once.

⊙ WHATEVER IT TAKES

World Enduro champion Stéphane Peterhansel simply can't cure himself of the Dakar bug, as he keeps coming back for more. Not satisfied with claiming a record six wins in the motorbike section between 1991 and 1998, all on Yamahas, he moved across to four wheels with a Nissan in 1999 and was then first home in 2004, 2005 and 2007, all in Mitsubishi Pajeros.

RIDER WITH MOST WINS – MOTORBIKES

1	Stéphane Peterhansel	6
2	Cyril Neveu	5
3	Edi Orioli	4
4	Cyril Despres	3
=	Richard Sainct	3
6	Hubert Auriol	2
=	Marc Coma	2
=	Fabrizio Meoni	2
=	Gaston Rahier	2
10	Gilles Lalay	1
=	Nani Roma	1

MANUFACTURER RECORDS

⊙ OUTSIDE ITS COMFORT ZONE

Porsche is synonymous with sports car racing, whether at Le Mans, Silverstone or Sebring. However, after dabbling with rallying in the 1970s, the German manufacturer decided to have a crack at the Paris–Dakar Rally as the event's profile grew. René Metge won in a four-wheel-drive 911 SC/RS in 1984, then again in a far more radical 959 two years later.

⊙ CITROËN STRIKES BACK

Held almost exclusively in Africa until it moved to South America in 2009, the Dakar is always thought of as a French event, since that is where it used to start, and event organizer Thierry Sabine filled the entry with French competitors. Consequently, it has always been a big event for the French manufacturers and Citroën had to respond to Peugeot's early dominance, scoring its first win in 1991, then enjoying a three-year run of wins from 1994 to 1996, with Pierre Lartigue winning each time in a ZX.

⊙ STOLEN IN THE NIGHT

Finland's Ari Vatanen gave Peugeot its first win, in 1987, but the hopes of the French manufacturer making it two wins on the trot were put in jeopardy when Vatanen's 405 Turbo 16, with which he was leading, was stolen. Fortunately for Peugeot, fellow rally driver, and compatriot, Juha Kankkunen came through to win in another 405 Turbo 16.

⊙ WHEN STANDARD WAS SUFFICIENT

In the days before specialist modified vehicles were created specifically for this event, rugged standard vehicles like Range Rovers could still succeed. Alain Genestier won the inaugural event with one in 1979 and René Metge gave Range Rover its second win in 1981. However, every event after this has been won by tailor-made machinery.

⊙ THE STRANGEST WINNER

VW's Race Touareg that won in 2009 and 2010 is a large, competition version of its standard four-wheel-drive SUV. However, its first winner, in 1980, the Iltis, was a very different piece of machinery. It was designed as a military vehicle and used an early Audi-developed four-wheel-drive system that would find fame on Audi's Quattro range.

⊙ A CHANGING OF THE GUARD

Yamaha, motorbike-class winner in the inaugural event, still leads the way with nine wins, but the most recent of these victories was Stéphane Peterhansel's in 1998. Austrian off-road bike manufacturer KTM has since cleaned up in the last seven runnings of the Dakar, with Cyril Despres triumphant in 2010 on a 690 Rally.

⊙ FROM TOP TO BOTTOM

The 1992 Paris–Dakar Rally was special, as the route was changed. It ran from Paris to the top of Africa and then right the way to the tip, to Cape Town. Italian all-terrain vehicle manufacturer Perlini made the most of this enlarged "shop window" and Francesco Perlini won the truck class, as he did in 1993 when the rally reverted to a Dakar finish.

⊙ SEVEN IN A ROW

Mitsubishi has a great record in the Dakar Rally and its four-wheel-drive vehicles have claimed seven wins. The first of these came in 2001 with Jutta Kleinschmidt – the event's only female winner – at the wheel. Mitsubishi Pajeros then won again in each of the next six events, with Stéphane Peterhansel the Japanese manufacturer's most recent winner, in 2007.

⊙ GOLD, SILVER AND BRONZE

VW scored a one-two-three finish in the 2010 Dakar Rally in Chile and Argentina, with Carlos Sainz leading home Nasser Al-Attiyah and, some way back, Mark Miller. Giniel de Villiers, winner in 2009, endured engine trouble after rolling his Race Touareg and finished back in seventh in the fourth of the team's entries.

MANUFACTURER WITH MOST WINS – CARS

1	Mitsubishi	12
2	Citroën	4
=	Peugeot	4
4	VW	3
5	Porsche	2
=	Range Rover	2
=	Schlesser Buggy	2
8	Mercedes	1
=	Renault	1

MANUFACTURER WITH MOST WINS – MOTORBIKES

1	Yamaha	9
=	KTM	9
3	BMW	6
4	Honda	5
5	Cagiva	2

⊙ FROM SUPPORT ACT TO A CLASS OF ITS OWN

The truck category was never part of the plan, trucks being entered in the inaugural event in 1979 simply as support vehicles. By 1980, however, they had a class of their own and Kamaz has overhauled Tatra as the most successful truck manufacturer in the event. Victory in the 2010 event in South America took its victory tally to nine.

MANUFACTURER WITH MOST WINS – TRUCKS

1	Kamaz	9
2	Tatra	6
3	Mercedes-Benz	5
4	Perlini	4
5	ALM/ACMAT	1
=	DAF	1
=	Hino	1
=	MAN	1
=	Sonacome	1

PART 4: INDYCAR

America's top category, IndyCar, ran from 1909 to 1979 without feeling the need to name a champion. It became more cohesive, as Championship Auto Racing Teams (CART), but that became divided when the Indy Racing League (IRL) split off in 1996 to focus on ovals. Over the years, some of the racing has been magnificent and it has produced the greats like AJ Foyt, Mario Andretti, Al Unser, Bobby Rahal and Rick Mears, with the Indianapolis 500 as the jewel in its crown.

DRIVERS

America has always been fond of sporting dynasties and the Andretti and Unser families have kept the IndyCar scene filled with generations of winners over the past half-century. However, big winners' purses have also attracted drivers from overseas. Sébastien Bourdais, Alessandro Zanardi, Gil de Ferran, Juan Pablo Montoya and Dario Franchitti are the recent interlopers who have been crowned champion.

CHAMPIONS

⊙ THREE FROM FOUR

Rick Mears was very much the pacesetter in the early years of the CART Championship, winning the inaugural title in 1979, and adding the 1981 and 1982 crowns. His three titles leaves him equal second with Bobby Rahal, behind only Sébastien Bourdais's four.

⊙ SEVEN UP FOR FOYT

America's senior single-seater championship was known as the AAA National Championship from 1909–55. It then became the USAC National Championship, until CART broke away to form its own series in 1979. AJ Foyt claimed seven USAC titles – 1960, 1961, 1963, 1964, 1967, 1975 and 1979 – a record not surpassed in either CART or the IRL since.

⊙ A LONG WAIT

Bobby Rahal, the 1982 Rookie of the Year, won his first two CART titles in consecutive seasons, 1986 and 1987, for Jim Trueman's Truesports team. However, Rahal then had to wait for five years before he claimed his third crown, this time with Rahal-Hogan Racing in 1992. This is the longest gap between titles in the history of the CART Championship.

⊙ JUST SHARP ENOUGH

The first IRL title, in 1996, was unique in that it was shared. Buzz Calkins and Scott Sharp ended the season tied on 246 points apiece. This was only a three-race trial series, though, with Sharp not even winning a round, although he put that right later in the year by winning the opening race of the second series that ran from August 2006 through 2007.

⊙ BRIDGING THE GAP

Al Unser was one of only two drivers who won a USAC title and became a champion again under the CART aegis (i.e. post-1979). He took the USAC crown in 1970 and was the CART champion in 1983 and 1985. The other driver to achieve this double was Mario Andretti, who won USAC titles in 1965, 1966 and 1969, then the CART title in 1984.

⊙ WATCH THOSE BOYS GO

The American racing dynasties of the Andrettis and the Unsers added an extra storyline when the race was on to see which of their second-generation racers, either Michael Andretti or Al Unser Jr, would be the first to become CART champion. Unser Jr won this challenge by landing the 1990 title, one year ahead of Andretti Jr.

⊙ VILLENEUVE CROSSES THE OTHER WAY

Michael Andretti, Juan Pablo Montoya and Cristiano da Matta have all tried, but Jacques Villeneuve remains the only CART champion to have transferred to F1 and become world champion. After claiming the CART crown in 1995, he came close at his first attempt with Williams in 1996, only to finish runner-up behind teammate Damon Hill. But Villeneuve went one better the following year and landed the world title.

⊙ FROM ONE DISCIPLINE TO ANOTHER

Six drivers – Mario Andretti, Bobby Rahal, Danny Sullivan, Emerson Fittipaldi, Nigel Mansell and Alessandro Zanardi – have moved from F1 to become CART champion. But it was Mansell who made the most immediate success of the transatlantic move, winning the F1 title in 1992 and the CART title the following year.

⊙ SAM'S THE MAN

Sam Hornish Jr leads the way in the most Indy Racing League championships won, having claimed three titles, in 2000, 2001 and 2006. Scott Dixon (champion in 2003 and 2008) and Dario Franchitti (2007 and 2009) are next up, with two apiece. The inaugural co-champions Buzz Calkins and Scott Sharp have been joined on one title by Kenny Brack, Tony Kanaan, Buddy Lazier, Greg Ray, Tony Stewart and Dan Wheldon.

⊙ FROM AMERICANS TO ALIENS

The IRL started life wishing to be more American than CART had become, and six US drivers were champions (two jointly) in the series' first seven years. However, apart from Sam Hornish Jr in 2006, every title since 2003 has gone to drivers born outside the USA, with Scott Dixon of New Zealand, England's Dan Wheldon and Scotsman Dario Franchitti matching Swede Kenny Brack's feat of 1999.

DRIVERS WITH MOST CART TITLES

1	Sébastien Bourdais	4
2	Rick Mears	3
=	Bobby Rahal	3
4	Gil de Ferran	2
=	Al Unser	2
=	Al Unser Jr	2
=	Alessandro Zanardi	2
8	Mario Andretti	1
=	Michael Andretti	1
=	Emerson Fittipaldi	1
=	Nigel Mansell	1
=	Juan Pablo Montoya	1
=	Johnny Rutherford	1
=	Danny Sullivan	1
=	Paul Tracy	1
=	Jimmy Vasser	1
=	Jacques Villeneuve	1

⊙ SACRÉ BLEU, IT'S SÉBASTIEN

America's CART series became increasingly cosmopolitan, with champions coming from Brazil, Canada, Colombia, Great Britain, France and Italy as well as the USA. The record for the most CART titles was claimed by Sébastien Bourdais in 2007 when he wrapped up his fourth, rounding out his season at Mexico City with his eighth win.

⊙ FROM SÃO PAULO TO THE USA

Brazilians have enjoyed a long love affair with American single-seater racing and both Emerson Fittipaldi and Nelson Piquet moved to the USA after becoming multiple F1 world champions. Fittipaldi fared better and was CART champion in 1989. However, the Brazilian with the most CART titles to his name is Gil de Ferran, champion in 2000 and 2001.

WINS

⊙ HITTING THE GROUND RUNNING

Italian racer Alessandro Zanardi never hit the high notes in F1, but he came alive when he moved to CART. He scored three wins in his debut season in 1996, at Portland, Mid-Ohio and Laguna Seca. He added two CART titles and another dozen wins, seven of which came in 1998. He lost both legs in a life-threatening accident at the Euro Speedway in 2001. Amazingly, he has since won races in the World Touring Car Championship.

⊙ THE KID DID WELL

After dipping his toe in the water in CART in 1982 and enjoying a single season in F1 in 1983, Danny Sullivan set into a lengthy and successful CART career, immediately winning races for Doug Shierson Racing. By 1988, "The Kentucky Kid" was champion after winning at Portland, Michigan, Nazareth and Laguna Seca. He won 17 races in all, placing him ninth on the CART all-time winners' list.

⊙ DOUBLE HAT-TRICK IS JUST THE TRICK

Reigning F3000 champion Juan Pablo Montoya claimed the 1999 CART title with a pair of hat-tricks. The Colombian won three in a row at Long Beach, Nazareth and Rio de Janeiro, then another three at Mid-Ohio, Chicago and Vancouver later in the year. Each was important, as he ended the year equal on points with Dario Franchitti and claimed the title only by having scored more wins, seven to three.

⊙ A KIWI THAT FLIES

Scott Dixon leads the way in terms of race wins in the IRL. The double champion's tally was 21 by the end of 2009, two ahead of Sam Hornish Jr. The Kiwi's first came on his IRL debut at Homestead in 2003 en route to his first title and his most recent at Motegi in Japan, as he was just edged out in the 2009 title race. He has raced for Chip Ganassi Racing since joining IndyCar.

⊙ FOYT LEADS THE WAY

Feisty Texan AJ Foyt is king of the pre-CART, pre-IRL days when IndyCar racing was run as the USAC National Championship. He won 67 races, his first at Du Quoin in an Offenhauser-powered Meskowski in 1960 and his last at Texas World Speedway in 1979 in a Parnelli-Cosworth. He also won a non-championship race at Pocono in 1981.

⊙ WARDING OFF HIS RIVALS

Two-time USAC champion Rodger Ward was the driver that the fans looked to when they were tipping a winner from the late 1950s to the early 1960s, and he had some increasingly fierce battles with AJ Foyt. His final win, at Trenton in a Lola-Offenhauser in 1966, was his 26th, with his best tally in one year coming in 1963 when he won five races.

⊙ OUT OF HIS FATHER'S SHADOW

Michael Andretti had a hard act to follow, as his father Mario had three USAC titles, a CART title and an F1 World Championship title to his name. However, Michael, who was CART champion in 1991, is the most successful driver in terms of CART wins, having claimed 42 between his first at Long Beach in 1986 to his last, also at Long Beach in 2002. His father took only 19 CART wins but also 33 USAC ones beforehand.

⊙ HORNISH FIRST TO HIT 10

Sam Hornish Jr was the first IRL driver to achieve 10 wins, hitting this target in his Panther Racing Dallara at Chicagoland towards the end of the series' eighth championship in 2003. It was in this season that the new hotshots really started to make their presence felt, demoting many of the drivers who had been with the series from its first campaign in 1996 to the sidelines.

⊙ A STYLE OF HIS OWN

Flamboyant Brazilian Hélio Castroneves ranks third in the all-time list of IRL race winners, with 16. Many have been memorable; such as his comeback win in the 2009 Indy 500 after missing races while being investigated for alleged tax evasion. However, what makes them all stand out is the way he celebrates. He scales the safety fencing to wave to the crowds. He's also well known for winning America's *Dancing with the Stars.*

DRIVERS WITH MOST CART WINS

1	Michael Andretti	42
2	Sébastien Bourdais	31
=	Paul Tracy	31
=	Al Unser Jr	31
5	Rick Mears	25
6	Bobby Rahal	24
7	Emerson Fittipaldi	22
8	Mario Andretti	19
9	Danny Sullivan	17
10	Alessandro Zanardi	15

DRIVERS WITH MOST IRL WINS

1	Scott Dixon	21
2	Sam Hornish Jr	19
3	Hélio Castroneves	16
4	Dan Wheldon	15
5	Dario Franchitti	13
=	Tony Kanaan	13
7	Scott Sharp	9
8	Buddy Lazier	8
9	Ryan Briscoe	5
=	Eddie Cheever	5
=	Gil de Ferran	5
=	Greg Ray	5

⊙ REGULAR WINNER, RARE CHAMPION

Canadian firebrand Paul Tracy sits equal second in the all-time CART race winners' table, despite having only one championship title to his name. He has 31 wins, equal with Al Unser Jr and Sébastien Bourdais. His first win was at Long Beach in 1993 for Penske Racing and his last at Cleveland for Forsythe Championship Racing in 2007.

⊙ UNSER GETS CART GOING

After single-seater racing was formalized into a championship by the formation of CART for 1979, Bobby Unser and Johnny Rutherford were the drivers on form. Unser was the first driver to score 10 CART wins, hitting this landmark in his Penske at the ninth round of the 1980 season at Ontario Speedway in California. For all of this success, he ended up as runner-up in both 1979 and 1980.

POLES AND FASTEST LAPS

⊙ FROM THE START
The driver with by far the greatest number of CART fastest laps to his name is Sébastien Bourdais. The four-time CART champion set the fastest lap in 34 races, putting him 16 fastest laps clear of Alessandro Zanardi, the next most successful driver in this department. French ace Bourdais was fast from the outset, setting four fastest laps in his first season in 2003.

⊙ BOAT CRUISES TO POLE
Billy Boat set nine IRL poles from his 63 IRL starts, to rank equal seventh, but two-thirds of these came in one season, in 1998, when he was on pole six times in the 11 rounds. However, proving that pole doesn't count for everything, he ranked only 13th overall that year after winning only once and missing two races.

⊙ SEVEN AND SEVEN
Hélio Castroneves and Scott Dixon share the record for the most IRL pole positions in a season, landing seven apiece in 2007 and 2008 respectively. Dixon is also at the top of the pile in the table for the most IRL fastest laps, with 14, ranking equal first with Tony Kanaan.

⊙ MEARS ALWAYS SEARS
Rick Mears had a habit of claiming pole position and his tally of 39 poles was greater than any of his rivals, with Michael Andretti having to make do with ranking second best on 32. In 1982 Mears enjoyed a best season of eight poles, with his career-best run of four in succession flowing through into 1983.

⊙ THE BOY FROM BRAZIL
Hélio Castroneves tops the table for the most IRL pole positions, with 30, 13 clear of Scott Dixon. But his single lap expertise isn't continued under race conditions as he ranks only eighth in terms of fastest laps set. However, his record of winning races and titles shows that this popular Brazilian racer has his priorities right.

⊙ RYAN'S FLYIN'

Team Penske's Australian racer Ryan Briscoe ranks only fifth in the all-time IRL fastest laps table, with 10, but he has been the driver in form during the races across the past two seasons. He ranked top in 2008 with four fastest laps and then shared top spot with Scott Dixon in 2009, this time with five fastest laps.

⊙ LEARNING FROM EXPERIENCE

Canadian racer Paul Tracy ranks equal fourth, with Michael Andretti, for most CART fastest laps – 13. He was instantly up to speed, setting the first three of these in his first full season, 1992, after running four races in 1991. He was, mind you, racing for the crack Penske squad, having the rough edges smoothed off his raw speed by veteran teammates Emerson Fittipaldi, Rick Mears and Al Unser.

⊙ RAY OF SUNSHINE

Greg Ray isn't the most heralded driver in IRL circles, despite being champion in 1999, but his record of qualifying on pole position is impressive. His tally of 14 poles places him third on the all-time IRL list. These were set predominantly in the series' early years, before the big-hitting drivers moved across from CART. The last of Ray's pole positions came for the Harrah's 200 at Nashville Superspeedway in 2001.

⊙ MARIO AND DANNY

Mario Andretti and Danny Sullivan share the record for the most pole positions in a CART season, with nine. Andretti achieved this in 1984 and Sullivan equalled it four years later. Andretti secured five of his nine poles in successive races mid-season, winning from three of these in his Newman/Haas Lola T800. Sullivan also had a five-pole streak in 1988 in the final five races, winning two to land the title in his Penske.

DRIVERS WITH MOST IRL POLES

1	Hélio Castroneves	30
2	Scott Dixon	17
3	Greg Ray	14
4	Dario Franchitti	12
5	Sam Hornish Jr	12

DRIVERS WITH MOST CART POLES

1	Rick Mears	39
2	Michael Andretti	32
3	Sébastien Bourdais	31
4	Mario Andretti	29
5	Paul Tracy	25
6	Danny Sullivan	19
7	Emerson Fittipaldi	17
=	Bobby Rahal	17
9	Gil de Ferran	16
10	Juan Pablo Montoya	14

DRIVERS WITH MOST CART FASTEST LAPS

1	Sébastien Bourdais	34
2	Alessandro Zanardi	18
3	Hélio Castroneves	14
4	Michael Andretti	13
=	Paul Tracy	13
6	Juan Pablo Montoya	12
7	Emerson Fittipaldi	11
=	Bruno Junqueira	11
9	Jimmy Vasser	9
10	Dario Franchitti	8

⊙ FASTEST LAPS NOT NEEDED

Sam Hornish Jr was completely overshadowed in terms of fastest laps when he collected his second consecutive IRL title in 2002, for he claimed just one, at Gateway International Raceway in St Louis, in his Panther Racing Dallara. In that same season Tomas Scheckter gathered seven fastest laps and yet failed to end the year in the top 10 overall on points.

DRIVERS WITH MOST IRL FASTEST LAPS

1	Scott Dixon	14
=	Tony Kanaan	14
3	Dan Wheldon	13
4	Tomas Scheckter	12
5	Ryan Briscoe	10

POINTS

⊙ EARLY STARTERS FAVOURED

There is a definite skew when you look at the table for points scored in CART, with the drivers from the early years dominating. The reason for this is that a victory in the first two seasons, in 1979 and 1980, was worth 300 points, but only 20 points thereafter. So, with CART failing by 2008, Rick Mears has cemented his place in history with his collection of 8,642 points.

⊙ A WINNER TO THE END

Bobby Unser already had 25 IndyCar wins to his name before CART formed, but his 10 wins, each in the points-generous early days of CART, elevated him to second in the all-time points table, 1,009 shy of Rick Mears. Then, after notching up two second places in 1981, he quit at the age of 47 to give the next generation of drivers a chance.

⊙ THE BEST OF THE REST

The driver who gathered the greatest number of points in a season after CART changed the points-scoring system for 1981 is Sébastien Bourdais. The French driver collected 387 points in the third of his four consecutive title-winning years, thanks to racing to seven wins in his Newman/Haas/Lanigan Racing Panoz in 2007.

⊙ CONSISTENCY PAYS FOR CARTER

Four of the top 10 points scorers in CART history failed to claim a single title. They were Bobby Unser (second on the list behind three-time champion Rick Mears), Tom Sneva (fourth), Gordon Johncock (fifth) and Pancho Carter (eighth). Carter owes his place in the list to racing in the first two CART seasons when points were generous, as he won only one round, at Michigan in 1981.

⊙ ON THE SLIDE

For so long a points machine in IndyCar racing, winning seven rounds in 1975, AJ Foyt never quite got to grips with CART in the twilight of his career. He scored just 190 points across 85 starts as he cherry-picked the races he wanted to contest in CART's early years, avoiding the street courses in favour of what he knew best: ovals.

⊙ BATTLE OF THE FAMILIES

The Unser family holds bragging rights over the Andrettis when their combined family points scores are totted up. The combined score for Bobby, Al and Al Jr comes to 13,809 points, with Johnny and Robby trying but failing to score. This is some 8,027 more than Mario, Michael, John and Jeff's total of 5,782.

⊙ NO HOME ADVANTAGE

The IRL was created to make America's top single-seater series more American after overseas drivers started filling the top places in CART. The races would almost all be held on ovals to favour drivers brought up on this style of racing. However, when you look at points scored, only three of the top 10 drivers (Sam Hornish Jr in fourth, Scott Sharp fifth and Buddy Lazier eighth) are American.

⊙ TONY KAN

Tony Kanaan, a fixture at Andretti Green Racing, owes his place at third in the all-time IRL points table to consistent competitiveness. He scored at least one win in every season since his first full year in the championship, 2003, before failing to win in 2009. Across these years, the Brazilian racer has been on the podium 46 times.

⊙ BEST IN ONE YEAR

Scott Dixon moved into second place in the all-time IRL points list when he finished as runner-up for Chip Ganassi Racing in the 2009 season. The New Zealander's most successful season in his seven-year IRL career in terms of points is 2008, when he landed the second of his pair of IRL titles with a record tally of 646 thanks to winning six of the 17 rounds.

⊙ GO JOHNNY GO

Johnny Rutherford retired from CART in 1992, but his constant gathering of points, plus the generous points allocation in the championship's first two seasons, have him still ranking third in the all-time points table, with 7,243. His tally of 4,723 in his title-winning 1980 campaign remains the highest points tally for a single season.

TOP 10 DRIVERS WITH MOST CART POINTS

1	Rick Mears	8,642
2	Bobby Unser	7,633
3	Johnny Rutherford	7,243
4	Tom Sneva	4,978
5	Gordon Johncock	4,194
6	Al Unser	3,923
7	Mario Andretti	2,979
8	Pancho Carter	2,701
9	Michael Andretti	2,492
10	Bobby Rahal	2,321

⊙ HÉLIO AGAIN

Hélio Castroneves has scored the most IRL points. His tally of 3,876 at the end of 2009 was 398 more than the next highest scorer, Scott Dixon. Despite this impressive tally the Brazilian has yet to win an IRL title. He has had to make do with ending the year as runner-up twice; to Sam Hornish Jr in 2002 and Scott Dixon in 2008.

TOP 10 DRIVERS WITH MOST IRL POINTS

1	Hélio Castroneves	3,876
2	Scott Dixon	3,478
3	Tony Kanaan	3,477
4	Sam Hornish Jr	3,412
5	Scott Sharp	3,338
6	Dan Wheldon	3,257
7	Dario Franchitti	2,537
8	Buddy Lazier	2,229
9	Vitor Meira	2,167
10	Tomas Scheckter	2,082

RACE STARTS

⊙ THREE HUNDRED AND MORE

If CART is considered alone, that's to say the period from 1979 to the demise of the series at the start of 2008, Michael Andretti has recorded the most race starts – 309. He made his first appearance three races from the end of the 1983 season and raced on in CART until one race short of the end of the 2002 season. Of these, he won 42.

⊙ TIME LOST IN EUROPE

Bobby Rahal didn't take the traditional route to IndyCar racing. He tried F1 first, fleetingly, via racing in Europe. However, after that failed to take off, he came home to the USA and started his IndyCar career in 1982, at the age of 29. He raced on until 1998, taking in the third-highest number of CART starts, 264, in that time.

⊙ SOME YOU WIN, SOME YOU LOSE

Paul Tracy has the fourth-highest number of CART starts, but he could have ranked higher were it not for misfortune. He didn't have a brilliant start to his CART career as he broke his leg on his debut in 1991. That cost him a few appearances, as did a back injury in 1996 and another in 2007. A poor disciplinary record also counted against him, such as being banned from the opening race of 1999.

⊙ HOME AND AWAY

If it hadn't been for continuing his F1 career through to the end of 1981, Mario Andretti would rank higher than sixth on the CART starts chart. Although he raced in CART in each of its first three seasons from 1979, taking in 12 races, he missed out on 25, which would have eased him one ahead of Jimmy Vasser on to 233 starts.

⊙ RACING ON FOR AMERICA

Few would have imagined it when Jimmy Vasser won the CART title in 1996, but he is the last American winner of the CART crown before drivers from overseas took over. Jimmy kept on trying for another nine full seasons after that, stretching his number of race starts to 232, but he gradually slid down the order.

⊙ WHO NEEDS RETIREMENT?

Double F1 world champion Emerson Fittipaldi is the driver with the greatest number of CART starts for someone who was having his second career. He had retired from racing after five years of disappointment with the family F1 team, but an invitation in 1984 to do a sports car race reignited the fire and he moved straight across to CART. He stayed on for 195 races and picked up the 1989 title along the way.

⊙ SECOND AND RISING

Hélio Castroneves joined the IRL in 2001, but he's already up to second place in the all-time race starts list with 130. Amazingly, all of these IRL race starts since his debut at Phoenix have been made for one team, Team Penske, for whom he raced in CART from 2000.

⊙ COMPLETING A CENTURY

Buddy Lazier holds a place in IRL history as the driver who started the series' first ever race from pole, at the Walt Disney World Speedway in 1996. He became a regular winner and raced on until the end of 2002 before losing a full-time ride. By picking up occasional drives, and always tackling the Indy 500, he made it to 100 IRL starts on his last outing, at Indianapolis in 2008.

⊙ STARTING HIGH

Buddy Rice is one of a cluster of drivers who have fallen just short of achieving their 100th IRL start, with his most recent being the 2008 season closer at Chicagoland. He would have expected more, as he started so impressively, finishing second on his series debut at Michigan in 2002 and he won three times for Rahal Letterman Racing in 2004, but the top rides have eluded him in recent times.

⊙ LIKE FATHER, LIKE SON

Al Unser Jr and Michael Andretti were brought up in the shadow of incredibly successful racing fathers. Six months apart in age, they hit CART within a year of each other and Unser Jr raced on to record the second-highest number of CART starts, behind Andretti, with 273 between his debut at Riverside in 1982 and his final race at California Speedway in 1999.

DRIVERS WITH MOST CART STARTS

1	Michael Andretti	309
2	Al Unser Jr	273
3	Bobby Rahal	264
4	Paul Tracy	261
5	Jimmy Vasser	232
6	Mario Andretti	208
7	Emerson Fittipaldi	195
8	Adrian Fernandez	179
9	Rick Mears	178
10	Raul Boesel	172

⊙ AT THE SHARP END

Scott Sharp was in at the start of the IRL in 1996, and was still racing in the series in 2009. So it comes as little surprise that he holds the record tally for IRL race starts, with 147. This figure would have been higher had he not made a career move to predominantly concentrate on the American Le Mans Series from 2008, coming back only for the Indy 500.

DRIVERS WITH MOST IRL STARTS

1	Scott Sharp	147
2	Hélio Castroneves	130
3	Sam Hornish Jr	116
4	Tony Kanaan	115
5	Dan Wheldon	114
6	Scott Dixon	113
7	Tomas Scheckter	109
8	Buddy Lazier	100
9	Ed Carpenter	99
10	Vitor Meira	97
=	Buddy Rice	97

CAREER DURATION

⊙ OVER HERE AND OVER THERE

Mario Andretti had a successful but fractured career and his sojourn in F1 in the 1970s interrupted his IndyCar career, costing him race starts. However, in terms of IndyCar career duration, he's second only to AJ Foyt. His career spanned 31 years, from his first start at Trenton in 1964 to his last at Laguna Seca in 1994, which brought down the curtain on his "Arrivederci Tour".

⊙ LONGTIME LONE STAR RACER

Johnny Rutherford was a racer with staying power, as he survived the rough and tumble of modified stock cars then sprint cars to hit the IndyCar ovals in 1963. The Texan then raced all the way through that year and the next 29, up to his final attempt on the Indy 500 in 1992, four years after his final full season of CART, when he failed to qualify, and thus failed to add to his three wins there.

⊙ HE KEPT ON RACING

Al Unser can't match AJ Foyt and Mario Andretti for top-level career longevity, but his tally of 29 years in IndyCar is remarkable nonetheless. It started with a bang, as he made his debut in 1965 and won that year's race at Pikes Peak. He was champion in 1970, 1983 and 1985, then picked when to race after that. But the speed was still there until his final race in 1993, the Indy 500, the day after his 54th birthday.

⊙ THIS IS THE END, AGAIN

Gordon Johncock enjoyed a 28-year IndyCar career. It kicked off in 1965, was given momentum by winning at Milwaukee that year and ran with great vigour and more wins through the 1970s. Success was harder to come by in the 1980s, with just one victory in 1982, albeit in the Indy 500. However, despite retiring in 1985, he returned and bowed out after the 1992 Indy 500.

⊙ STOPPING BEFORE SLOWING DOWN

Bobby Unser is five years older than his brother Al, so he was the first of the pair to make it to IndyCar racing, doing so in 1963. He too was successful, with two drivers' titles and three Indy 500 wins, but he called it a day earlier than his brother, at the end of the 1981, after 19 seasons. However, second place in his final outing, at Phoenix, proved that the speed was there if he wanted to continue.

⊙ TRACY STILL PACY

Paul Tracy was the fresh-faced teenager who travelled from Canada to try his hand at Formula Ford in Britain. Now, though, his hair is greying and he has 19 years of IndyCar racing under his belt since his debut at Long Beach in 1991 when he stepped up to the category as American Racing Series champion. His record may stretch further, but rides are getting harder to come by for the 2003 CART champion.

⊙ STAYING ON FOR MORE

Tom Sneva had an IndyCar racing career that lasted 19 years. It began at the Indy 500 in 1974 and stretched all the way through to the same race in 1992 when he bowed out a week short of his 44th birthday. This exemplified the role of the Indy 500 in keeping drivers in the cockpit "for one last crack at big the one" after their regular drives had dried up. Sneva's last full season of CART was in 1986.

⊙ COLLECT AND CRUISE

Short but generally sweet is one way of describing Nigel Mansell's two-year whirlwind CART career. Champion at his first attempt in 1993, fresh from winning the F1 drivers' title, the Englishman then failed to add to his tally of five wins. He was often a factor in races in 1994 in his second campaign for Newman/Haas Racing, but following this season he decided to retire.

⊙ FROM BOY TO MAN

As long as wins were a possibility, AJ Foyt kept on racing. His IndyCar career is the longest of all, at 35 years. He started in 1958 and was a winner in 1960, taking his first victory at Du Quoin. But, as the wins kept on coming, another 65 in all, he raced on until 1992. He made his final outing at the Indy 500, showing well to finish ninth.

DRIVERS WITH LONGEST INDYCAR CAREERS (YEARS)

1	AJ Foyt	35
2	Mario Andretti	31
3	Johnny Rutherford	30
4	Al Unser	29
5	Gordon Johncock	28
6	Michael Andretti	25
7	John Andretti	23
=	Al Unser Jr	23
9	Pancho Carter	19
=	Tom Sneva	19
=	Paul Tracy	19
=	Bobby Unser	19

⊙ MICHAEL'S QUARTER CENTURY

Swapping neatly from the CART series to the IRL worked well for Michael Andretti. Not only does he now run a very successful team in the IRL, but as a driver his time in the IRL stretched his IndyCar career to 25 years, from 1983–2007. He did have a certain amount of time out in 1993 when racing for McLaren in F1.

⊙ JOHN THE ONE

John Andretti – son of Aldo, nephew of Mario, cousin of Michael – is a driver who slips under the radar despite having spent 23 years on the IndyCar scene. His IndyCar career began in 1987 and he won once, at Surfer's Paradise in 1991, before turning his attention to NASCAR from 1993, but the lure of the Indy 500 kept him coming back until 2009.

DRIVER RECORDS

⊙ SWAPPING ONE CROWN FOR ANOTHER
When he found out that Williams was going to dispense with his services, even while he was homing in on his F1 title in 1992, Nigel Mansell turned his attention to CART and signed to drive for Newman/Haas Racing for 1993. After winning on his debut in Surfer's Paradise, he added four more wins to make it two titles in two years by becoming CART champion in his rookie season.

⊙ FATHER SHOWS SON
If two generations race, it's rare that they compete against each other, as the father has usually retired before their son or daughter starts racing. Thus the Unsers, Al and Al Jr, achieved something unique when Al was still on the pace as Al Jr started in CART. They scooped a family one-two in 1985, with Senior beating Junior into second place.

⊙ FOYT'S YEAR OF YEARS
AJ Foyt is a driver dripping with titles and records, but no season has been more successful for the Texan on the IndyCar trail than his record-breaking 1964 campaign. He won 10 of the 13 rounds, achieving the highest winning average in IndyCar history, at 76.923 per cent after kicking off the year by winning the first seven rounds.

⊙ MR VERSATILE
Tony Stewart is best known for his successes in NASCAR's Winston Cup, having been champion in 2001, but he has the distinction of being a single-seater champion too, having won the second IRL crown that ran from 1996 into 1997. His talents are further emphasized by that fact that he won the 1995 Triple Crown for winning all USAC's disciplines in the same year: Silver Crown, Sprint Cars and Midgets.

⊙ THE SMALLEST OF FRACTIONS
The closest finish in IRL history came at Chicagoland in 2002 when Panther Racing's Sam Hornish Jr beat Al Unser Jr by just 0.0024 sec. Six years later, at the same venue, Team Penske's Hélio Castroneves came close to beating that, but his winning margin was a fraction larger, at 0.0033 sec over Scott Dixon.

⊙ LOOK TO UNSER

Al Unser hit IndyCar racing's most purple patch, scorching a winning streak that started at Indianapolis Raceway Park midway through the 1970 season in his Vel's Parnelli Colt. He added seven more victories in the next eight races, Jim McElreath winning at Ontario Speedway in the other one. Then, although Swede Savage won the season finale, Unser continued winning as soon as the 1971 season commenced, triumphing in the first three races of the campaign. Mike Mosley won the fourth race, at Trenton, but Unser got back to winning ways, with a pair of back-to-back victories, giving him an unprecedented run of 13 successes in 16 races.

⊙ YOUNG AND FAST

Three-time IRL champion Sam Hornish Jr is also the youngest driver to win an IRL race. He was just 21 years and 259 days old when he was first to the finish in the 2001 season-opening race at Phoenix in his Panther Racing Dallara. Tomas Scheckter is the second youngest, being just 50 days older when he won at Michigan in 2002.

⊙ FROM ROOKIE TO CHAMPION

Only one IRL Rookie of the Year has gone on to become champion. This was former British Formula Ford champion Dan Wheldon, who arrived in the IRL after finishing as the runner-up in Indy Lights in 2001. He was top rookie in 2003 with Andretti Green Racing and then champion with the same team just two years later.

⊙ MICHAEL MAKES THE MOVES

Michael Andretti holds the record for the most laps led in CART, having totalled 6,607 laps in front between his series debut at Las Vegas in 1983 and his last race at California Speedway in 2002. He raised the amount achieved in one season to 965 in 1991 then raised it again to 1,136 in 1992. He has also been the driver to lead the most laps in a single race 57 times.

TOP 10 DRIVERS WITH MOST LAPS LED IN CART

1	Michael Andretti	6,607	6	Bobby Rahal	3,034
2	Paul Tracy	4,240	7	Emerson Fittipaldi	2,635
3	Rick Mears	3,243	8	Sébastien Bourdais	2,100
4	Al Unser Jr	3,134	9	Juan Pablo Montoya	1,774
5	Mario Andretti	3,054	10	Alessandro Zanardi	1,467

TEAMS AND TRACKS

The variety of circuits that are or were visited by IndyCar racing is vast, from the ovals such as Indianapolis to the rolling road courses at Laguna Seca and Road America, and the contrasting street tracks at Long Beach and Toronto. It is from these circuits that the great teams have emerged, such as Penske Racing, Newman/Haas, Chip Ganassi and Andretti Green Racing.

TEAM RECORDS

⊙ PENSKE WEARS THE MOST CROWNS

Roger Penske's team has long been an example to the others, for its considerable success as well as its professionalism. Not surprisingly, Penske Racing has accumulated the most CART titles, nine, one more than Newman/Haas/Lanigan Racing. The team's titles were won by Rick Mears (in 1979, 1981 and 1982), Al Unser (1983 and 1985), Danny Sullivan (1988), Al Unser Jr (1994) and Gil de Ferran (2000 and 2001).

⊙ TWO IN A ROW

Winning consecutive CART team titles is a tough proposition, so Jim Trueman had reason to be an extremely proud man at the end of the 1987 season as his Truesports entry for Bobby Rahal achieved just that. Rahal and Truesports edged out Michael Andretti in 1986 and then enjoyed a greater margin over him the following year, having changed from a March to a Lola chassis.

⊙ FROM SPORTS CARS TO SINGLE-SEATERS

Racer, team owner and inspired engineer, Jim Hall was a busy man. Sports cars were his first love, but he tried F1 and moved his Chaparral team from sports cars to F5000 to IndyCar, running his own chassis. Quick from the outset, Johnny Rutherford claimed the second ever CART title, in 1980, with a record number of points, 4,723, before the points system was changed.

⊙ BREAKING AWAY FOR SUCCESS

After a brief spell as Forsythe-Green Racing, Barry Green went his own way in 1995 with driver Jacques Villeneuve and had an incredible year. They kicked off with a win at Miami in the opening round, scored a dramatic win in the Indy 500 and then Villeneuve added further wins at Elkhart Lake and Cleveland to land the drivers' title.

⊙ FROM CHAMP TO CHAMP

Bobby Rahal is the only CART champion to go on and become champion with his own team. After bagging titles in 1986 and 1987 with Truesports, Bobby formed Rahal-Hogan Racing with Carl Hogan at the end of 1991, absorbing Truesports. They won the CART title at their first attempt in 1992. Then, in 1986, the team became Rahal-Letterman Racing when top TV chat show host David Letterman bought a share.

⊙ YEARS OF WINNING

Newman/Haas/Lanigan Racing holds the record as the team with the most CART race wins, with a tally of 107, 24 ahead of Penske. The first of these came when Mario Andretti won at Elkhart Lake in 1983, but it was the final years of CART when the team was at its most competitive. Sébastien Bourdais won four titles in succession and personally added 31 wins to the team's total.

⊙ PENSKE PUTS DOWN A MARKER

Penske enjoyed a quite remarkable campaign in the first CART championship in 1979 when its chassis won 11 of the 14 races. Two were won by McLarens and the final round by a Chaparral. However, unusually, only nine of those wins belonged to Penske Racing, as Gordon Johncock won the opening round and another in mid-season in a Penske run by Patrick Racing.

⊙ FORZA FORSYTHE

Forsythe Racing ranks fourth on team wins and, after scoring the first of its 34 wins through Hector Rebaque at Elkhart Lake in 1982, it had its most successful season in 2003 when its drivers won eight rounds. Paul Tracy won seven en route to being a dominant champion and fellow Canadian Patrick Carpentier picked up the other win.

⊙ LOLA REIGNS SUPREME

Lola is the manufacturer with the greatest number of CART titles to its name, 13, six ahead of both Penske and Reynard. It also holds the record for the most races won, 196, helped in 2005 and 2006 by being the provider of the series' standardized chassis. Fellow British chassis manufacturer Reynard is second on 95.

⊙ BLUE OVAL ON THE OVALS

Ford can claim the glory for building the most successful CART engine, with cars carrying its engines winning 17 titles. The Cosworth-developed DFX, a turbocharged derivative of the successful DFV F1 engine, landed the title each year from 1979–87. In terms of race wins, the blue oval also comes out at the top of the pile, with 251 to Chevrolet's 82.

⊙ FOUR FROM FOUR

Former racer Chip Ganassi's team got the hang of winning the CART title as it backed up its first title, won by Jimmy Vasser in 1996, with three more over the next three years – through Alessandro Zanardi in 1997 and 1998 then Juan Pablo Montoya in 1999. In the space of four years, the team vaulted to third in the overall table for titles won.

⊙ FROM SHOPPING TO LAPPING

Bradley Motorsports had the shortest route to IRL championship glory when it won the inaugural title in a series of just three races at Walt Disney World's Speedway, Phoenix and the Indy 500. Set up by supermarket owner Brad Calkins, it ran his son Buzz to a share of the 1996 title, tied on points with AJ Foyt Racing's Scott Sharp.

⊙ FIRST BLOOD TO PENSKE

The first team which managed to enjoy the novelty of winning the CART championship was Penske Racing. This was in 1979 and Rick Mears was the winning driver. He tasted success three times, claiming victories at Indianapolis, Trenton and the season-closer at Atlanta Motor Speedway.

TEAMS WITH MOST CART TITLES

1	Penske Racing	9
2	Newman/Haas/Lanigan Racing	8
3	Chip Ganassi Racing	4
4	Truesports	2
5	Chapparal Racing	1
=	Forysthe Racing	1
=	Galles-Kraco Racing	1
=	Team Green	1
=	Patrick Racing	1
=	Rahal-Hogan Racing	1

⊙ STAR OF TRACK AND SCREEN

Legendary film actor Paul Newman was passionate about his racing and no fool behind the wheel. He demonstrated this when he finished second in the Le Mans 24 Hours in 1979. However, he'll be remembered most in American racing circles for the hugely successful team he ran with Carl Haas – Newman/Haas Racing – with Mike Lanigan buying a share in 2007. The team collected the second-highest haul of CART titles, eight, from Mario Andretti's crown in 1984 to Sébastien Bourdais's fourth championship in 2007.

⊙ COMBINE AND SHINE

It took Rick Galles's eponymous team from 1980 to 1990 to land the CART title. Al Unser Jr's success in winning the races at Long Beach, Milwaukee and then four in a row at Toronto, Michigan, Denver and Vancouver came a year after Galles had merged with Maurice Kranes's team to form Galles-Kraco Racing. However, it was never to run as strongly again apart from Unser Jr's win in the 1992 Indy 500.

⊙ THREE TITLES FOR TWO

Armed with the knowledge of what it took to win a CART title, Barry Green joined forces with Michael Andretti in 2003 and their team – Andretti Green Racing – has since moved to the top of the table for the most IRL titles. These came through Tony Kanaan in 2004, Dan Wheldon in 2005 and Dario Franchitti in 2007. Chip Ganassi Racing equalled this record in 2009 when Franchitti gave the team its third title.

⊙ HONDA MOVES IN FRONT

Oldsmobile's Aurora engine set the early pace in the IRL, powering the champion's car five years in a row from the 1996/97 series. However, Honda passed it in 2009 to become the most successful engine manufacturer when Dario Franchitti helped it to its sixth title. It should be pointed out that Honda has been the standard engine since 2006.

⊙ TOUGH AT THE TOP

John Menard's team ranks equal third on IRL titles won, with two. The first was with Tony Stewart, in 1996/97, and the second was in 1999 with Greg Ray. The owner of a chain of home-improvement stores, John found it increasingly hard to keep up as the top teams moved across from CART, so Team Menard merged with Panther Racing in 2004.

⊙ ITALIAN CARS, AMERICAN OVALS

Italian chassis manufacturer Dallara is the manufacturer with the greatest number of IRL titles to its name – 11 – including every one since 2004. It also holds the record for the most number of IRL races won, with 167 wins, 90 ahead of G-Force, helped hugely by its chassis being the standardized one since 2007.

⊙ WIN THEN LOSE

Patrick Racing is one of six teams that have claimed a solitary CART title. This came in 1989, when double F1 world champion Emerson Fittipaldi showed that he was still competitive in the second part of his career and edged out Rick Mears thanks to three wins in a row in the first half of the year. Then it all went wrong as Fittipaldi took the Marlboro money to Penske and new partner Chip Ganassi left to form his own team.

⊙ PANTHER STRIKES

John Barnes's Indianapolis-based Panther Racing team had a proud record in the early days of the IRL series as it guided Sam Hornish Jr to two titles in a row, in 2001 and 2002, winning eight rounds across those two seasons.

⊙ FOYT RACING DOUBLES UP

Having shared the inaugural IRL title with Bradley Motorsports, inveterate winner AJ Foyt enjoyed his team becoming the first two-time IRL champions when Swedish driver Kenny Brack delivered the 1998 title. He did it thanks to a winning streak of three straight races at Charlotte, Pikes Peak and Atlanta in the second half of the season.

TEAMS WITH MOST IRL TITLES

1	Andretti Green Racing	3
=	Chip Ganassi Racing	3
3	AJ Foyt Racing	2*
=	Team Menard	2
=	Panther Racing	2
6	Bradley Motorsports	1*
=	Hemelgarn Racing	1
=	Penske Racing	1

One shared title

TRACK RECORDS

◉ MICHIGAN THE MOST

Michigan has hosted more rounds of the CART series than any other circuit, having held 33 between 1979 and 2001 thanks to hosting a second round each year between CART's inaugural season in 1979 and 1986, in addition to the Michigan 500. No doubt the attraction was that it was the fastest of them all, until the California Speedway was built at Fontana in 1997.

◉ NEW YORK, NEW TRACK

CART's attempts to crack New York never took off, but the Meadowlands circuit, close to Manhattan, had a go at enticing the city's petrolheads from 1984–91 but failed. Mario Andretti was the first winner, but his average speed of 80.742mph wasn't enough to excite the fans, so a modified "oval" was introduced. However, the fastest average there, set by Al Unser Jr in 1988, was still only 99.352mph.

◉ OVER AND BLACK OUT

Texas Motor Speedway first hosted a round of the CART series in 2001. It was a circuit that frightened the drivers. The reason for their concern was that several drivers found the centrifugal forces on the 24-degree banked turns too much for them and they started to black out. They duly refused to race and CART never returned.

◉ QUICK IN THE HOOD

When it comes to street circuits built on a temporary arrangement of regular streets, Al Unser Jr has the best record, as he has won 18 times on them. This started with his win at Meadowlands in his Shierson Racing Lola in 1985 and continued with further wins at Miami, Long Beach (six times), Toronto and Vancouver.

◉ FOYT BEST ON THE BANKING

Banked ovals remain the type of circuit most associated with IndyCar racing in all of its forms and incarnations, and AJ Foyt is the driver with the greatest number of wins on these, with 40 over his lengthy career. The first of these came back in 1961 when he won the Indy 500 no less, having previously won four times in 1960 on dirt ovals.

⊙ FLAT BUT NOT FLAT-OUT

The variety of circuits raced on by CART is shown by the one laid out at Cleveland's Burke Lakefront Airport. It was flat and wide, as one would expect in such a setting, with the track marked out by cones and its width offering endless overtaking possibilities. Emerson Fittipaldi, Danny Sullivan and Paul Tracy all collected three wins here.

⊙ TWISTS AND TURNS

Mid-Ohio is the polar opposite of any of the ovals and superspeedways. It's a difficult twisting and undulating road circuit set in woodland near Lexington. Bought by Truesports team owner Jim Trueman, it became a fixture from 1980, then continued to be used through to the demise of CART before the IRL took over the race.

⊙ NORTH OF THE BORDER

Canada has held IndyCar races (USAC then CART) at six different circuits. They are Edmonton, the Circuit Gilles Villeneuve in Montreal, Mosport Park, St Jovite at Mont-Tremblant, Toronto and Vancouver. Edmonton is a temporary circuit at the airport, Toronto and Vancouver are temporary street circuits and the other three all permanent road courses.

⊙ CALIFORNIA FLYER

California Speedway at Fontana has a notable claim to fame. It was here that the fastest ever qualifying lap in any form of motor sport was set. Gil de Ferran's flying lap in 30.255 secs set in 2000 equated to 241.428mph. And anyone who has had the pleasure of meeting the effervescent Brazilian will know there couldn't be anyone better suited to describing the lap.

⊙ RIGHTS AS WELL AS LEFTS

Mario Andretti showed his ability at turning right as well as left by proving to be the king of all sorts of circuits, not just ovals. He holds the record for the most wins on road circuits, with 17, including wins at Indianapolis Raceway Park, St Jovite, Seattle, Riverside, Castle Rock, Elkhart Lake, Mid-Ohio and Portland.

TOP 10 FASTEST CART CIRCUITS

	Circuit	Driver	Year	Speed
1	Fontana	Gil de Ferran	2000	241.428mph
2	Michigan	Paul Tracy	2000	234.970mph
3	Texas	Kenny Brack	2001	233.344mph
4	Indianapolis	Roberto Guerrero	1992	232.483mph
5	Motegi	Gil de Ferran	1999	218.922mph
6	Homestead	Greg Moore	1998	217.519mph
7	Rockingham	Kenny Brack	2002	213.742mph
8	Pocono	Emerson Fittipaldi	1989	211.716mph
9	Lausitzring	Tony Kanaan	2001	209.549mph
10	Las Vegas	Patrick Carpentier	2004	206.184mph

These are qualifying lap records.

⊙ VICTORY BY A NOSE

The closest finish in a CART race came at Portland in 1997 when Mark Blundell carried more momentum out of the final corner to outdrag and get his Pac West Racing Reynard's nose in front of Gil de Ferran's Walker Racing Reynard as he took the chequered flag. His margin in winning the Budweiser GI Joe's 200 was 0.027 sec.

⊙ LONG BEACH, LONG RECORD

The circuit around the streets of the Californian city of Long Beach has been used by four international racing series: F5000 in 1975, F1 from 1976–83, CART from 1984–2008 and, most recently, by the IRL from 2009. Al Unser Jr enjoyed six wins here and Alessandro Zanardi (1997/98), Paul Tracy (2003/04), Sébastien Bourdais (2005/06) and Will Power (2007/08) have all taken doubles.

⊙ EUROPE JOINS THE FAST SET

Racing ovals are few and far between in Europe after the demise of Brooklands in England, Sitges in Spain and the banked oval at Monza in Italy. However, modern ovals at Rockingham in England and the Lausitzring (also known as the Euro Speedway) in Germany both break into the top 10 fastest CART circuits, with the fastest lap around the former being 213.742mph.

⊙ COVERED BY A BLANKET

The Chicagoland Speedway oval is the circuit that clearly lends itself most to tight finishes, as it can claim four of the top 10 closest finishes. The closest ever was in 2002, the second closest in 2008, the fifth closest in 2003 and the ninth closest in 2005. The margins of these wins ranged from 0.0024 sec to a scarcely comprehensive 0.0133 sec. The first three finishers in 2003 were covered by one-tenth of a second.

⊙ TWO FOR T

Texas Motor Speedway has hosted more rounds of the IRL than any other circuit, outstripping the series' talismanic home, the Indianapolis Motor Speedway by 20 races to 14. This is because the Texas circuit hosted two rounds each year between 1998 and 2004, after which no circuit was granted a second round.

⊙ A DIFFERENT SORT OF HORSEPOWER

The state of Kentucky is best known for horse racing and bourbon, but it is becoming known in motor-racing circles because of its smart tri-oval speedway that opened in 2000. It has bragging rights over neighbouring state Tennessee because its speedway is faster than the one in Nashville.

⊙ TWO ROLLS OF THE DICE

There can be no mistaking the difference between the venue at Caesar's Palace when Las Vegas hosted F1 in the 1980s and the Las Vegas Speedway, home when the IRL visits. The former was a twisting track marked out in a casino car park with a qualifying record of 106.931mph. The other is a purpose-built speed oval with a lap speed more than 100mph faster.

⊙ MILWAUKEE MOST VISITED

The Indianapolis Motor Speedway has hosted the Indy 500 on 93 occasions, but the Milwaukee Mile at the Wisconsin State Fair Park – the world's oldest permanent racing circuit – is the most visited circuit across the spread of the AAA National Championship, USAC, CART and IRL series, having hosted 112 races between 1903 and the end of 2009.

⊙ SAVE THE BEST FOR LAST

The fastest lap recorded at the tri-oval Pocono Raceway was 211.716mph, set by Emerson Fittipaldi in his Penske-Chevrolet PC18 during qualifying in 1989. This turned out to be CART's final visit to the Pennsylvanian circuit as the teams said the track was simply too bumpy for them to want to lap at more than 200mph around it.

⊙ BEAUTY AND THE BEAST

If prizes were handed out for beauty, the Road America circuit at Elkhart Lake in upcountry Wisconsin would win every time. There's more to the road circuit's allure than appearance alone, as the challenge its dipping, turning, 5.3-mile lap presented was one of CART's toughest. It also had the appeal of throwing up the odd shock result, such as wins for Hector Rebaque in 1982 and then Jacques Villeneuve Sr in 1985.

⊙ RAY GUNS IT

Chiefly a NASCAR circuit, the Atlanta Motor Speedway was used by CART from 1979–83. However, the IRL has embraced it more, racing there since 1998. Greg Ray made it the third-fastest IRL circuit behind Indianapolis and the California Speedway Fontana when he qualified on pole at the Georgia circuit in 224.049mph in 2001 in his Team Menard Dallara-Aurora.

TOP 10 IRL CIRCUITS LAP RECORDS

	Circuit	Driver	Year	Speed
1	Indianapolis	Tony Stewart	1996	233.102mph
2	Fontana	Hélio Castroneves	2003	226.778mph
3	Atlanta	Greg Ray	2001	224.049mph
4	Chicagoland	Richie Hearn	2003	223.140mph
5	Texas	Gil de Ferran	2003	222.902mph
6	Michigan	Tomas Scheckter	2003	222.478mph
7	Kentucky	Sam Hornish Jr	2003	219.629mph
8	Homestead	Sam Hornish Jr	2006	218.549mph
9	Kansas	Scott Dixon	2003	218.067mph
10	Las Vegas	Sam Schmidt	1999	209.463mph

These are qualifying lap records.

INDIANAPOLIS 500

Dating back to 1911, the Indianapolis 500 is America's big one. The Daytona 500 NASCAR race has grown in recent years, but the Indy 500 is the one with the clearest claim to the title of "the greatest". It is a race that has had more than its share of drama and its participants over the years are a roll-call of the great and the good, including AJ Foyt, the Unsers, the Andrettis and Rick Mears.

DRIVER RECORDS

⊙ TWO ON THE SPIN
Only five drivers to date have managed to win the Indy 500 two years in succession. The first to do so was Wilbur Shaw, who won in 1939 in the Boyle Special – a Maserati 8C – and then repeated the feat in 1940 in the same dark red car. The other repeat winners are: Mauri Rose (1947 and 1948), Bill Vukovich (1953 and 1954), Al Unser (1970 and 1971) and Hélio Castroneves (2001 and 2002).

⊙ ENJOYING LIFE AT THE FRONT
Ralph de Palma ranks second behind Al Unser for the most laps led in the Indy 500, with 612. When the Italian-born driver did his leading, he did so with a riding mechanic alongside, as was mandatory until 1937. No doubt de Palma enjoyed the race, which is more than can be said for his riding mechanic in 1920, who had to climb on to the bonnet while racing to extinguish flames.

⊙ NO RESPECT FOR AGE
Racing drivers tended to have a higher average age in the 1950s, so Troy Ruttman must have been considered almost a babe in arms when he turned up to race in the Indy 500 for the first time in 1949 aged just 18. He failed to go the distance but kept coming back and won on his fourth visit in the JC Agajanian Kuzma-Offenhauser in 1952 aged just 22 years and 80 days. The record still stands.

⊙ NEAR TOTAL DOMINATION
Billy Arnold nearly achieved the ultimate Indy 500 performance in 1930. He started his front-wheel-drive Miller-Hartz from pole position and raced to victory, leading all but two of the 200 laps, having had to follow fellow front-row starter Lou Meyer's Sampson for laps one and two.

⊙ WOMEN TO THE FORE
In 1977 aerospace engineer Janet Guthrie was the first female racer to qualify for the Indy 500. She finished ninth the following year in her Texaco Star Wildcat. However, the best finish by a female racer in the Indy 500 was in 2009, when Danica Patrick finished third for Andretti Green Racing, advancing from 10th on the grid.

⊙ OVERCOMING A PENALTY

The Indy 500 is tough to win, but Jacques Villeneuve certainly did it the hard way in 1995 when he overcame a two-lap penalty to come out on top after taking the lead on lap 195 from 200. The setback came on lap 37 when his Player's Reynard overtook the safety car, not realizing that he was leading the race as others had pitted. The penalty dropped him to 24th and he had to advance from there.

⊙ NO SIGN OF SLOWING DOWN

Al Unser was a driver who just kept on going, and he became the oldest ever winner of the Indianapolis 500 in 1987, when he was just five days short of his 48th birthday. Despite starting from 20th place on the grid, he guided his bright-yellow Penske Racing March up through the field to finish 4.487 secs clear of Roberto Guerrero's Vince Granatelli Racing March.

⊙ 12 SHARE THE LEAD

Emerson Fittipaldi was in front when it mattered most as he claimed victory for Penske Racing in 1993. It had been a race of considerable change at the front, with 12 of the 33 starting drivers taking a turn in the lead. The others were: Arie Luyendyk, Raul Boesel, Stephan Gregoire, Kevin Cogan, Al Unser, Mario Andretti, John Andretti, Robby Gordon, Scott Goodyear, Nigel Mansell and Al Unser Jr.

⊙ ATTACK FROM THE BACK

Ray Harroun and Louis Meyer share the record for achieving the greatest advance through the field in the history of the Indy 500, both rising from 28th on the grid to first. Harroun's charge came in the first race, in 1911, when he guided his Marmon Wasp to win from Ralph Mulford who had started just one place further back. It should be noted that there had been no qualifying for the inaugural race and the grid had been decided according to the order in which the cars had been entered. Meyer's climb came in 1936 and he hit the front by half-distance before motoring on to beat Ted Horn by 2 mins 17.15 secs.

⊙ THREE WIN FOUR

AJ Foyt, Al Unser and Rick Mears share the record for the most Indy 500 victories, having taken four apiece. Foyt was the first to achieve this, wrapping up his fourth in 1977, having won in 1961, 1964 and 1967. Unser was next, winning in 1970, 1971, 1978 and 1987 before Mears matched them with wins in 1979, 1984, 1988 and 1991.

DRIVERS WITH MOST INDIANAPOLIS 500 WINS

1	AJ Foyt	4
=	Rick Mears	4
=	Al Unser	4
4	Hélio Castroneves	3
=	Louis Meyer	3
=	Mauri Rose	3
=	Johnny Rutherford	3
=	Wilbur Shaw	3
=	Bobby Unser	3
10	Emerson Fittipaldi	2
=	Gordon Johncock	2
=	Arie Luyendyk	2
=	Tommy Milton	2
=	Al Unser Jr	2
=	Bill Vukovich	2
=	Rodger Ward	2
=	Howdy Wilcox	2

55 drivers have one win, some of which were shared.

⊙ REAR-ENGINED REVOLUTION

The writing was on the wall for the front-engined roadsters as soon as Jack Brabham ran well with a Cooper in 1961, and Lotus came within an ace of winning with Jim Clark in 1963. Clark was on pole in 1964 then claimed the first rear-engined win in 1965. While the American teams got to grips with this new sort of car, Clark's fellow F1 racer Graham Hill scored the second rear-engined win, in a Lola, in 1966.

TEAM RECORDS

▶ PENSKE ON POLE

Penske's table-topping record of 15 wins in the Indy 500 is matched precisely by its record tally of 15 pole positions. Tom Sneva claimed the first of these, in 1977, qualifying his McLaren-Cosworth M24 at 198.884mph. He went on to finish second in the race behind AJ Foyt's Coyote.

▶ THE OLD ONE-TWO

The first team one-two finish came in 1947 when Mauri Rose led home Bill Holland for Lou Moore's team. its Blue Crown Spark Plug Specials started third and eighth, but they picked their way past pole-sitter Ted Horn's Maserati. It should have been Holland ahead of Rose, for Moore had signalled them to "go easy", but Rose ignored this and caught Holland with seven laps to go who let him by, thinking he was a lap down.

▶ RETURN OF THE EUROPEANS

Apart from Peugeot, Delage and Mercedes winning from 1913 to 1919, and Maserati taking the race in 1939 and 1940, it was American cars and teams in front all the way until the Europeans struck a mortal blow to the front-engined roadsters. Team Lotus used its F1 experience to win in 1965 and come second in 1966 behind Englishman Graham Hill in his British-built, American-run John Mecom Lola.

▶ FOUR FOR FOYT

AJ Foyt drove to victory in the Indianapolis 500 on four occasions, and all but the first of his triumphs, in 1961, were in his own team's car. He won in 1964 and 1967, under the banner of Ansted-Thompson Racing, in deference to sponsors, and then in 1977, as the Gilmore Racing Team in partnership with Jim Gilmore. After retiring, he ran a car under his AJ Foyt Enterprises label, with which Swedish driver Kenny Brack triumphed in 1999.

⊙ THREE WINS FOR THE THREE WS

Racer Rodger Ward formed Leader Card Racing with greetings card manufacturer Bob Wilke and mechanic/designer AJ Watson for the 1959 season. Their reward was instant as Ward won easily ahead of Jim Rathmann. They won again in 1962 and raced to their third win in 1968 when Ward had retired and Bobby Unser was at the wheel of the team's Eagle-Offenhauser.

⊙ RAIN HELPS PATRICK BLOSSOM

Patrick Racing spread its three Indy 500 wins across 17 years, with Emerson Fittipaldi's win in 1989 moving it into equal fourth place in the all-time wins chart. Pat Patrick's team's first two victories were scored by Gordon Johncock in 1973 and 1982, with the former clinched after only 133 of the scheduled 200 laps as rain brought the race to a halt.

⊙ PLEASING THE BOSS

Seven drivers have had the distinction of winning in a car they owned. The first of the owner/driver winners was Jimmy Murphy (1922), followed by Kelly Petillo (1935), Wilbur Shaw (1937), AJ Foyt (1967 and 1977) and Eddie Cheever (1998). Parnelli Jones and Bobby Rahal did it differently; they won the race as drivers then entered cars with which Al Unser (1970 and 1971) and Buddy Rice (2004) took victory.

⊙ MEAN AND GREEN

Barry Green and his brother Kim ran Jacques Villeneuve in Formula Atlantic and graduated with him to CART in 1994 as Team Green. They won both the Indy 500 and the CART title. Michael Andretti raced for Kim in 2001 and this led to the formation of Andretti Green Racing, which took two Indy 500 wins in 2005, with Dan Wheldon, and 2007, with fellow Brit Dario Franchitti. Marco Andretti was pipped by 0.0635 secs in the intervening year.

⊙ ALL-ROUND SUCCESS

Firestone is the tyre manufacturer with the best record in the Indy 500, with 62 wins to its credit. Its first came in the inaugural race in 1911. The next was Jimmy Murphy's victory in 1922, with this run going through 25 consecutive races to 1948. Further wins were picked up over the next 25 years, then the manufacturer took a 20-year break from the race. It returned in 1993 and carried on winning, with the latest victory being with Hélio Castroneves in 2009.

TEAMS WITH MOST INDIANAPOLIS 500 WINS

1	Penske Racing	15
2	Lou Moore	5
3	AJ Foyt Enterprises	4
4	Andretti Green Racing*	3
=	Leader Cards Racing	3
=	Patrick Racing	3
7	JC Agajanian	2
=	Boyle Racing	2
=	Chaparral Cars	2
=	Duesenberg Automobile	2
=	Harry Hartz	2
=	Howard Keck	2
=	McLaren Cars	2
=	Louis Meyer	2
=	Peugeot	2
=	George Salih	2
=	Vel's Parnelli Jones Racing	2
=	John Zink	2

* Ran as Team Green in 1995

⊙ THE FLYING DUTCHMAN

Shierson Racing won the Indy 500 only once, in 1990 with Arie Luyendyk at the wheel of its Lola-Chevrolet T90/00. However, team owner Doug Shierson can lay claim to the proud boast that the Dutchman's winning average speed was a record: 185.981mph across the 500 miles.

MISCELLANEOUS RECORDS

⊙ END OF A CHAPTER

The arrival of F1-inspired cars at the Indy 500 in the 1960s triggered a revolution: their engines were behind the drivers rather than in front. Their handling was vastly superior to the IndyCar roadsters and AJ Foyt laid down another claim to fame in 1964 when he became the last driver to win the race in a front-engined car, the Ansted-Thompson Racing Watson-Offenhauser.

⊙ HOME AND HOSED

Jules Goux enjoyed the largest ever winning margin in 1913 when he brought his works Peugeot home 13 mins 08.40 secs ahead of Spencer Wishart's Mercer. Before 1966, the clock was left running to allow the drivers to complete the 500 miles. The Frenchman was the first non-American winner of the race and the first to win without the help of a relief driver. Allegedly, he slaked his thirst at pit stops with champagne.

⊙ STARTING FROM A LOW BASE

The lowest winning average speed was set, not surprisingly, in the first Indianapolis 500, back in 1911. Ray Harroun's self-designed yellow and black Marmon Wasp averaged just 74.602mph. It would have been higher but for a blown tyre that left Harroun to limp back to the pits.

⊙ MAKE THAT THE OFFENHAUSER

The Offenhauser engine is almost as much a symbol of the Indy 500 as the line of bricks across the main straight. There's good reason for this in that the mighty Offy has powered more winners than any other type of engine, winning 27 times between 1935 (Kelly Petillo's Wetteroth) and 1976 (Johnny Rutherford's McLaren).

TOP 10 DRIVERS WITH MOST LAPS LED

1	Al Unser	644	6	Emerson Fittipaldi	505
2	Ralph de Palma	612	7	Parnelli Jones	492
3	Mario Andretti	556	8	Bill Vukovich	485
4	AJ Foyt	555	9	Bobby Unser	440
5	Wilbur Shaw	508	10	Michael Andretti	431

⊙ THE WORST POSITION OF ALL

Five drivers have suffered the fate of being runner-up at the Indy 500 on three occasions: Harry Hartz (1922, 1923 and 1926), Wilbur Shaw (1933, 1935 and 1938), Jim Rathmann (1952, 1957 and 1959), Al Unser (1967, 1972 and 1983) and Tom Sneva (1977, 1978 and 1980). Of these, only Hartz never went one place better.

⊙ IN FRONT BUT BEHIND

Rodger Ward achieved a remarkable record when he hit the front 10 times in the 1960 Indy 500 in his Leader Card-Offenhauser, yet he failed to win the race. He came home second behind Jim Rathmann's Ken-Paul Special after an enthralling duel in which the lead changed hands between the pair eight times in the final 31 laps. Rathmann took the lead for good with three laps to go as Ward's tyres lost their grip.

⊙ ITALIAN FLIERS

Dallara is the chassis manufacturer that has scored the most Indy 500 wins – nine. It triumphed in 1998 (driven by Eddie Cheever), 1999 (Kenny Brack), 2001 and 2002 (Hélio Castroneves), 2005 (Dan Wheldon), 2006 (Sam Hornish Jr), 2007 (Dario Franchitti), 2008 (Scott Dixon) and 2009 (Hélio Castroneves). It must be pointed out that the Italian company was appointed the supplier of the standard chassis in 2007.

⊙ FALLING AT THE LAST

A driver can suffer heartache at any stage of a race, but disaster when the race is all but won is the most soul-destroying. Take Ralph de Palma. He was leading on lap 198 in 1912, with two laps to go, when his Mercedes threw a con rod, leaving Joe Dawson to motor past to victory. Eight years later, de Palma's engine caught fire, this time on lap 186.

⊙ DASH FOR THE LINE

The tightest Indy 500 finish came in 1992 when Galles-Kraco Racing's Al Unser Jr beat Scott Goodyear by just 0.043 secs. A yellow flag period ended on lap 194, giving them six laps to sprint to the finish. Unser Jr made a mistake at the final corner so Goodyear dived down his inside, but came up agonizingly short. This beat the previous record set in 1982 when Gordon Johncock beat Rick Mears by 0.16 secs.

PART 5: OTHER OPEN WHEEL FORMULAE

Now more than ever, there are myriad single-seater formulae, whereas once it used to be simply F3, F2 and, if you were good enough, F1. However, it's in these training categories that drivers mark themselves out as ones to watch and present their calling card, as anyone who watched the likes of Jackie Stewart, Jochen Rindt, Ayrton Senna, Michael Schumacher and Lewis Hamilton on the way up will attest.

FORMULA TWO

Although first raced in 1948, Formula Two became a serious feeder category for Formula One in 1967 when the European Championship was created and it ran until 1984. It was the springboard to Formula One, the final step before the big time. It was where Jacky Ickx, Clay Regazzoni, René Arnoux and a host of others sprung from. It was also a category to which Formula One drivers stepped back on their spare weekends, providing a useful yardstick for up-and-coming drivers.

DRIVER RECORDS

⊙ MR F2

To many people, Jochen Rindt was the face of F2. He burst on to the scene in 1964 at Crystal Palace and kept on winning in the category all the way through his F1 career, which started in earnest in 1965. It also kept his competitive edge sharp when his F1 machinery was less than satisfactory, as in the first year of the European F2 Championship in 1967 when he won the opening three rounds, beating F1 rivals Graham Hill, Jack Brabham and John Surtees.

⊙ STARTING FROM THE FRONT

Bruno Giacomelli – F2 champion in 1978 – holds the record for taking the most F2 pole positions. Moving up to F2 in 1977 after a title-winning year in British F3, Bruno was run by March Engineering and advanced through the year, taking his first pole at the fifth round. He went on to collect 10 more by the end of 1978, when he became F2 champion. Jochen Rindt has the next most poles, 10, with Mike Thackwell third on nine.

⊙ MAKING THE GRADE

If F2 was a springboard for some, it also proved a graveyard for others, the final resting place for their F1 dreams. Italian Alberto Colombo is the ultimate proof of this. He registered 74 F2 starts between 1973 and 1980, but he tried to qualify three times in F1 in 1978, all without success. Then again, as his highest ranking in F2 was seventh overall in 1977, and he never finished higher than third in any of those races, he didn't really deserve to graduate.

⊙ VALUE OF EXPERIENCE

Graham Hill was one of the F1 drivers who most frequently made time to step down to F2. He didn't just do it for fun either. Prize money was a factor and the 1962 and 1968 F1 world champion collected plenty of it. However, he wasn't eligible to collect any points as he was a graded driver. Hill seemed to adjust with ease to a car with less power than his F1 mount and he became the oldest ever F2 winner aged 42 years and 56 days when he triumphed at Thruxton in 1971.

⊙ OVER AND OUT

F2 came to an end, to be superseded by F3000, in 1985, at a very wet Brands Hatch. Philippe Streiff claimed a dominant victory in the two-part race, scoring his only win in the formula and giving his French team, AGS, only its third victory. Neither driver nor team would succeed in F3000.

⊙ KEEPING SCORE

Mike Thackwell enjoyed being competitive in every one of his F2 campaigns (bar 1982 when he was dropped from the Ralt team as team boss Ron Tauranac felt that he hadn't recovered full fitness after being injured in a huge crash at Thruxton in 1981). As a result, he clocked up a record 164 points across his five years in F2. Brian Henton ranks second on points scored, with 123, with Patrick Depailler third on 119 and Bruno Giacomelli fourth on 114.

⊙ WINNING BY A NOSE

Two races – Snetterton in 1967 and Enna-Pergusa in 1968 – tie for the closest finish in F2 history with a winning margin of 0 secs. How so? Because stopwatches weren't as accurate in the 1960s and several cars were credited with the same time. In the Snetterton race, Jochen Rindt was judged to have pipped Graham Hill. While, in the Enna race, a slipstreaming pack were given the same time, but that man Rindt got the nod again, ahead of Piers Courage, Tino Brambilla and Clay Regazzoni.

⊙ IMPRESS AND LEAVE

It's often said in sport that a competitor should leave before they are asked to, before their form drops. However, Pierluigi Martini took this to extremes. He finished second on his F2 debut for Minardi at Misano in 1983 but never raced in F2 again, therefore ensuring his scoring average of six points a race in F2 history.

⊙ STILL BABY-FACED

Eddie Cheever holds the record for being the youngest winner in F2 history, triumphing at Rouen-les-Essarts in 1977 when aged just 19 years and 168 days. Mike Thackwell was also a winner when still just 19 (he was 20 the following day), with Corrado Fabi scoring the first of his six wins when just 42 days past his 20th birthday.

⊙ WIN AND MOVE ON

As befits a stepping-stone formula, drivers who won the F2 title moved on up to F1. In fact, some like Ronnie Peterson – champion in 1971 – had already dabbled in F1 so they simply stepped back up. So, across the history of the European F2 Championship, there were 18 champions across its 18 seasons, from Jacky Ickx in 1967 to Mike Thackwell in 1984.

DRIVERS WITH MOST F2 WINS

1	Jochen Rindt	12
2	Bruno Giacomelli	11
3	Mike Thackwell	9
4	Jean-Pierre Jarier	7
=	Jacques Laffite	7
6	René Arnoux	6
=	Corrado Fabi	6
=	Emerson Fittipaldi	6
=	Brian Henton	6
=	Jonathan Palmer	6
=	Ronnie Peterson	6
12	Thierry Boutsen	5
=	Jean-Pierre Jabouille	5
=	Hans-Joachim Stuck	5

⊙ A KIWI WHO COULD FLY

Mercurial teenager Mike Thackwell set more fastest laps in F2 than any other driver. He did so 15 times between 1980 and F2's final year, 1984. He would have set more, but for a huge accident at Thruxton in 1981 that temporarily halted his career. British driver Brian Henton was the next most successful at setting fastest race laps, doing so 12 times, with most of these coming in 1980, his title-winning year with Toleman.

TEAM RECORDS

⊙ IT WORKS FOR ME
Although March supplied chassis to anyone who wanted to buy one, it also ran a works team – March Engineering – and this accounted for 57 wins between 1971 and 1982, after which the works team was disbanded. Ralt Racing was second most successful, harnessing 20 wins, with privateer teams claiming three more for Ralt.

⊙ RALT'S NEAR DOMINANCE
Ralt scored nine wins from 11 rounds in 1984 for the best ever strike rate, with its Honda engines a real boon for drivers Mike Thackwell and Roberto Moreno after Jonathan Palmer had come on strong through 1983 to take the crown. March Engineering's 1978 record of eight wins from 12 is the next best strike rate, with a further win taken by March privateer Alex Ribeiro.

⊙ SHORTLIVED CHALLENGERS
German constructor Maurer showed promise in 1981 and threatened to take control of F2 at the start of the 1982 season. Stefan Bellof and Beppe Gabbiani finished first and third in the opening round at Silverstone and Bellof won the second round at Hockenheim. However, March and Spirit won the remaining rounds, and the Maurer marque went no further after 1983.

⊙ BMWS HORSES PROVE TO BE THE BEST
BMW engines scored the most wins in F2, outscoring early dominant force Ford by 94 to 60. The company scored its breakthrough win at Rouen-les-Essarts in 1970 through Jo Siffert and continued winning regularly until the final F2 race in 1984. Honda came on strong in the 1980s to rank third with 23 wins, outstripping Hart, which won 17 times, mainly with Toleman in 1980.

⊙ STRENGTH IN DIVERSITY
Although March dominated and Ralt shone late on in F2's history, 21 other racing car constructors entered cars that won F2 races between 1967 and 1984. Among those that scored four wins or fewer, Spirit, AGS, Osella and Minardi all stepped up to F1, with one-time F2 winners McLaren – Jody Scheckter at Crystal Palace in 1972 – electing to continue concentrating on F1 and CanAm instead.

⊙ FERRARI'S FLEETING ROLE

When racing fans think of Ferrari, they think of F1 and of sport car racing successes in the early 1960s in particular. However, Ferrari also dabbled in F2 and collected three victories. The first two of these came at the end of the 1968 season, when Tino Brambilla triumphed at Hockenheim then Vallelunga. The third followed in 1977 when Italian Lamberto Leoni won on home soil, at Misano, with a Ferrari engine fitted to his Scuderia Everest Chevron.

⊙ A SPONSOR'S DREAM

Having spent a lot of money sponsoring French drivers in F2, French fuel company Elf decided to lend its name to Jean-Pierre Jabouille's team (Elf Switzerland) for its Alpine-based 2J. This was developed through 1975 and Jabouille went on to lead a three-car attack in 1976, taking his Elf 2J to wins at Vallelunga and Hockenheim to claim the championship title, with teammate Michel Leclere winning once in his Elf.

⊙ TAKING ON THE BIG BOYS

In the 1960s when the German GP was run at the Nürburgring Nordschleife, F2 cars were allowed to enter alongside the F1 cars as the 14-mile track could accommodate them. The F2 cars' best showing came in 1967 when Lotus Components ran an F2 Lotus for Jackie Oliver, who finished fifth overall, equal with Henri Pescarolo's result for Matra two years later.

⊙ F2'S EARLY STAR TEAM

Roy Winkelmann Racing was one of the most successful teams in the history of the formula – ranking fourth overall with 11 wins – and this was almost solely due to Jochen Rindt in his Brabham in the first few years of the European F2 Championship. He won 23 races for the American-owned team, 11 of which were in the European F2 series. Then, when the team closed, Rindt's manager Bernie Ecclestone kept him on in F2 driving a Lotus in 1970 for the last of the Austrian's F2 wins.

CONSTRUCTOR WHO WON MOST RACES IN F2

1	March	77
2	Ralt	23
3	Brabham	18
4	Martini	14
5	Lotus	10
=	Matra	10
7	Toleman	8
8	Chevron	6
9	Elf	5
=	Surtees	5
=	Tecno	5

⊙ MOTORBIKE MEN

John Surtees is the most famous motorbike-racing convert to cars, adding the 1964 F1 title to his seven motorcycle world crowns. Although his own race team never won in F1, Surtees won the 1972 F2 constructors' title when fellow motorcycle crossover Mike Hailwood won at Mantorp Park and the Salzburgring. Surtees himself set the ball rolling that year by winning at Imola, although he was a graded driver so he didn't collect anypoints.

⊙ A SPRINGBOARD TO F1

Several racing-car constructors built on their successes in F2 to advance to F1. Among these were Toleman, F2 champions in 1980 when Brian Henton and Derek Warwick ranked first and second in their works cars, with further wins coming from the privately entered Docking Spitzley Racing Tolemans of Huub Rothengatter and Siegfried Stohr.

FORMULA 3000

Following the demise of Formula Two, Formula 3000 was created for 1985 and for the next 20 years it was the entry point for Formula One. The racing used to be great but for some reason its champions never went on to become Formula One world champions. Juan Pablo Montoya was the most successful in terms of Formula One wins, with seven. In 2005, Formula 3000 was superseded by GP2 Series.

DRIVER RECORDS

⊙ WINNERS ONE AND ALL

Twenty different drivers won the championship in F3000's 20 years, but 77 different drivers won races. Future F1 grand prix winners Fernando Alonso, David Coulthard, Johnny Herbert and Eddie Irvine were among the ranks of those who racked up only one F3000 victory before going on to achieve greater things in F1.

⊙ F3000'S SPECIALIST FLIERS

Vitantonio Liuzzi and Juan Pablo Montoya share the record for achieving the most pole positions in F3000, with 10 apiece. As with his wins, Montoya shared his between the 1997 and 1998 seasons, while Liuzzi claimed his first pole late in 2003 then rattled off pole in nine of 2004's 10 rounds, qualifying second behind Enrico Toccacelo in the second race of the year.

⊙ DOWN TO THE WIRE

The 1989 F3000 series ended up as a deadheat, with both Jean Alesi and fellow French racer Erik Comas scoring 39 points. However, the title went to Eddie Jordan Racing's Alesi as he had three race wins to his name compared with Comas's pair for DAMS, scored in the last two races. Comas would go on to be champion in 1990.

⊙ CLOSEST FINISH

Uruguayan racer Gonzalo Rodriguez claimed the record for winning the closest F3000 finish when he triumphed at Spa-Francorchamps in 1998. His Team Astromega Lola nosed across the finish line just 0.035 secs ahead of Juan Pablo Montoya's Super Nova Racing Lola. The next closest finish was when Frenchman Olivier Grouillard was 0.22 secs in front of Mark Blundell at Zolder in 1988.

⊙ SHOULD YOU BE HERE?

F3000 was always intended to be a category for up-and-coming drivers, but that didn't stop Fritz Glatz, who raced under the pseudonym "Pierre Chauvet", racing in it until past his 45th birthday. The oldest F3000 winner was Philippe Alliot, who was 31 years and 300 days when he triumphed at Spa-Francorchamps for ORECA in 1986 after stepping back from F1 (to which he returned later that year).

⊙ FAST, BUT NEVER A CHAMPION

Czech driver Tomas Enge was very competitive through the 2001 and 2002 campaigns, winning six times, but the only F3000 record that he can lay claim to is that of having set the most fastest laps. He did this 10 times, adding the final three in 2004. This took him past Nick Heidfeld who set the fastest lap on nine occasions and Juan Pablo Montoya who did it eight times.

⊙ ECONOMY OF EFFORT

The drivers to land the F3000 championship with the fewest wins were Ivan Capelli in 1986 for Genoa Racing, Christian Fittipaldi in 1991 for Pacific Racing and Jorg Muller in 1996 for RSM Marko. All scored only two wins in their title-winning year, emphasizing how competitive this category was.

⊙ HE CERTAINLY TRIED

Marco Apicella spent years trying to win a race in F3000. He qualified on pole twice and finished on the podium 10 times, but never as a winner. After a record 52 starts, he headed for the Japanese F3000 series in 1992 and it was there that he finally claimed an F3000 win, going on to win the Japanese title two years later.

⊙ FIRST AMONG EQUALS

F3000 became a one-make formula in 1996 in the name of keeping costs in check. Every driver was at the wheel of a Zytek-powered Lola T96/50. So, it was a prestigious year to win the title and the honour went to Jorg Muller of the RSM Marko team.

⊙ WITH YOUTH COMES SPEED

Not only did Fernando Alonso score one of the most impressive F3000 wins ever when he sped away from all of his rivals at Spa-Francorchamps in 2000 for Team Astromega, but this also marked him out as F3000's youngest winner, at just 19 years and 27 days. He lowered the mark set five years earlier at Estoril by DAMS driver Tarso Marques.

⊙ BY THE WIDEST MARGIN

Sweden's Bjorn Wirdheim scored only three wins from 10 starts in 2003, but he still became the F3000 champion and enjoyed the widest points advantage ever achieved in F3000. He won for Arden International by 35 points, three more than British driver Justin Wilson's title-winning margin for Nordic Racing in 2001.

DRIVER WITH MOST F3000 WINS

1	Nick Heidfeld	7
=	Vitantonio Liuzzi	7
=	Juan Pablo Montoya	7
4	Erik Comas	6
=	Tomas Enge	6
=	Giorgio Pantano	6
7	Bruno Junqueira	5
=	Roberto Moreno	5
=	Emanuele Naspetti	5
=	Ricardo Zonta	5
11	Luca Badoer	4
=	Sebastien Bourdais	4
=	Kenny Brack	4
=	Christian Danner	4
=	Franck Lagorce	4
=	Pierluigi Martini	4
=	Nicolas Minassian	4
=	Luis Perez Sala	4
=	Mike Thackwell	4
=	Jason Watt	4
=	Mark Webber	4
=	Bjorn Wirdheim	4

⊙ CHRISTIAN WAS THE FIRST

The honour of having his name on F3000's first championship trophy was claimed by Christian Danner in 1985 when he won four of the opening season's 11 rounds in his BS Automotive-entered March 85B, picking off the Ralt of early season pacesetter Mike Thackwell. Nineteen other drivers would follow in his wheel tracks in becoming F3 champion.

TEAM RECORDS

⊙ F3000's BRIGHTEST STAR

Super Nova Racing was the pre-eminent F3000 team, taking a record 37 wins. Its first was in the 1995 season opener at Silverstone, with Ricardo Rosset leading home Vincenzo Sospiri for a Super Nova one-two. The team's last victory was when Enrico Toccacelo won at the Nürburgring in 2003. The next most successful F3000 team was DAMS, with 21 wins, mainly in the early 1990s.

⊙ MANAGEMENT TRAINING GROUND

Christian Horner is now best known as the team principal of the Red Bull Racing F1 team, but his transition from F3000 racer to that lofty position came via running a team – Arden International. It really came on strong in F3000's final years, guiding Bjorn Wirdheim to the 2003 title, and following it up with the 2004 crown for Vitantonio Liuzzi. These successes brought the team's total wins to 15.

⊙ ON THE SLIDE

March, the most successful marque by far in F2, started F3000 well in 1985, with seven wins in the category's inaugural season as Christian Danner raced to the title. However, it stopped winning after Fabrizio Giovanardi triumphed at Vallelunga at the start of 1989. This was its 18th win and March had to watch as Reynard collected win after win, reaching 59 before F3000 became a one-make category in 1996, with Lola building all the chassis thereafter and ending up with a final haul of 116 wins.

⊙ TEAM TITLE HONOURS

Super Nova Racing came out on top, with four championships, through Vincenzo Sospiri (1995), Ricardo Zonta (1997), Juan Pablo Montoya (1998) and Sebastien Bourdais (2000). DAMS bagged three titles, through Erik Comas (1990), Olivier Panis (1993) and Jean-Christophe Boullion (1994).

⊙ AMBITIONS REALIZED

Eddie Jordan was always an ambitious man. Once he realized that he would not make it to the top as a driver, he started his own team. Successful in F3, he guided it into F3000 in 1985 and was rewarded with the 1989 title for Jean Alesi, with Martin Donnelly also a race winner. Bolstered by this, Eddie Jordan Racing became Jordan Grand Prix and graduated to F1 in 1991.

⊙ F1's MINI ME

McLaren considered that the best way to help its junior drivers develop was to run its own team in F3000. McLaren's F1 engine supplier Mercedes wanted Nick Heidfeld to be on McLaren's books, so he was given a drive for West Competition in F3000 in 1998 and 1999, coming away with the title in the second year. The cars were painted to look like little McLaren F1 cars, sporting the same silver-grey West livery.

⊙ UNDER THE ENGINE COVER

Had it not been for the transformation of F3000 into a one-make formula from 1986, the Cosworth would have remained the category's most successful engine-supplier. However, this opened the door for Zytek to take over and it ended up with 84 wins to its credit, four more than Cosworth, when F3000 was replaced by GP2 at the end of 2004. Japanese Mugen engines scored the third most wins – 20.

⊙ COSMOPOLITAN MIXTURE

No less than 36 different teams enjoyed watching their drivers standing on the top step of the podium during F3000's 20 years. Emphasizing the international nature of the series, these winners came from six countries – Austria, Belgium, France, Great Britain, Italy and Spain. British-based teams dominated, though, accounting for half of these winners.

⊙ FASTEST F3000 RACE

Arden International holds the record for the fastest F3000 victory. This came at Monza in 2003, when Bjorn Wirdheim triumphed at the high-speed circuit through the Italian parkland, with little more than a few chicanes to slow the otherwise flat-out blast. His winning average was 127.271mph.

⊙ PIECES OF EIGHT

Lola holds the record as the top point-scoring constructor, but seven others scored points. They were, in descending points order: Reynard, March, Ralt, AGS, Williams, Tyrrell and Dallara. Williams and Tyrrell scored their points in F3000's first season in 1985, when former F1 chassis were run by some teams before bespoke F3000 chassis were built.

⊙ SLOW PROGRESS

A winning average of just 77.005mph was the slowest ever recorded in F3000, and this occurred in Monaco in 2001 when Mark Webber guided his Super Nova Racing Lola to victory on the famous street circuit. He finished less than a second ahead of title rival Justin Wilson's Nordic Racing entry.

MOST WINS BY MANUFACTURER

1	Lola	116
2	Reynard	59
3	March	18
4	Ralt	13

⊙ WITH A LITTLE HELP FROM THEIR FRIENDS

F3000 was largely a customer formula, that's to say one in which teams bought cars from the constructors and ran them themselves. Some teams were works entries, and others were at some point in between. An example of the latter was Mike Earle's Onyx Race Engineering, which guided Stefano Modena to the 1987 title in a March, with a little works assistance. Onyx went on to try F1 in 1989.

MOST WINS BY ENGINE MAKE

1	Zytek	84
2	Cosworth	80
3	Mugen	20
4	Judd	7
5	Honda	3

OTHER FORMULAE

At the start of the 21st century it seemed as if a new single-seater formula came into being every year. The expansion was mad, diluting the racing "gene pool". GP2 is the feeder formula for Formula One, A1GP brought novelty by pitching nation against nation and F3 remains the first international category in which the hottest teenage hopefuls can be compared.

DRIVER/TEAM RECORDS

⊙ BREEDING GROUND FOR CHAMPIONS

Where its predecessor F3000 failed, for reasons unknown, to produce a single F1 world champion, GP2 has, in its five-year existence, already beaten that. Lewis Hamilton came within a point of becoming world champion just a year after landing the 2006 GP2 title, and in 2008 he won the coveted F1 crown.

⊙ PERSEVERANCE WINS THE DAY

Natural speed and longevity are the keys to Giorgio Pantano being the driver with the most GP2 wins – nine. He arrived in GP2 in 2005 after racing briefly in F1 with Jordan. His plans to quickly bounce back to F1 didn't work and it took four years for him to become GP2 champion, and even that didn't reopen the door to F1. Timo Glock is next up on seven victories, followed by Lucas di Grassi, Lewis Hamilton, Nico Hülkenberg, Heikki Kovalainen, Nelson Piquet Jr and Nico Rosberg, all of whom have recorded five successes.

⊙ SIX, SIX, SIX

When it comes to setting fastest laps, the honours up to the end of 2009 were split between Lucas di Grassi, Romain Grosjean and Lewis Hamilton, with six apiece. However, Hamilton holds the bragging rights as he took just one campaign to achieve this, whereas Grosjean spread his across 2008 and the first half of 2009, while di Grassi took four years for his six.

⊙ YOUTH WINS THE DAY

Sébastien Buemi is the youngest driver to win a race in GP2, making his mark at Magny-Cours in 2008 at the age of 19 years and 244 days. Javier Villa had held the record previously, having won at the equivalent race at Magny-Cours a year earlier when he was aged 19 years and 291 days.

⊙ FLYING EVERY YEAR

Nico Hülkenberg's five GP2 fastest laps in 2009 were the latest additions to ART Grand Prix's record tally of fastest laps. This stands at 29, emphasizing the team's continued excellence, especially when the team with the next highest tally after the first five years of GP2 is iSport International with 15. Piquet Sports has 10.

⊙ BY THE SMALLEST OF MARGINS

The closest finish in GP2 history happened at Istanbul Park in 2005 when French driver Alexandre Prémat edged home his ART Grand Prix entry just 0.336 secs ahead of Giorgio Pantano, driving for Super Nova Racing.

⊙ POLE IS WHERE THE ART IS

ART Grand Prix is the team most frequently seen on pole position. The team's total of 10, at the end of 2009, was one more than iSport International and two ahead of Piquet Sports. Behind them, Racing Engineering had set seven, though Barwa Addax was fast gaining ground on the teams above them by scoring five in its maiden season in 2009.

⊙ LEADER OF THE PACK

When it comes to the gathering of points, ART Grand Prix's GP2 success is amazing. Its five-year tally is 881 points, more than double its closest challenger, iSport International, on 425.5. Incredibly, the next three teams are covered by just half a point, with Campos Racing (now called Barwa Addax) on 324.5, then both Arden International and Super Nova Racing on 324.

⊙ ON A DIFFERENT CONTINENT

There is also a GP2 Asia Series, which has been running for two seasons. Romain Grosjean and the ART Grand Prix team won the titles at the beginning of 2008 and Kamui Kobayashi and DAMS claimed the 2008–09 series.

⊙ THREE FROM FIVE

Of the five GP2 titles from 2005–09, ART Grand Prix has proved itself as the team to beat. It has won three drivers' titles – with Nico Rosberg in 2005, Lewis Hamilton in 2006 and Nico Hülkenberg in 2009 – and also won the teams' title in those same years.

⊙ THE ART OF WINNING

ART Grand Prix holds the record for the most GP2 wins by a team. By the end of the 2009 season, the French team, owned by Frederic Vasseur and FIA president Jean Todt's son Nicolas, had collected 23 wins. The first of these victories came on the team's home soil, at Magny-Cours in 2005, through Nico Rosberg, who went on to be the inaugural GP2 champion. And the wins kept flowing up to Nico Hülkenberg's victory at Algarve International Circuit in Portugal in 2009.

⊙ BEST PLACE TO START

Giorgio Pantano holds the record for claiming the most GP2 poles, seven, with Nelson Piquet Jr second on six. Timo Glock, Romain Grosjean and Nico Rosberg all started from pole on four occasions. Note that this takes into account only the first GP2 race at each meeting, as pole for the second race is simply awarded to the driver who finished in eighth place in the first race.

DRIVERS WITH MOST GP2 POINTS

1	Giorgio Pantano	228
2	Lucas di Grassi	221
3	Nelson Piquet Jr	148
4	Timo Glock	146
5	Alexandre Prémat	133
6	Adam Carroll	122
7	Pastor Maldonado	121
8	Nico Rosberg	120
9	Lewis Hamilton	114
=	Vitaly Petrov	114

DRIVER/TEAM RECORDS

⊙ SWISS PRECISION

Pitting nation against nation was A1GP's founding principle, with the national teams bringing through a host of their best young drivers in a quest for glory. Neel Jani was a near regular in the Swiss team and holds the record faor the most wins – 10. This is one more than Nico Hülkenberg's tally when he dominated the 2006–07 series for Germany.

⊙ FRANCE AND SWITZERLAND ON TOP

The British team missed one of the 39 A1GP rounds, this being the first of the fourth series when not all of the new Ferrari-powered cars were ready. However, its red, white and blue-liveried car still ranks third in the table of most points scored, with 343. These points were scored chiefly by Robbie Kerr and Oliver Jarvis. However, this tally is no match for Switzerland and France, whose teams have scored 438 and 404 points respectively.

⊙ THEY ALWAYS SHOW UP

Twelve national teams attended each of the 39 rounds held across the four seasons from 2005 to 2009: Australia, China, France, Holland, Ireland, Italy, Lebanon, Malaysia, New Zealand, South Africa, Switzerland and the USA. Of these, four countries were crowned champions: France, Germany, Switzerland and Ireland.

⊙ NEW CAR, NEW CHAMPIONS

The fourth A1GP series – 2008–09 – introduced new chassis and a new engine from Ferrari in place of the Lola-Zytek combination. The Irish team proved the most proficient at making it competitive and Adam Carroll claimed four wins en route to the title, finishing off Switzerland's hopes of making it two titles in a row at the Brands Hatch finale.

⊙ UNFURL THE STARS AND STRIPES

Jonathan Summerton demonstrated ever-improving form for Team USA, and he helped it become a winning team for the first time when he triumphed in the feature race (the longer of the two at each meeting) at Shanghai in 2008. It was a career-boosting way of celebrating his 20th birthday the following week.

⊙ GIVING YOUTH A CHANCE

Promoting youth was always one of the aims of A1GP from its foundation, but the Indian team took this to an extreme level when it promoted Armaan Ebrahim to its race seat for the third round of the inaugural series after Karun Chandhok moved on. Ebrahim was just 16 years and 159 days old when he made his A1GP race debut at Estoril.

⊙ GOING UP, COMING DOWN

Sébastien Buemi, Nico Hülkenberg, Nelson Piquet Jr, Scott Speed and Adrian Sutil have all used A1GP on their way up to F1. However, even more drivers have used it on their way down from the big time, namely Robert Doornbos, Ralph Firman, Christian Fittipaldi, Narain Karthikeyan, Franck Montagny, Hideki Noda, Max Papis, Jos Verstappen and Alex Yoong, while Vitantonio Liuzzi used it to keep himself sharp before returning to F1.

⊙ SONS OF FAMOUS FATHERS

Numerous offspring of former F1 world champions have raced in A1GP. The first brace of wins was scored at Brands Hatch in 2005 by Nelson Piquet Jr for Brazil, while Mathias Lauda, son of Niki, competed for the Austrian team. Alan Jones, F1 world champion in 1980, ran the Australian team and his son Christian had a cameo role, Jody Scheckter's son Tomas appeared for South Africa, Mario Andretti's son Marco raced for the USA and Alain Prost's son Nicolas drove for France.

⊙ KING OF EVERYTHING

There's scarcely a driver record in A1GP that Switzerland's Neel Jani doesn't hold. As well as having made the most starts and scored the most wins, he has claimed the most pole positions, set the most fastest laps, raced the most laps, led the most races, led the most laps, appeared on the podium the most times and scored the most points.

⊙ INTERNATIONAL VARIETY

A1GP's idea of giving developing motor sport nations a chance
to take on the established racing nations on a level playing field
by using the same equipment certainly worked. Malaysia scored
the first of its wins in the inaugural series, thanks to Alex Yoong
winning at Shanghai in 2006. The Malaysian team went on to score
four more victories.

TEAM WITH MOST A1GP WINS

1	France	15
2	Germany	11
3	Switzerland	10
4	New Zealand	7
5	Ireland	6
6	Great Britain	5
=	Malaysia	5
8	Holland	4
9	South Africa	3
10	Brazil	2
=	Canada	2
=	India	2
=	Mexico	2

⊙ VIVE LA FRANCE

France holds the record as the most successful nation in A1GP.
Alexandre Prémat and Nicolas Lapierre claimed 13 wins from 22
starts to win the 2005–06 championship, although the French team
added just two more victories over the next three seasons, both
courtesy of Loïc Duval.

⊙ THE MAIN MAN

Most teams in A1GP either rotated their drivers or tried another
when the first wasn't winning on a regular basis. However, the
Swiss team stuck by Neel Jani in 30 of the 39 rounds (Sébastien
Buemi was tried in the second series) and it paid off as he won the
2007–08 series.

DRIVER/TEAM RECORDS

⊙ WAY OUT WEST

The F3 team with the best record of producing F1 world champions is West Surrey Racing, a team run by Dick Bennetts. The team ran Ayrton Senna in 1983 and Mika Hakkinen seven years later. It also guided future F1 racers Mauricio Gugelmin (1985) and Rubens Barrichello (1991) to the British F3 crown.

⊙ BEST ALMA MATER

With 11 future F1 world champions – Jenson Button, Emerson Fittipaldi, Mika Hakkinen, Damon Hill, James Hunt, Alan Jones, Nigel Mansell, Nelson Piquet, Jody Scheckter, Ayrton Senna and Jackie Stewart – having passed through its ranks, the British F3 Championship is the one through which most F1 champions have been channelled. Other multiple F1 grand prix winners to have raced in British F3 include 1991 contemporaries Rubens Barrichello and David Coulthard.

⊙ JAN'S THE MAN

Jan Magnussen set a record for the number of wins in a campaign in the British F3 Championship in 1994 when he blitzed the opposition by taking his Paul Stewart Racing Dallara-Mugen Honda to 14 wins from 18 races. This outstripped Ayrton Senna's 12 wins from 20 in 1983, the year he fought tooth and nail with Martin Brundle.

⊙ F3's SHOP WINDOW

The F3 Monaco GP was the most prestigious of the season, as it was held under the noses of the F1 team managers. Since 1964, when Jackie Stewart won it, the race has been won by no fewer than 10 drivers who would go on to win F1 grands prix plus another 10 who raced in F1. The F3 Monaco GP was stopped after 1997, save for one running in 2005.

⊙ RISING IN THE EAST

The eastern equivalent of the F3 Monaco GP is the race around the streets of Macau. Ayrton Senna won here in 1983, and Michael Schumacher raced to victory in 1990, after famously clashing with Mika Hakkinen on the final lap.

⊙ SEVEN STRAIGHT IN FRANCE

ORECA is the most successful team in the history of the French F3 Championship, with its drivers winning seven titles. Its dominance was so marked that Hughes de Chaunac's team won it in seven consecutive years, from 1983–89, through Michel Ferte, Olivier Grouillard, Pierre-Henri Raphanel, Yannick Dalmas, Jean Alesi, Erik Comas and Jean-Marc Gounon respectively. Of these, only 1983 champion Ferte failed to graduate to F1.

⊙ USING HIS KNOWLEDGE

Bertram Schafer won the German F3 title in 1976 and 1978, but his connection went on for another quarter of a century, thanks to him moving into team ownership and guiding these teams to the title. He did this eight times, starting with Frank Jelinski in 1980 and 1981, and finishing with Toshihiro Kaneishi in 2001.

⊙ RISE OF THE EURO

The F3 Euroseries is now the most highly favoured F3 series. Since being revamped for 2003 it can already claim to have been the training ground for one F1 world champion, Lewis Hamilton, who won the F3 Euro series at his second attempt in 2005.

⊙ FOUR TITLES APIECE

Two teams shared the Italian F3 Championship between 1982 and 1989, with Enzo Coloni Racing and Forti Corse taking four titles each. Coloni drove the winning car in 1982 for his own team, then ran it for others in 1983 (Ivan Capelli), 1984 (Alessandro Santin) and 1986 (Nicola Larini). RC Motorsport also won four Italian F3 titles, all in the 1990s.

MONACO F3GP WINNERS BY CHASSIS

1	Martini	10	=	Tecno	2
2	Dallara	8	9	Alpine	1
3	Lotus	2	=	Brabham	1
=	March	2	=	Chervon	1
=	Matra	2	=	Cooper	1
=	Ralt	2	=	GRD	1
=	Reynard	2			

PART 6: SPORTS CARS AND TOURING CARS

Sports car racing and touring car racing are branches of motor sport that have their own passionate fans who revel either in the guile and tactics of long-distance racing or the short sprints packed with door-banging action. Each branch of competition has its heroes, from Tom Kristensen and Jacky Ickx in sports cars, to Bernd Schneider and Peter Brock in touring cars, and manufacturers invest millions in adding sporting allure to their road-car ranges.

LE MANS 24 HOURS

The Le Mans 24 Hours is the pinnacle of sports car racing, the one race that carries global prestige. A win will be trumpeted in the media the following day. Manufacturers have invested millions chasing glory, with Audi Ferrari, Ford, Jaguar and Porsche all enjoying periods of dominance. However, for every success in this car-breaker of a race there are tales of heartache.

DRIVER RECORDS

⊙ THE DRIVER ON POLE IS...

Jacky Ickx is the driver with the most Le Mans pole positions to his name. The Belgian started from the front five times – in 1975, 1978, 1981, 1982 and 1983. Rinaldo Capello, Stéphane Sarrazin and Bob Wollek have claimed three poles apiece. Pole was decided on qualifying speed only from 1963 onwards. Prior that it was done on engine capacity, with the largest lining up at the front of the grid.

⊙ GREATEST FIGHTBACK

Jacky Ickx staged the greatest fightback to victory. His Porsche 936 dropped as low as 41st out of the 55 starters after just two hours of the 1977 race following fuel pump problems. However, he and co-drivers Jurgen Barth and Hurley Haywood managed to drive the car back up the order.

⊙ RALLY STAGE TO RACE TRACK

The most successful of the five World Rally champions who have taken part in the Le Mans 24 Hours is Sébastien Loeb, who finished second for the Pescarolo team in 2006. Marko Alen, Colin McRae, Walter Rohrl and Bjorn Wöldegård were the four other World Rally champions to attempt this change of discipline.

⊙ PRIZE FOR PERSEVERANCE

These days, Henri Pescarolo enters a team of cars at Le Mans, but this four-time winner of the race holds the record for the most starts – 33. Bob Wollek is next up, with 30. He suffered the frustration of never winning but finishing second four times. Japanese veteran Yojiro Terada has 27 starts to his name, one more than five-time winner Derek Bell.

⊙ END OF THE "LE MANS START"

A long-standing tradition at Le Mans was its start. The drivers lined up on the side of the track opposite the pits. When given the signal the drivers sprinted across to their cars, climbed aboard and sprinted off, doing up their seatbelts in later years as they sped away. Since a protest from Jacky Ickx in 1969, when he walked instead of ran, the race has been started with drivers onboard since 1970.

⊙ F1 CHAMPIONS AT LE MANS

Nineteen drivers who were already or would be an F1 world champion have contested the Le Mans 24 Hours. They are: Mario Andretti, Alberto Ascari, Jack Brabham, Jim Clark, Juan Manuel Fangio, Giuseppe Farina, Mike Hawthorn, Damon Hill, Graham Hill, Phil Hill, Denny Hulme, Alan Jones, Nelson Piquet, Jochen Rindt, Keke Rosberg, Michael Schumacher, Jackie Stewart, John Surtees and Jacques Villeneuve. Of these, only four have won: Mike Hawthorn (1955), Graham Hill (1972), Phil Hill (1958, 1961 and 1962) and Jochen Rindt (1965). And of these four, only Graham Hill and Phil Hill won it after becoming F1 world champion.

⊙ MOST HOURS DRIVEN IN WINNING THE LE MANS 24 HOURS

Louis Rosier drove all but two hours in 1950 when sharing his Talbot Lago with son Jean-Louis. Alfa Romeo racer Raymond Sommer had set a precedent in 1932 by driving 20 hours through the race, leaving his co-driver Luigi Chinetti precious little to do. However, "Pierre Levegh" (born Pierre Bouillin) looked set to beat both these records in 1952 when he attempted to drive his Talbot single-handed. He was leading by four laps with less than two hours to go when he fluffed a gear change and damaged the engine.

⊙ BRITISH DRIVERS RULE THE ROAD

More British drivers have experienced victory at Le Mans than those of any other nationality, including the race's host nation, France. The tally is 32 to 27 in Britain's favour. One typically patriotic response from the tens of thousands of British fans came in 1988 when Johnny Dumfries and Andy Wallace took Jaguar to its first Le Mans win since 1957, helped by Dutchman Jan Lammers.

⊙ FAMOUS LE MANS PARTICIPANTS

Film actor Paul Newman was more than just a wealthy guy playing at racing. In 1979 he finished second overall, sharing a Porsche 935 with Rolf Stommelen and Dick Barbour, finishing only seven laps down on the winning Porsche. Much of that time was lost to a jammed wheel nut in the closing stages.

TOP DRIVERS WITH MOST WINS

1	Tom Kristensen	8	1997, 2000, 2001, 2002, 2003, 2004, 2005, 2008
2	Jacky Ickx	6	1969, 1975, 1976, 1977, 1981 1982
3	Derek Bell	5	1975, 1981, 1982, 1986, 1987
=	Frank Biela	5	2000, 2001, 2002, 2006, 2007
=	Emanuele Pirro	5	2000, 2001, 2002, 2006, 2007
6	Yannick Dalmas	4	1992, 1994, 1995, 1999
=	Olivier Gendebien	4	1958, 1960, 1961, 1962
=	Henri Pescarolo	4	1972, 1973, 1974, 1984
9	Woolf Barnato	3	1928, 1929, 1930
=	Rinaldo Capello	3	2003, 2004, 2008
=	Luigi Chinetti	3	1932, 1934, 1949
=	Hurley Haywood	3	1977, 1983, 1994
=	Phil Hill	3	1958, 1961, 1962
=	Al Holbert	3	1983, 1986, 1987
=	Klaus Ludwig	3	1979, 1984, 1985
=	Marco Werner	3	2005, 2006, 2007
17	Henry Birkin	2	1929, 1931
=	Ivor Bueb	2	1955, 1957
=	Ron Flockhart	2	1956, 1957
=	Jean-Pierre Jaussaud	2	1978, 1980
=	Gerard Larrousse	2	1973, 1974
=	JJ Lehto	2	1995, 2005
=	Allan McNish	2	1998, 2008
=	Manuel Reuter	2	1989, 1996
=	Andre Rossignol	2	1925, 1926
=	Raymond Sommer	2	1932, 1933
=	Hans-Joachim Stuck	2	1986, 1987
=	Gijs van Lennep	2	1971, 1976
=	Jean-Pierre Wimille	2	1937, 1939
=	Alexander Wurz	2	1996, 2009

Ninety drivers have won once.

⊙ NOT A MALE PRESERVE

Fifty female drivers have competed in the race, starting with Marguerite Maurese and Odette Siko who brought their Bugatti home seventh out of nine finishers in 1930. Siko's fourth place in 1932 in her Alfa Romeo 6C shared with Louis Charaval remains the best female result. Annie-Charlotte Verney takes the prize for trying, as she made 10 appearances between 1974 and 1983, with a best finish of sixth in 1981. She shared a Cooke-Woods Racing Porsche 935 with Bob Garretson and Ralph Kent-Cooke.

⊙ HIGHEST WIN RATE

Woolf Barnato won three from three for Bentley between 1928 and 1930. Jean-Pierre Wimille also hit 100 per cent with two wins from two starts driving Bugattis in 1937 and 1939. Four drivers have tasted victory in their one and only appearance: Tazio Nuvolari (Alfa Romeo) in 1933, Luis Fontes (Lagonda) in 1935, Hermann Lang (Mercedes) in 1952 and AJ Foyt (Ford) in 1967.

⊙ MEN WITH THE WINNING TOUCH

Jacky Ickx was the master of Le Mans, with six wins between 1969 and 1982, then along came Tom Kristensen, who won at his first attempt in 1997. That was with TWR, but his great move was to join Audi as it hit the top, helping it to victory in 2000. This started a six-year run of glory through to 2005 for Kristensen, all with Audi except in 2003 when he drove for Bentley. He won again in 2008 and his eight wins in just 12 years will probably never be beaten.

TEAM RECORDS

⊙ BEST RESULT FOR A MANUFACTURER

Jaguar occupied first, second, third, fourth and sixth places in 1957, with only Audi getting close to matching that with first, second, third and fifth places in 2004. Porsche had a podium clean sweep (first, second and third places) in 1982, something that Peugeot matched in 1993, then Audi in both 2000 and 2002.

⊙ FASTEST LE MANS 24 HOURS CIRCUIT

The 8.369-mile layout used from 1968–71, on which Jackie Oliver recorded a race record lap of 3 mins 18.4 secs in 1971, was for many years the fastest in the race's history, equating to 151.855mph. This race speed was finally bettered 37 years later when works Peugeot driver Stéphane Sarrazin set the race's fastest lap at 3 mins 19.394 secs around the most recent 8.469 mile circuit layout for a new lap record speed of 152.899mph.

WORST RACING ACCIDENT EVER

"Pierre Levegh" (born Pierre Bouillin) and more than 80 spectators were killed at Le Mans in 1955 when there was a collision by the start of the pit lane, which then was separated from the circuit by just a painted line. The Frenchman's works-entered Mercedes clipped the back of Lance Macklin's Austin-Healey and was catapulted over the fence into the crowds on the opposite side of the track. This was motor racing's worst ever accident.

⊙ NAMED ON THE FLANK AND THE NOSE

The only Le Mans success by a driver in a car bearing his name came in 1980 when Le Mans-born Jean Rondeau guided his Rondeau M379B to victory. He was partnered by Jean-Pierre Jaussaud, with the team's sister car driven by Gordon Spice and the Martin brothers (Jean-Michel and Philippe) following up in third place.

⊙ IMPROVING THE BREED

Competition is a great proving ground for new technology and Jaguar racers Duncan Hamilton and Tony Rolt broke new ground when they brought their XK120C home three laps ahead of its sister car, driven by Stirling Moss and Peter Walker, in 1953. The car was fitted with disc brakes whereas previously all cars had been stopped by drum brakes.

⊙ HIGHEST SPEED RECORDED

If straight-line speed is everything at Le Mans, then WM would have won, as its Peugeot turbo-engined WM P88 driven by Roger Dorchy, Claude Haldi and Jean-Daniel Raulet – with Dorchy behind the wheel – hit 251.7mph in 1988. The car's speed wasn't matched by its reliability, however, and it covered just 59 laps before overheating led to its retirement. However, the insertion of a pair of chicanes on the previously 3-mile long Mulsanne Straight for 1990 has meant that no car has had a chance of beating this record since then.

⊙ THE MOST AND THE LEAST

The highest number of cars to start a Le Mans 24 Hours was 60 – in 1950, 1951 and 1953. The lowest number to start the race was just 17 in 1930 when, not surprisingly, the figure for the fewest finishers, only nine, was recorded. Cars were certainly more fragile in the early years and there were 40 retirements on three occasions – in 1952, 1959 and 1966. The years with the most cars circulating at the finish were 1983, 1993 and 1997– when 31 were still lapping.

⊙ SPEED AND DISTANCE

A record 3,315.193 miles were covered in 1971 by the Porsche 917K of Helmut Marko and Gijs van Lennep, at the astonishing average speed of 138.133mph. With Jackie Oliver setting a fastest race lap of 151.855mph, also in a Porsche 917, it was decided that speeds had got too high to be safe and so the circuit was remodelled for 1972. The Porsche Curves were inserted, removing the track from the public road after Arnage up to the Ford Chicane.

⊙ GERMAN METAL PROVES SUPREME

With Audi, BMW and Mercedes bolstering Porsche's 16 wins, German manufacturers are at the top of the pile for Le Mans wins, with a combined tally of 26. This outstrips the efforts of Aston Martin, Bentley, Jaguar, Lagonda, McLaren and Mirage who have given British manufacturers 17 victories, three more than Bugatti, Chenard & Walcker, Delahaye, Lorraine Dietrich, Matra Simca, Peugeot, Renault, Rondeau and Talbot have managed for France. Ferrari's nine wins take Italy only to fourth in the rankings, with four wins provided by Alfa Romeo.

⊙ WINNING BY A FRACTION

It seems unfair that either the Ford pairing of Jacky Ickx and Jackie Oliver or the Porsche duo of Hans Herrmann and Gerard Larrousse had to come away as losers in 1969. After 24 hours of racing the Ford GT40 was ahead of the Porsche 908 by just a few seconds. It had been even closer three years earlier when Ford tried to celebrate its first win here by staging a deadheat, but the organizers insisted that the Chris Amon/Bruce McLaren GT40 had travelled further than the Denny Hulme/Ken Miles sister car as it had started further back on the grid.

⊙ MOST SURPRISING WIN

Mazda had always been in the shadow of Toyota and Nissan in the quest to become the first Japanese automotive manufacturer to win the Le Mans 24 Hours, and was operating with a considerably smaller budget to finance its campaigns. However, it all came right for Mazda in 1991. There's no doubt that having six-time Le Mans winner Jacky Ickx managing its attack was a huge plus, and Johnny Herbert, Volker Weidler and Bertrand Gachot guided their rotary-engined 787B home two laps clear of the best of the faster but thirstier Jaguars.

TOP MANUFACTURERS WITH MOST WINS

1	Porsche	16
2	Ferrari	9
3	Audi	8
4	Jaguar	7
5	Bentley	6
6	Alfa Romeo	4
=	Ford	4
8	Matra Simca	3
=	Peugeot	3
10	Bugatti	2
=	Lorraine Dietrich	2

⊙ BET YOUR SHIRT ON IT

If you'd bought a Porsche T-shirt to celebrate Derek Bell and Jacky Ickx's win in 1981 you could have worn that shirt for a further six years and still shown your allegiance to the winning manufacturer as Porsche dominated Le Mans. Mind you, an Audi T-shirt from 2000 would have been the one to have right through to 2008, except for 2003, when the Bentley driven by Rinaldo Capello, Tom Kristensen and Guy Smith won.

SPORTS CARS

Loyalty to a manufacturer rather than to a particular team is the way that sports car racing works, with the current array of races around the globe offering interest for those who support famous sporting marques, Aston Martin, Audi, Ferrari, Jaguar, Peugeot and Porsche alike, as they do battle on some of the world's classic racing circuits. There are many different categories of sports cars too, with the CanAm series of the late 1960s and early 1970s standing out.

DRIVER RECORDS

⊙ BEFORE DRIVERS WERE HONOURED

The World Sports Car title was only for manufacturers until 1981. However, Derek Bell was one of the drivers who stood out before then, helping Alfa Romeo in 1975 to the first of its two sports car titles. He is generally associated with Porsche, though, and won 17 sports car races for the German manufacturer, including four at Le Mans, taking his overall tally to 21.

⊙ THREE-WAY TIE

Although there was a World Sports Car Championship from 1953, running under assorted names, there was no drivers' title until 1981, when American racer Bob Garretson was the first champion. From then until its final year in 1992, a trio of drivers won two titles apiece. They were Jacky Ickx (1982 and 1983), Derek Bell (1985 and 1986) and Jean-Louis Schlesser (1989 and 1990).

⊙ BROUGHT TO A CLOSE

With the number of works entries depleted and fields dwindling, 1992 was the final year for the World Sports Car Championship. Peugeot's works entries were the best cars, and they ought to have won every round, but they crashed out of the opener. Wins in three of the rounds, including the Le Mans 24 Hours, left Yannick Dalmas and Derek Warwick as the final champions.

⊙ WINNER BY A DISTANCE

The greatest winning margin was in the 1979 Daytona 24 Hours when the winning Interscope Porsche 935 of Ted Field, Hurley Haywood and Danny Ongais finished 49 laps clear of the Ferrari 365 GTB4 Daytona of Tony Adamowicz and John Morton, equating to a winning margin approaching 1 hr 40 mins.

⊙ SO CLOSE AND YET SO FAR

The closest competitive finish, as opposed to team-orchestrated one-twos, came at Spa-Francorchamps in 1986 when Thierry Boutsen and Frank Jelinski brought their Brun Motorsport Porsche 962C home just 0.8 secs clear of the works Jaguar XJR-6 of Jan Lammers and Derek Warwick. This was after more than 5½ hours of racing, and the Porsche coasted to the finish line, out of fuel.

◉ SPICE OF LIFE

Between 1985 and 1989, a subsidiary class was run in the World Sport-Prototype Championship: Group C2. This was won in all but the final year by Gordon Spice, first in a Tiga, then thereafter in one of his own Spice chassis, sharing with fellow Briton Ray Bellm in 1986 and 1988, and Spaniard Fermin Velez in 1987.

◉ FINDING A WINNING CAR

Bernd Schneider was the first driver to win the FIA GT Championship on his own. This was in 1997 when Mercedes introduced its pace-setting CLK-GTR and he used the rule that a driver could change car at any stage of a race, doing so when the car he shared with Alex Wurz hit trouble at the A1-Ring and Suzuka and he jumped into one of the other works entries. His eventual haul was six wins from 11 starts.

◉ WENDING HIS WAY

Former F1 driver Karl Wendlinger is the driver with the most FIA GT race wins – 16. They run from his title-winning 1999 campaign – with a win at the opening race at Monza with Olivier Beretta, sharing an ORECA Chrysler Viper GTS-R – to victory in the 2009 season opener at Silverstone in a KplusK Saleen. Mike Hezemans is second with 14, with Michael Bartels having 13 and Jamie Campbell-Walter 12.

◉ THE START OF SOMETHING BIG

Sports car racing became fractured after the World Sports Car Championship collapsed in 1992. By 1994, there were green shoots of revival and GT racing kicked off again, becoming a championship for 1995. John Nielsen won twice with Thomas Bscher in a McLaren F1 GTR to become champions as sports car racing found its feet again.

◉ TANGERINE DREAM

McLaren, with its Chevrolet-engined racers, dominated the Canadian-American Challenge (CanAm) series from its second season. Marque founder Bruce McLaren followed John Surtees as champion in 1967 and won again in 1969, with teammate Denny Hulme champion in 1968 and 1970. McLaren died when testing at Goodwood in 1970, but the team's dominance lived on, with Peter Revson champion in 1971.

SECOND PLACE GOES TO...

Jochen Mass kept his sports car racing career going from 1972 to 1991, ending on a high when Mercedes made a major push from the late 1980s. His first win came at Enna-Pergusa in 1975, his last at Mexico City in 1990, where he shared his Mercedes with Michael Schumacher. Mass is second in all the sports car rankings, with 32 wins, 14 poles and 12 fastest laps, with Jacky Ickx topping each of these tables.

MEET MR SPORTS CAR

Jacky Ickx was not only World Sports Car champion twice, in 1982 and 1983, both times for Porsche, but he won more races at World Championship level than any other sports car driver ever. He won for the first time at Spa-Francorchamps in 1967 in a Mirage then added another 36 wins, the last of which was in 1985 at Shah Alam in Malaysia, for Porsche. He also tops the tables for most pole positions (19) and most fastest laps (25).

DRIVERS WITH MOST WORLD SPORTS CAR RACE WINS

1	Jacky Ickx	37
2	Jochen Mass	32
3	Derek Bell	21
=	Henri Pescarolo	21
5	Mauro Baldi	17
=	Brian Redman	17
7	Jean-Louis Schlesser	15
8	Phil Hill	14
=	Jo Siffert	14
10	Gerard Larrousse	12
=	Stirling Moss	12

Note: World Sports Car races were held from 1953–92.

TEAM RECORDS

⊙ WIN AND MOVE ON
Aston Martin had been gunning to win the World Sport Car Championship since the outset in 1953, but it all came good in 1959. Amazingly, despite winning the last three of the five races and taking the title, the team closed at the year's end. The English sports car manufacturer elected to concentrate on F1, only to quit that as well a year later.

⊙ THEY'RE ALL MINE
The 1962 sports car series contained only four races: Sebring, Nürburgring, Le Mans and the Targa Florio road race. Ferrari won them all. The only other manufacturers to take a clean sweep are Porsche in 1977 (World Championship of Makes), 1978 and 1983, and Alfa Romeo in 1977 (World Championship for Sports Cars).

⊙ THE JOY OF SIX
Porsche has the greatest record of domination, as its cars have filled the top-six finishing positions a record 16 times. This happened at Daytona in 1975, at Mugello in 1976, at Mugello, Watkins Glen and Brands Hatch in 1977, at Daytona in 1978, at Sebring in 1981, at Monza, Le Mans and Fuji in 1983, at Le Mans, Brands Hatch, Spa, Imola and Sandown Park in 1984 and at Le Mans in 1986.

⊙ FORZA FERRARI
Ferrari has claimed more FIA GT Championship race wins than any other marque, taking 24 between 2001, when Peter Kox and Rickard Rydell won in a 550 Maranello at Austria's A1-Ring, to Dubai in 2005 when Gabriel Gardel and Pedro Lamy won in a similar car. Its recent success has been in the GT2 junior class. Chrysler has one win fewer, with a recent run for Maserati propelling it past Mercedes to be third on 20.

⊙ TAKING TITLES TWO BY TWO

Audi and Pescarolo Sport rank equal top in the table for the most senior class (LMP1) teams' titles in the Le Mans Series, with two apiece. Audi won in the inaugural season, 2004, and 2008, then Pescarolo in 2005 and 2006. Larbre Compétition has won twice in the GT1 class and both Sebah Automotive and Virgo Motorsport twice in GT2.

⊙ PENSKE'S POWERFUL PORSCHES

The most powerful sports car ever is the turbocharged Porsche 917/30, which had 1500bhp when it ran at full boost. With Penske Racing running it and Mark Donohue driving it, no one else got a look-in at the 1973 CanAm series. Two 1972 vintage 917/10s won the first two rounds, then Donohue and Penske won the remaining six.

⊙ TRIDENT CARRIERS

The most successful team in FIA GT history is the Vitaphone Racing Team, led by Michael Bartels. This Maserati MC12-equipped outfit has landed the senior teams' title every year from 2005–09. Its drivers also claimed the drivers' title four times, being edged out in 2005 by only a point by Larbre Compétition's Gabriel Gardel.

⊙ BMW WINS BMW SERIES

BMW's M1 sports car had a series of its own in 1979 and 1980, supporting grands prix around Europe, with F1 drivers invited to take part. Double world champion Niki Lauda won the first title for Project 4 Racing, but BMW Motorsport was more successful in 1980. Its drivers – Carlos Reutemann, Didier Pironi and Nelson Piquet – won five of the nine races. Piquet was crowned champion after winning the last three.

⊙ ALL BUT ONE

The Sauber-run Mercedes team came very close to completing a clean sweep in 1989 when it won every round, except one – at Dijon-Prenois – when Porsche edged it out. Porsche's Jean-Louis Schlesser finished second on that occasion, but he won at Suzuka, Jarama, the Nürburgring, Donington Park and Mexico City to secure the drivers' title.

PORSCHE'S PROWESS

With an incredibly successful run through the 1970s and early 1980s, Porsche is way out clear as the manufacturer with the most race wins in the World Sports Car Championship (1953–92), even though its last win was early in 1989. It has 126 wins, precisely double Ferrari's tally, with Mercedes-Benz and Jaguar on 25 and 23 respectively.

TEAMS WITH MOST WORLD SPORTS CAR RACE WINS

1	Porsche	126
2	Ferrari	63
3	Mercedes-Benz	25
4	Jaguar	23
5	Alfa Romeo	19
6	Matra	15
7	Ford	13
8	Lancia	11
9	Peugeot	8
10	Aston Martin	7

Note: World Sports Car races were held from 1953–92.

⊙ THE BIG CAT POUNCES

Jaguar was able to win the Le Mans 24 Hours five times in the 1950s, but it seemed as if it may never claim the World Championship. However, that was put right when Tom Walkinshaw Racing guided Jaguar to the manufacturers' title in 1987. And, for good measure, Walkinshaw's team did it again in 1988 and 1991, scoring 18 of its 23 wins across that five-year period.

PORSCHE SUPERCUP

ALTFRID THE FIRST

Altfrid Heger was the first driver to be crowned Porsche Supercup champion at the end of the 1993 inaugural season. This one-make series for Porsche's 911 Carrera ran as the support for the European-based F1 grands prix. The 35-year-old German won three rounds to shade compatriot and teammate Uwe Alzen by 154 points to 152. Alzen would bounce back to win the following year.

THE OLD BOYS FIGHT BACK

The oldest average age of the first three finishers in a Supercup race came at one of the races supporting the Bahrain GP in 2007. Damien Faulkner (then aged 31), Uwe Alzen (39) and Alessandro Zampedri (37) stepped up to the podium, together making an average age of 36 years 1 month and 11 days.

GIVE THE KIDS A CHANCE

The youngest average age of the three drivers on the podium came at one of the two Supercup races supporting the 2008 Spanish GP. Winner Jan Seyffarth (then aged 21) was joined by Jeroen Bleekemolen (26) and Martin Ragginger (20) for an average age of just 22 years 9 months and 17 days.

FARNBACHER LEADS THE WAY

The most successful team in Porsche Supercup history is Farnbacher Motorsport, with 33 wins to its name, a dozen wins more than Manthey Racing's tally of 21, and a further five wins better than Kadach Racing's 16.

WHO INVITED THIS GUEST?

Porsche has always asked one or two guest drivers to compete in each race. F1 driver Mika Hakkinen set the bar high in the inaugural season, 1993, when he needed something to do as McLaren found itself with three drivers until Michael Andretti quit F1. He turned up twice and won twice, much to the chagrin of the regulars.

⊙ GERMAN CARS, GERMAN WINNERS

German drivers, as one would expect, have dominated the Porsche Supercup since its inception in 1993. Between them they have scored 87 wins over the 17 years, 50 more than the next most successful nation, the Dutch. The French have taken 25 wins, the British 11 and the Italians five.

⊙ AS CLOSE AS IT GETS

The closest ever finish in the Supercup came in the second of two races supporting the Bahrain GP in 2009. Jeroen Bleekemolen had wrapped up the title in the first, but he still wanted to win the second. However, he was barged out of the way by René Rast with two corners to go, to lose out by 0.157 secs. Then the stewards reversed the positions as the move had been overly robust.

⊙ FIRST FRANCE THEN EUROPE

The Supercup has long been the pinnacle of Porsche's racing ladder, with junior series being staged in Britain, France, Germany and, more recently, Asia, Australia and Italy. Jean-Pierre Malcher is an example of how this works, stepping up to the Supercup after four years in the French Carrera Cup in which he was champion in 1991 and never ranked below third. Third in his first Supercup foray, Malcher nailed the title in 1995.

⊙ A ROUTE OUT OF SINGLE- SEATERS

Emmanuel Collard had hopes of racing in F1, but he stalled in F3000 and so the chance to race in the Supercup gave him a lifeline. He grasped it with both hands in 1994, adapting fast to sports cars and, despite failing to win a race, just lost out to Uwe Alzen for the title. Three wins followed in 1995, then five wins and the title in 1996. Since then, "Manu" has been a Porsche-favoured driver in GT racing.

⊙ A RARE SUCCESS

British success in the Supercup has been scarce, save for Kelvin Burt's win in a Porsche-entered guest car in 1994. Richard Westbrook (British Porsche Carrera Cup Champion in 2004) put that record right in 2006 when he won at Imola. He then won three more races to lift the title, repeating the feat in 2007 with wins in Spain and Hungary. A third Brit, Sean Edwards, won twice in 2008.

⊙ THE OTHER DUTCHMAN

Patrick Huisman isn't the only Dutch driver to win the Porsche Supercup crown, as compatriot Jeroen Bleekemolen came good after several years of dabbling at it alongside his involvement in other sports car series and in A1GP. Three wins in 2007, his first full season, were followed by three more and the title in 2008, then five wins in 2009 and a second title, with Huisman trailing far behind.

⊙ SPLITTING 10 BETWEEN FIVE

Displaying an impressive level of competition, five teams have shared the Porsche Supercup teams' title that runs alongside the drivers' championship in the 2000s. Team Farnbacher wo ns three titles, in 2001, 2003 and 2004, while Lechner Racing (2005 and 2007) and Konrad Motorsport (2008 and 2009) are two-time champions. Kadach Tuning (in 2002) and Tolimit Motorsport (2006) won the other teams' championships.

PORSCHE SUPERCUP RACE WINS

1	Patrick Huisman	25
2	Wolf Henzler	14
3	Uwe Alzen	13
4	Jeroen Bleekemolen	11
5	Jorg Bergmeister	8
=	Emmanuel Collard	8
=	Richard Westbrook	8
8	Stephane Ortelli	7
9	René Rast	6
=	Marco Werner	6

⊙ WOLF'S YEAR OF YEARS

The record for the most wins in a Supercup season is held by Wolf Henzler, with the nine victories he secured out of a dozen starts in 2004. Driving for the Farnbacher Motorsport team, the 29-year-old German won races at Imola, Barcelona, the Nürburgring, two at Indianapolis, Magny-Cours, Silverstone, the Hungaroring and Spa-Francorchamps. Needless to say, he was a dominant champion.

AMERICAN LE MANS SERIES

⊙ WINNER WITHOUT A WIN

Veteran racer Elliott Forbes-Robinson did precisely what he needed to do to win the inaugural American Le Mans Series (ALMS) title in 1999: he finished consistently. By the year's end, he had never finished higher than second in his Dyson Racing Riley & Scott, but this was enough to outscore the drivers of the faster BMWs, who skipped one race and boycotted another, and Panozes.

⊙ THE ENEMY WITHIN

The smallest title-winning margin was in 2002 when Tom Kristensen beat Dindo Capello to the title by just two points, 232 to 230. They spent the most of the year sharing one of Audi North America's two Audi R8s, but the difference arose in the opening two races. Capello had a winning start at Sebring, with Kristensen fifth, before Kristensen bounced back to finish second at Sears Point with Johnny Herbert, while Capello partnered Frank Biela and Emanuele Pirro and ended up 15th.

⊙ CAPELLO POWERS IN FRONT

JJ Lehto was the first driver to win more than one ALMS race, winning four for BMW in the inaugural ALMS season in 1999. Although he went on to win 19 races in all, he has been eclipsed as the driver with the most wins by Dindo Capello as the Audi racer's win at Sebring in 2009 was his 26th. Fellow Audi racers fill the next five places in the table of winners.

⊙ A BOW TIE FOR THE WINNERS

Corvette Racing has wielded Chevrolet's famous bow-tie-shaped emblem with enormous success in the ALMS, with its Corvettes dominating the GT1 class. The yellow and black cars have taken that class title eight times, with drivers Olivier Beretta, Oliver Gavin, Ron Fellows and Johnny O'Connell claiming three crowns apiece before the class was scrapped for 2009 due to a lack of competition.

⊙ A CHANGE OF FACE

With long-time champions Audi and 2008 rivals Porsche having quit the ALMS, it was the turn in 2009 for Honda's Acura arm to take the spoils, with David Brabham and Scott Sharp taking the crown in the Highcroft Racing entry. Acura also pulled off the unique feat of winning the LMP2 class in the same season, through Adrian Fernandez and Luis Diaz.

⊙ FOUR BY TWO

Jorg Bergmeister shares the record for the most class titles, four, with fellow German Lucas Luhr. Bergmeister's all came in the GT (later GT2) class for Porsche, sharing with Patrick Long in 2005 and 2009 and Wolf Henzler in 2008, and claiming it alone in 2006. Luhr is the only driver to have won titles in three classes, having been crowned in the GT class in 2002 and 2003, LMP2 in 2006 and LMP1 in 2008.

⊙ SHARING IT AROUND

Not only has German sports-car specialist Marco Werner won the main LMP1 (née LMP900) class title three times for Audi, but he has done so with three different partners: Frank Biela in 2003, JJ Lehto in 2004 and Lucas Luhr in 2008.

⊙ JOHNNY O'WINNER

Chevrolet's domination of the GT1 class, which ran as GTS until 2004, led to Johnny O'Connell taking the most wins in any ALMS class, amassing 36. This is one more than fellow Chevrolet driver Olivier Beretta, who had a strong 2000 campaign with a Dodge Viper in which he won nine of the 12 rounds, before joining the Chevrolet attack.

⊙ FORMULA AUDI

Audi finished third in the first ever ALMS race in 1999, the Sebring 12 Hours, then returned a year later, also at Sebring, where Frank Biela, Tom Kristensen and Emanuele Pirro were victorious. Audi has carried on winning ever since to take its wins tally to 63. The next most successful manufacturer, Porsche, has 11.

⊙ AS EASY AS ONE, TWO, THREE

The first hat-trick of wins in ALMS history was claimed by Allan McNish and Dindo Capello at Laguna Seca in 2000 where they took their works Audi R8 to victory over Frank Biela and Emanuele Pirro's sister car, following on from wins at Portland and Road Atlanta.

⊙ PENSKE POWERS ON

Successful in F1, IndyCar and NASCAR, the Penske team has been a hit since joining the ALMS in 2006 and won the LMP2 class first time out, even taking an outright win over the LMP1s. Lucas Luhr and Sascha Maassen drove the class-winning Porsche RS Spyder, but it was the drivers of the sister car, Timo Bernhard and Romain Dumas, who won the crown in 2007 (with six outright wins) and 2008, adding to Bernhard's GT title from 2004.

DRIVERS WITH MOST WINS

1	Dindo Capello	26
2	Frank Biela	21
3	Marco Werner	20
4	JJ Lehto	19
5	Allan McNish	18
6	Emanuele Pirro	16
7	David Brabham	10
=	Tom Kristensen	10
9	Timo Bernhard	9
=	Romain Dumas	9

TOURING CARS

Much as it's NASCAR that draws the most fans in the USA, touring cars have fervent supporters in pretty much every other country. The British Touring Car Championship (BTCC) has always drawn great crowds, Germany's Deutsche Tourenwagen Masters (DTM) packs the grandstands and Australia's V8 Supercar fans, thronging the hillsides at Bathurst, echo this passion. The racing is seldom less than dramatic.

DRIVER RECORDS

⊙ FIRST, BEAT THE OLD GUY

Staying power was very much part of John Cleland's arsenal when he raced in the BTCC from 1989–99. He won the title at his first attempt in a Class C Vauxhall Astra at the age of 37, taking 11 class wins from 13 starts. Once the class structure was removed, he started winning outright for Vauxhall and notched up 17 wins, landing his second title in 1995.

⊙ LAYING DOWN A MARKER

The first driver to win any championship is always guaranteed a place in history and Jack Sears won the inaugural BTCC in 1958 in an Austin A105 Westminster. He won the title for a second time in 1963, in a campaign during which he drove both a Lotus Cortina and a giant American Ford Galaxie.

⊙ TRIO OF HAT-TRICKS

Three drivers have claimed BTCC title hat-tricks. Bill McGovern won three in a row from 1970 in his Class D Sunbeam Imp. Win Percy matched this from 1980, winning the first two in a Class B Mazda RX7 and the third in a Class C Toyota Corolla. Andy Rouse followed on directly from Percy's run to score his trio from 1983. Rouse stands out as he won each title in a different car: first in a Class B Alfa Romeo GTV6, then in a Class A Rover Vitesse and, finally, in 1985, in a Class A Ford Sierra Turbo.

⊙ F1 DRIVERS PLAY AROUND

One of the greatest features of racing in the 1960s was that the top drivers raced whatever they could get their hands on, looking to pocket prize money every weekend from spring to autumn. This is why Lotus's 1963 F1 world champion Jim Clark raced in the BTCC in 1964 and he drove to the title in a Lotus Cortina.

⊙ TOM'S DOUBLE DELIGHT

Future team entrant Tom Walkinshaw secured a record that is unlikely ever to be beaten when he scored class wins in different cars on the same day. This came when the BTCC visited Ingliston in his native Scotland in 1974 and he won his class in a Ford Capri 3000GT, then later in the day did so again in a Ford Escort RS2000.

⊙ MR COSMOPOLITAN

If Fabrizio Giovanardi was disappointed when his single-seater career stalled at F3000 level, he needn't have been, because his move to touring cars after 1991 was the start of great things. Class winner in the Italian Touring Car Championship in 1992, he went on to be the champion in Spain in 1997, the Italian champion again in both 1998 and 1999, the European champion from 2000 to 2002 and British champion in both 2007 and 2008.

⊙ BEST OF THE BEST

New Zealander Paul Radisich can say that he was once the world's best touring car racer. When the majority of the touring car series were run to 2-litre Super Touring rules in the 1990s, the Touring Car World Cup was held to unite the best drivers. He won both races at Monza in 1993 in his Ford Mondeo, and then further enhanced his reputation by winning in 1994 when the event was held as a single race at Donington Park. Frank Biela won the 1995 Touring Car World Cup at Paul Ricard for Audi.

⊙ THE DOMINATOR

The FIA World Touring Car Championship had a problem when it started its fourth season in 2008. Crowds were good, race entries were strong and the racing was exciting, but Andy Priaulx had claimed the 2005, 2006 and 2007 crowns, all for BMW. He didn't always take the titles by a clear margin, winning the 2006 championship by just one point over Jorg Müller, but it was enough to frustrate his rivals. Priaulx's run ended in 2008, when SEAT León driver Yvan Müller was champion.

⊙ FIVE MAKE IT THREE

The European Touring Car Championship ran from 1963–88, with an upgraded Italian series carrying the title from 2000–04. Five drivers have won three outright or class titles: Dieter Quester, Toine Hezemans, Umberto Grano, Helmut Kelleners and Fabrizio Giovanardi, who won the first three years of the revived ETCC, from 2000 to 2002.

⊙ A BIT OF A WINNER

Andy Rouse sits at the top of the table for the most British Touring Car Championship wins, with 60, seven clear of Jason Plato. However, the 1983–85 champion holds another record, that of the most wins in succession. The Ford Sierra RS500 driver enjoyed a run of eight wins in a row in 1988, though he finished only third in the final BTCC standings, behind champion Frank Sytner and Phil Dowsett. Robb Gravett's run of seven in a row in his Trakstar Ford Sierra Cosworth in 1990 is the next best sequence.

⊙ SWISS ON A ROLL

Alain Menu had a magnificent season in the BTCC in 1997. Not only did the Swiss driver start his campaign for the Williams-run Renault team with four straight wins, but he added another eight wins in his Laguna and lifted the title by the record margin of 110 points, with a total of 281. Audi Sport UK's Frank Biela was runner-up.

DRIVERS WITH THE MOST BTCC RACE WINS

1	Andy Rouse	60
2	Jason Plato	53
3	Alain Menu	36
=	Yvan Muller	36
=	James Thompson	36
6	Frank Gardner	35
7	Matt Neal	31
8	Gordon Spice	27
9	Brian Muir	23
10	Fabrizio Giovanardi	22

TEAM RECORDS

⊙ FORD'S VARIETY SHOW
Both Ford and Vauxhall have won four BTCC drivers' titles in a row, from 1965–68 and 2001–04 respectively, but when Ford scored its run it did so with different cars. The first was Roy Pierpoint's title in a Mustang in 1965, then John Fitzpatrick's in a Broadspeed Anglia in 1966. Frank Gardner then bagged the next two for Alan Mann Racing, in a Falcon in 1967, and then in both an Escort and a Cortina in 1968.

⊙ SCHNITZER RULES THE WORLD
Motor racing has an ability to confuse by moving the goalposts. The ETCC decided to add a few races out of Europe – in Australia, New Zealand and Japan – in 1987 so that it could become the World Touring Car Championship. Roberto Ravaglia won this for the Schnitzer BMW team, but it reverted to the ETCC in 1988 and Ravaglia, Schnitzer and BMW won that as well, making it a hat-trick as they'd also won in 1986.

⊙ BMW BEST IN THE WORLD
The manufacturer with the greatest number of race wins in the World Touring Car Championship since the latest incarnation of the series kicked off in 2004 is BMW, with 45 from the 110 races, never scoring fewer than six wins in a season. The most successful of BMW's works teams is Team BMW Germany, run by Schnitzer Motorsport, with 25 wins to its name.

⊙ TITLE AND OUT
SEAT campaigned five works-run Leon TDIs in the 2009 FIA World Touring Car Championship and Gabriele Tarquini ended up as champion ahead of teammate Yvan Müller. However, with the global economic downturn still biting hard, the Spanish manufacturer then closed its works team.

⊙ BAVARIAN MOTORS WORK

BMW's 3.0 CSL holds the greatest record in the history of the ETCC: it helped five drivers in succession claim the title between 1975 and 1979, having already helped Toine Hezemans land the 1973 title. BMW then went on to claim the next four drivers' crowns with its 320i, 635CSi and 528i models.

⊙ WHEN BIG CATS ROARED

Jaguar was almost unbeatable in the early days of the British Touring Car Championship, winning every race, except one, in the first five seasons, 1958–62, albeit with not one of its drivers landing the overall title. The lone non-Jaguar winner was Doc Shepherd in a little Austin A40. He broke the run at Snetterton in 1960.

⊙ DOMINANT BUT BEATEN

The longest winning streak by a model of car in the BTCC is Ford's run of 40 victories between September 1987 and October 1990 when its Sierra RS500 dominated. The class system obscured this as only Robb Gravett was champion for Ford in that time, with the 1987 title going to Chris Hodgetts's Class D Toyota Corolla, the 1988 title to Frank Sytner's Class B BMW M3 and the 1989 title to John Cleland's Class C Vauxhall Astra GTE.

⊙ TWR MAKES ITS MARK

Tom Walkinshaw was a racer and then a team boss. He enjoyed more success in the latter guise, and went on to run teams in sports cars and F1. However, Tom Walkinshaw Racing's first big success was in the BTCC when Win Percy gave it back-to-back crowns in 1980 and 1981, beating the ranks of Ford Capris by taking 18 class wins in his Class B Mazda RX7.

⊙ WINNING THE CLASS WAR

The BTCC underwent a major change for 1991, with the scrapping of the class system. From then on, all cars ran with the same-size engine and Vauxhall's John Cleland was runner-up in 1991 but landed Vauxhall's first crown in 1995. However, Vauxhall's prime came between 2001 and 2004 when Jason Plato, James Thompson (twice) and Yvan Müller helped it to four titles in succession.

⊙ NO EGG ON ITS FACE

Swiss team Eggenberger Motorsport had a very strong period in the ETCC in the early 1980s, winning three titles in a row from 1980. Helmut Kelleners won in 1980 and he shared with Sigi Müller Jr then with Umberto Grano in 1981 and 1982, all with BMWs. Eggenberger added a fourth title in 1985 when Gianfranco Brancatelli and Thomas Lindstrom shared one of its Volvo 240 turbos.

⊙ BLUE OVAL BEATS BMW

Some of the most exciting racing in the history of the ETCC was in the early 1970s when Ford Deutschland pitched its "Cologne" Capri RS2600s against BMW's 3.0 CSLs. Ford won the title in 1972 with Jochen Mass – the first year without smaller classes confusing the order – and did so again in 1974 when Hans Heyer raced both a Capri and an Escort RS.

MANUFACTURERS WITH MOST BTCC TITLES

1	Ford	9
2	Vauxhall	8
3	BMW	5
=	Mini	5
5	Sunbeam	3
=	Toyota	3
7	Alfa Romeo	2
=	Austin	2
=	Chrysler	2
=	Honda	2
=	Mazda	2

PART 7: MISCELLANEOUS MOTOR SPORTS

No sport has as much sheer variety as motor sport, ranging from regular circuit racing to extreme off-road competition. Some of the myriad forms, such as NASCAR's Camping World Truck Series, are a twist on the regular series, whereas drag racing is something completely different. Yet, one look at those brave, intensely focused drivers chasing the world land speed record and it's clear that they are even further out on a limb, with the next target being 1,000mph...

WORLD LAND
SPEED RECORDS

⊙ AND THEY'RE OFF...

The first recorded attempt to set a land speed record came in 1898 when Gaston de Chasseloup-Laubat set his electric-powered Jeantaud Duc off in a straight line at Achères in his native France. He was timed at an average speed of 39.24mph over a kilometre. Within six months, that record had changed hands five times and been extended to 65.79mph by Belgian Camille Jenatzy in a car fittingly called *La Jamais Contente* (The Never Content).

⊙ SHEDDING A WHEEL

Craig Breedlove caused a bit of a stir when he turned up for a record attempt with Spirit of America in 1963, as the car had only three wheels, one at the nose and two at the rear. Furthermore, its wheels weren't driven, with all motivation coming from its jet engine. He became the first man over 400mph, but it took a long while before his record was ratified, during which time Donald Campbell held the record temporarily.

⊙ DRY SAND IS BEST

With British beaches not offering a run that was long, flat or dry enough, British hopefuls headed for North America and Utah's Bonneville Salt Flats. It was here that Captain George Eyston took his Thunderbolt in 1937 and bettered Malcolm Campbell's 1935 record of 301.129mph, taking it up to 311.41mph.

⊙ BRITAIN FIGHTS BACK

Richard Noble became the first British driver to hold the land speed record in 33 years when he took Thrust2 to Black Rock Desert in north-western Nevada in 1983. He wound up its Rolls-Royce Avon jet engine and hit a top speed of 650.88mph and achieved a run average of 633mph.

⊙ BATTLE OF BONNEVILLE

The autumn of 1964 was a time of tit-for-tat land speed record breaking at the Bonneville Salt Flats as Americans Tom Green, Art Arfons and Craig Breedlove all took turns to be the world's fastest man. Arfons signed out with a new mark of 536.71mph in his turbojet-powered Green Monster. Then, in 1965, they would start all over again and go faster still.

⊙ COMING BACK FOR MORE

Malcolm Campbell is the driver who has held the most land speed records, having raised the level six times after his first record of 146.16mph set in Bluebird on Pendine Sands in 1924. His final mark of 301.129mph was set on the Bonneville Salt Flats in 1935 in his fourth and final Bluebird, the most powerful version with a supercharged Napier Lion engine producing 1450bhp.

⊙ DEATH OR GLORY

John Parry-Thomas was the first driver to be killed in pursuit of the land speed record, meeting his death at Pendine Sands in his native Wales. This happened in 1927 when he was attempting to regain his record that had been taken by Malcolm Campbell the year before. Parry-Thomas pushed his car above 174mph and was partially decapitated when one of the chains driving the aero-engine broke. His car, Babs, was buried on the beach.

⊙ A BRIEF MOMENT OF GLORY

The shortest amount of time for which a record setter has held the land speed record is less than 24 hours, when Camille Jenatzy set a record, only to have it taken back later that same day by Gaston de Chasseloup-Laubat in 1899. More recently, the record changed hands four times between three drivers in a month, in October 1964, with Art Arfons at least getting to hold the record until the following autumn.

⊙ A TON AND A HALF

British attempts on the land speed record were set at the Pendine Sands in south Wales back in the 1920s. It was here that Malcolm Campbell set his first land speed record in his aero-engined Bluebird. This was in 1924 and he came back the following summer to add another 4.6mph to his timed run over a mile, becoming the first driver to top 150mph.

TOP 10 FASTEST RUNS

	Speed	Driver	Vehicle	Year
1	763.035mph	Andy Green	ThrustSSC	1997
2	714.144mph	Andy Green	ThrustSSC	1997
3	633.000mph	Richard Noble	Thrust2	1983
4	622.407mph	Gary Gabelich	Blue Flame	1970
5	600.601mph	Craig Breedlove	Spirit of America – Sonic 1	1965
6	576.553mph	Art Arfons	Green Monster	1965
7	555.485mph	Craig Breedlove	Spirit of America – Sonic 1	1965
8	536.710mph	Art Arfons	Green Monster	1964
9	526.277mph	Craig Breedlove	Spirit of America	1964
10	468.719mph	Craig Breedlove	Spirit of America	1964

⊙ GOING SUPERSONIC

Richard Noble was the mastermind behind the 1997 land speed record attack at Black Rock Desert with ThrustSSC. The aim was to go supersonic – faster than the speed of sound, 768mph – and Royal Air Force pilot Andy Green was brought in to drive this twin-engined projectile, its engines the same as those used on a Phantom F4 fighter. Green harnessed the 110,000bhp to do a run of 714.144mph, then bettered that to average 763.035mph in both directions over a 1-mile course 20 days later.

⊙ HEADLINE NEWS

The most important and imagination-catching landmarks come when a driver breaks into another 100mph segment. This is what happened when Craig Breedlove returned to the Bonneville Salt Flats in 1965 and took Spirit of America past 600mph. This was 24mph faster than arch-rival Art Arfons had travelled a week earlier.

NASCAR TRUCK
SERIES RECORDS

⊙ TAKING IT TO THE WIRE

The closest race finish in NASCAR Truck Series history came in the inaugural season. Mike Skinner edged his Richard Childress Racing Chevrolet ahead out of the final corner of the Total Petroleum 200 at Colorado National Speedway in 1995, but Butch Miller got his Liberty Racing Ford's nose back in front on the finish line and won by 0.001 secs after 1 hr 20 mins of racing.

⊙ SNEAKING HOME

Four of the 15 NASCAR Truck Series champions to date have clinched the title with an advantage of fewer than 10 points over their closest rival. These are Ron Hornaday Jr (1998), Jack Sprague (1999), Travis Kvapil (2003) and Johnny Benson (2008). Hornaday Jr's title was claimed by just three points, 4,072 to Sprague's 4,069, by following him home in the final round at Las Vegas.

⊙ ONE IS ENOUGH

Two Truck Series champions have managed to lift the crown despite winning only one race in their campaign. They were Travis Kvapil of Xpress Motorsports in 2003 and Ted Musgrave for Ultra Motorsports, two years later, both from 25 starts, stressing how the points-scoring system favours consistency above all else.

⊙ ONE YEAR ON, ONE YEAR OFF

Jack Sprague has a trio of Truck Series titles to his name. He claimed all of these with Hendrick Motorsports, taking the first in 1997, the second in 1999 and the third in 2001. None came with many wins, as he scored three from 26, three from 25 and then four from 24, respectively, but that 1997 title was achieved with the largest ever winning margin of 232 points, over Rich Bickle.

⊙ SUCCESS BREEDS SUCCESS

Echoing its numerous successes in the Sprint Cup series, Hendrick Motorsports also is the most successful team in NASCAR Truck Series history, the team having collected three championship titles. There are three teams who are just behind Hendrick, with two wins apiece, those of Dale Earnhardt, Steve Coulther and Kevin Harvick.

⊙ ON THE WAY DOWN

Some drivers use the Truck Series as a way to climb up NASCAR's ladder, others use it on the way down. Todd Bodine is a prime example of the latter. He made his Winston Cup debut in 1992 and took occasional pole positions, but he tried his hand in the Truck Series in 2004 and has regularly enjoyed being among the front-runners. He claimed the title in 2006 in a Germain Racing Toyota.

⊙ THE TRIPLE CROWN

Twenty drivers have won races in the Truck Series as well as winning races in the Sprint Cup and the Nationwide Series. Leading the way in this is Mark Martin, whose 95 wins are split as follows: 40 in the Sprint Cup, 48 in the Nationwide Series and seven in the Truck Series. Kyle Busch is second in this hybrid ranking, with his 62 wins shared 16, 30 and 16 respectively.

DRIVERS WITH MOST TRUCK SERIES WINS		
1	Ron Hornaday Jr	45
2	Mike Skinner	28
=	Jack Sprague	28
4	Todd Bodine	17
5	Ted Musgrave	17
6	Dennis Setzer	17
7	Greg Biffle	16
8	Kyle Busch	16
9	Johnny Benson	14
10	Mike Bliss	13
=	Joe Ruttmann	13

⊙ MEET MR TRUCK RACING

Ron Hornaday Jr has won Truck Series titles in 1996, 1998, 2007 and 2009. He is the most garlanded driver since NASCAR launched the series in 1995. He has amassed 45 victories, some 17 more than his next most successful rivals Mike Skinner and Jack Sprague.

DRAG RACING RECORDS

⊙ FATHER OF DRAG RACING

"Big Daddy" Don Garlits remains the most famous drag racer of all time. He was dubbed "King of the Dragsters". These nicknames aren't without substance as he won a record 144 events in his black Swamp Rat Top Fuel dragsters. The last of his 17 NHRA titles came in 1987 when he was 54. He also changed the shape of Top Fuel dragsters, opting to put the engine behind the driver after losing part of his right foot as a result of a transmission failure in 1970.

⊙ IN THE BEGINNING

America was and always will be the home of drag racing. Back in 1955, the National Hot Rod Association (NHRA) held its first meeting at Great Bend in Kansas. Calvin Rice emerged the winner, taking 10.30 secs and averaging 143.95mph over the quarter-mile course to become the first Top Fuel champion.

⊙ BEATING THE CLOCK AND BIGOTRY

Known as "The First Lady of Drag Racing", Shirley Muldowney worked her way through the Top Gas then Funny Car classes to reach Top Fuel in 1973. She then won three Top Fuel Championship titles, in 1977, 1980 and 1982. However, she had to fight against resistance from the NHRA all the way.

⊙ MOVING IN AN UNUSUAL WAY

Gary Scelzi became the second driver after Kenny Bernstein to win titles in both of the NHRA's nitro classes. He was Top Fuel champion in 1997, 1998 and 2000 before unusually crossing over to the Funny Car class. Most drivers graduate in the opposite direction. However, he did that to please his sponsors and became Funny Car champion in 2005.

⊙ TONY'S LUCKY SEVEN

Second-generation drag racer Tony Schumacher holds the record for the most Top Fuel wins, 61, and the most titles, seven. Even more impressively, he won six of these titles in succession from 2004 to 2009, and had a record-breaking run of winning 10 events in a season in 2004. He also achieved the largest championship-winning margin of 415 points that year.

⊙ FAST, FASTER, FASTEST

Tony "The Sarge" Schumacher holds the record for the top speed achieved by a Top Fuel dragster down a quarter-mile course. He achieved this when guiding his US Army-sponsored rail to a new mark of 336.15mph at Columbus in 2005, lowering the Top Fuel elapsed time record by 0.004 secs to 4.437 secs.

⊙ TOP FUEL'S TOP RACER

Tony Schumacher held the elapsed time Top Fuel record for the quarter-mile, set at 4.428 secs at Pomona in 2006. However, this was bettered by Doug Kalitta, who lowered the mark to 4.420 secs. Schumacher also holds the record on the increasingly used shorter courses (1,000 ft) of 3.771 secs, with Larry Dixon hitting the highest speed on one of these courses, managing 321.58mph, also in 2009.

⊙ GET CARTER

The most successful Top Fuel racer in Europe in the past decade has been England's Andy Carter, who was FIA European champion in 2001, 2004, 2008 and 2009. Sweden's Jimmy Alund has been the Pro Stock champion six years in a row from 2004 to 2009.

⊙ ONE SHORT OF THE TON

Joe Amato came within a whisker of making his 100th Top Fuel final, eventually retiring with 99 appearances in finals, out of which he took 52 wins. Tony Schumacher, still competing, is closing in fast, with 95 appearances in finals by the end of 2009, and Larry Dixon also still gunning for glory on 92.

⊙ GOING FASTER DOWN UNDER

The late Scott Kalitta holds the Top Fuel speed record for Australia, hitting 332.84mph in a run in his Rapisarda Racing rail in Western Sydney at the end of 2006. The Australian Top Fuel elapsed time record was a 4.563-secs run by multiple Australian champion Phil Read at Willowbank in 2008.

⊙ CHAMPIONS MAKE CHAMPIONS

Larry Dixon, Top Fuel champion in 2002 and 2003, who achieved a then record-equalling nine wins in 2002, had a great teacher in his father, also Larry, who was a successful drag racer. However, he spent his early years at drag events learning his craft under none other than multiple Funny Car champion Larry "The Snake" Prudhomme, who then ran his title attacks for him.

⊙ FASTEST SHOOT-OUT

They say that second is the first of the losers, and in drag racing
this is more obvious than in any other branch of motor sport.
However, in Chicago in 2004 Dave Grubnic had every reason to feel
that this was a harsh judgement as he was edged out 4.497 secs
to 4.477 secs by Tony Schumacher in the fastest shoot-out in NHRA
history.

TOP 10 DRIVERS WITH MOST NHRA TOP FUEL WINS

1	Tony Schumacher	61
2	Joe Amato	52
3	Larry Dixon	48
4	Kenny Bernstein	39
5	Don Garlits	35
6	Doug Kalitta	31
=	Cory McClenathan	31
8	Gary Scelzi	25
9	Gary Beck	19
10	Darrell Gwynn	18

⊙ A IS FOR AMATO

Joe Amato wasn't flash, but he was fast and he was effective, being
the first driver to top 260mph then 280mph and claiming 52 wins.
He became the first driver to win five Top Fuel titles, taking drag
racing's most senior crown in 1984, 1988, 1990, 1991 and 1992.
An eyesight problem led to Joe retiring at the end of 2000, but
it wasn't until Tony Schumacher landed his sixth Top Fuel title in
2008 that his record fell.

OTHER CAR RACING RECORDS
(INCLUDING FUNNY CAR AND PRO STOCK RACING)

⊙ NOT FUNNY FOR THE OTHERS

Don Prudhomme was the man to beat in Funny Cars – dragsters topped by a carbon-fibre body shell to give them the appearance of a road car – from 1975 to 1978, winning four titles in a row. Having been the first Funny Car driver under 6 secs in 1975, he set another record in 1982 when he became the first Funny Car driver to break the 250mph mark.

⊙ FORCE OF NATURE

John Force is a man who is fast standing still. He's a wisecracking, story-telling entertainer. In a Funny Car, he's been all but unbeatable. NHRA champion in 1990 and 1991, if it hadn't been for Cruz Pedregon winning the Funny Car title in 1992, Force would have won the title for 13 straight years. Then, after Tony Pedregon won in 2003, John won again in 2004 and 2006. That's 14 titles in 17 years.

⊙ THE SNAKE VS THE MONGOOSE

Drag racing's most famous rivalry came in the 1960s and 1970s between Don "The Snake" Prudhomme in his yellow Plymouth Barracuda and Tom "The Mongoose" McEwen in his red Plymouth Duster. It was a set-up, as McEwen called himself "Mongoose" to take on "The Snake". Unlike in real life, The Mongoose invariably got beaten, taking only five wins in his career. Their fame was so great that Mattel sponsored them both and they had a pair of Hot Wheels cars made to commemorate their showdowns.

⊙ GLIDDEN ALONG...

Bob Glidden clocked up 85 NHRA wins, which at the time was a record, but John Force and Warren Johnson have since roared past him and Frank Manzo pulled level. A greater sign of his dominance of the Pro Stock scene is that he was first crowned in 1974 and went on to be champion nine more times before he retired in 1995. He notably claimed five titles in a row from 1985 to 1989.

⊙ JOHNSON THE PRO IN PRO STOCK

Warren Johnson's ranking in Pro Stock couldn't be higher, which is why the six-time champion is known as "The Professor of Pro Stock" and tops the table for the drivers with the most wins. He accrued 96 wins, moving past Bob Glidden's previous record of 85. Greg Anderson has the third-highest tally, 60, with Jeg Coughlin fourth on 47 and Kurt Johnson fifth on 39 wins.

⊙ THE HIGHT OF SUCCESS

The Funny Car quarter-mile record is 4.646 secs, set by Robert Hight. The record top speed is 334.32mph, hit by Mike Ashley. On the 1,000-ft course, the record is 4.023 secs, set by Don Capps in 2009, with Ashley Force Hood hitting a record top speed of 312.13mph a couple of months later. Both of these records were set at Chandler in Arizona.

⊙ ON THE STRIPS AND THE OVALS

Raymond Beadle made a considerable mark on two branches of American motor sport. Having won three NHRA titles from 1979–81 in his Blue Max Funny Car, he branched out into owning a NASCAR team in 1983 and helped guide Rusty Wallace to the 1989 Winston Cup title in his No. 27 Pontiac. He became the only entrant to achieve that double.

⊙ SHOWING THE YOUNG GUNS

In a career that passed 500 starts back in 2006, Warren Johnson demonstrated that age was no impediment and that drag racing was second nature to him as he was still able to be a frontrunner in his 60s. At the Mopar Parts Mile High Nationals in 2007, he became the oldest driver to win an NHRA event, aged 64.

⊙ STRAIGHT DOWN THE LINE

The lowest ever elapsed time for a Pro Stock run down a quarter-mile track is three-time champion Greg Anderson's 6.536-secs blast at Gainesville early in the 2007 season. However, he's only second-fastest in top speed achieved, managing a best of 211.49mph to 2006 champion Jason Line's 211.69mph in a record run in 2007.

DRIVERS WITH MOST NHRA FUNNY CAR TITLES SINCE 1974

1	John Force	14
2	Kenny Bernstein	4
=	Don Prudhomme	4
4	Raymond Beadle	3
5	Frank Hawley	2
=	Cruz Pedregon	2
=	Tony Pedregon	2
8	Shirl Greer	1
=	Robert Hight	1
=	Bruce Larson	1
=	Mark Oswald	1
=	Gary Scelzi	1

⊙ CHAMPION IN TWO DISCIPLINES

Budweiser-backed Kenny Bernstein enjoyed a run of four straight
Funny Car titles from 1985 to 1988. He then moved on to the
Top Fuel class and became the first driver to break 300mph in a
standing-start quarter-mile sprint, then later became the champion,
in 1996 and 2001. He was the first driver to win titles in both of
NHRA's nitro categories.

⊙ FORCING HIS WAY TO THE FRONT

John Force is by far the most successful driver in Funny Cars, as
he had 126 wins to his name by the end of the 2009 season. The
next most successful driver, Tony Pedregon, has 43. Both Force and
Pedregon easily outstripped earlier top performers Don Prudhomme
and Kenny Bernstein, who have 35 and 30 wins respectively.